English Brushup

Sixth Edition

John Langan
Atlantic Cape Community College

Janet M. Goldstein

Mc
Graw
Hill
Education

ENGLISH BRUSHUP, SIXTH EDITION

Published by McGraw-Hill Education, 2 Penn Plaza, New York, NY 10121. Copyright © 2015 by McGraw-Hill Education. All rights reserved. Printed in the United States of America. Previous editions © 2011, 2007 and 2003. No part of this publication may be reproduced or distributed in any form or by any means, or stored in a database or retrieval system, without the prior written consent of McGraw-Hill Education, including, but not limited to, in any network or other electronic storage or transmission, or broadcast for distance learning.

Some ancillaries, including electronic and print components, may not be available to customers outside the United States.

This book is printed on acid-free paper.

2 3 4 5 6 7 8 9 0 DOC/DOC 1 0 9 8 7 6 5 4

ISBN-13 (Student Edition):   978-0-07-351360-7
ISBN-10 (Student Edition):   0-07-351360-1
ISBN-13 (Instructor's Edition): 978-0-07-777634-3
ISBN-10 (Instructor's Edition): 0-07-777634-8

Vice President, General Manager, Products & Markets: *Michael Ryan*
Vice President, Content Production & Technology Services: *Kimberly Meriwether David*
Managing Director: *David S. Patterson*
Director: *Paul Banks*
Brand Manager: *Kelly Villella-Canton*
Executive Director of Development: *Lisa Pinto*
Managing Editor: *Penina Braffman*
Marketing Specialist: *Alexandra Schultz*

Brand Coordinator: *Adina Lonn*
Director, Content Production: *Terri Schiesl*
Content Project Manager: *Lisa Bruflodt*
Buyer: *Susan K. Culbertson*
Cover Illustration: *Paul Turnbaugh and Judith Ogus*
Media Project Manager: *Jennifer Bartell*
Compositor: *MPS Limited*
Typeface: *11/13 Times LT Std*
Printer: *R. R. Donnelley*

All credits appearing on page or at the end of the book are considered to be an extension of the copyright page.

Library of Congress Cataloging-in-Publication Data
Langan, John.
  English brushup/John Langan, Atlantic Cape Community College, Janet M. Goldstein.—Sixth Edition.
      pages cm.—(English Brushup)
  Includes index.
  ISBN-13: 978-0-07-351360-7 (Student Edition : acid-free paper)
  ISBN-10: 0-07-351360-1 (Student Edition : acid-free paper)
  ISBN-13: 978-0-07-777634-3 (Instructor's Edition : acid-free paper)
  ISBN-10: 0-07-777634-8 (Instructor's Edition : acid-free paper)
    1. English language—Rhetoric—Problems, exercises, etc. 2. English language—Grammar—Problems, exercises, etc. I. Goldstein, Janet M. II. Title.

PE1413.L28 2014
428.2—dc23
                                                        2013043698

The Internet addresses listed in the text were accurate at the time of publication. The inclusion of a Web site does not indicate an endorsement by the authors or McGraw-Hill Education, and McGraw-Hill Education does not guarantee the accuracy of the information presented at these sites.

www.mhhe.com

Contents

Part Two: Extending the Skills   183

Part Three: Applying the Skills   229

To the Instructor

English Brushup is a quick and practical guide to the grammar, punctuation, and usage skills that students most need to know. The book contains features that distinguish it from other grammar texts on the market:

1   *Three-part format.*   In order to highlight the most vital skills, the book is divided into three parts. Part One presents primary information about sixteen key skills. Part Two includes secondary information about these skills and also covers topics not discussed in Part One. Part Three tests students' mastery of the skills taught in Part One.

2   *Self-teaching approach.*   The *first page of every chapter* in Part One begins with an informal test—and then provides the answers and explanations. Students can quickly see what they know and don't know about the skill in question. In some cases, they may learn what they need to know about the skill without going any further in the chapter.

    The *next three to five pages* of each chapter present the basics about the skill. Lively examples and brief exercises give students the chance to practice the grammatical principle involved. Answers at the back of the book allow students to correct their own work, teaching themselves as they go.

    The *last six pages of each chapter* consist of six tests on the skill. Half of the items in Tests 1, 3, and 5 are accompanied by *hints*—shown in smaller type—which are designed to guide students in thinking through each kind of correction. More self-teaching is therefore ensured.

    In addition, as students work through the tests, they master the skills in progressively longer passages. In Tests 1 and 2, students practice the skills in sentences; in Tests 3 and 4, they work with short passages; finally, in Tests 5 and 6, they apply the skills to entire paragraphs. Step by step, then, their mastery of the skills advances from the sentence to the paragraph level.

3   *Manageable size.*   The book's compact size and short chapters will not overwhelm students. In addition, *English Brushup* does not discourage or confuse students by offering an equal amount of coverage for every grammar rule. Instead, Part One of the book presents only those rules that students actually *need to know* to write well. Additional useful information about many skills appears in Part Two.

4   *Invaluable supplements.*   An *Instructor's Edition* consists of the student text, as well as answers to all the practices and tests. An *Instructor's Manual and Test Bank,* one of several resources available online for instructors at

http://www.mhhe.com/langanbrushup6e, contains a diagnostic test and an achievement test as well as four additional mastery tests for each of the skills in Part One of the book. To provide for a range of student needs, the first two tests are relatively easy, and the second two are more difficult.

Other features of the book include the following:

- Simple language rather than traditional grammatical terminology.
- Examples and practice materials that are "real-life," high-interest, sometimes amusing, and always *adult*.
- An insistence that students play an active role in the learning process, not just "correcting," as in so many grammar books, but actually *writing out* corrections.

In short, *English Brushup* offers a combination of appealing features not found in other texts. Its focus on important skills, self-teaching approach, reasonable size, and outstanding supplements may prompt you to decide that *English Brushup* is the grammar book best suited to the needs of today's students.

Changes in the Sixth Edition

- New practice items have been added throughout Part Two.
- Also, practice materials and tests have been freshened throughout the book.

Acknowledgments

Reviewers who have provided helpful suggestions for this edition include Kathleen Andrew, Springfield Tech Community College; Douglas Barrett, Western Nevada College; Ashley Boswell, Western Nevada College; Maria Buchta, Norwalk Community College; Cindy Dupre, Shasta College; Joseph Fly, South Plains College; Lilian Gamble, Delgado Community College; Wanda Gilbert, Stanly Community College; Catherine Heath, Victoria College; Forrest C. Helvie, Norwalk Community College; Kimberly Hilton, Ivy Tech Community College; Cindy Howe, Lassen College; Michelle Paulsen, Victoria College; Denise M. Rogers, University of Louisiana at Lafayette; Karen Waska, Cuesta College.

We also owe thanks to Casey Furlong, for providing additional practice materials for this edition, and to Penina Braffman, Maureen Spada, and Lisa Bruflodt at McGraw-Hill.

John Langan
Janet M. Goldstein

Introduction

WHY BRUSH UP YOUR ENGLISH?

Suppose you saw the following sign in a convenience store:

- Please dont put children in our shopping carts, they are unstable. And can fall over easily.

… or read the following line in a student's history paper:

- The soldiers in the civil war often weared rags, on there feet that were torn from scraps of old clothing.

… or read the following sentence in a business memo:

- Profit's at the company has doubled in the passed 3 months its been our best sales performance in several yrs.

… or read the following paragraph in a job application:

- This June I will graduate. With twenty-four hours of courses in accounting. I have alot of previous experience. One was as a clerk in the school bookstore, the other doing data entry for ryder truck rental.

Chances are that the writers of the above lines felt vaguely uneasy about their sentences. They may have had doubts about whether their English was correct and clear. However, they went ahead because their work or school situation required them to put words on paper.

Here is what the four writers above should have written:

- Please don't put children in our shopping carts. The carts are unstable and can fall over easily.

- On their feet, the soldiers in the Civil War often wore rags that were torn from scraps of old clothing.

- Profits at the company have doubled in the past three months. It's been our best sales performance in several years.

- This June I will graduate with twenty-four hours of courses in accounting. I have a lot of previous experience. One position I have held was as a clerk in the school bookstore; the other was doing data entry for Ryder Truck Rental.

1

If you were uncertain about the corrections needed for the above sentences, then this book is for you. *English Brushup* is a guide to the essentials of English: the grammar, punctuation, and usage skills that you most need to write clearly and effectively.

HOW *ENGLISH BRUSHUP* WORKS

Here is one way to use the book:

1 **Look at the table of contents.** You'll see that *English Brushup* is divided into three parts. Part One presents sixteen key skills you need in order to write well. Part Two includes more information about some of the skills in Part One; it also covers some areas not included in Part One. Part Three contains a series of tests you can take after you have studied the skills in Part One.

2 **Turn to the first page of any chapter in Part One.** Take the "Seeing What You Know" test. Then check your answers. If you have a problem with the skill, you'll know it right away. In some cases, you may learn what you need to know about the skill without going any further in the chapter.

3 **Work through the rest of the chapter.** The next three to five pages of each chapter present the basics of the skill. The examples and brief exercises will give you the chance to practice the skill. The answers at the back of the book will allow you to correct your own work, teaching yourself as you go.

4 **Test yourself.** The last six pages of each chapter contain six tests on the skill. Tests 1, 3, and 5 usually include hints that will help you understand and answer half of the items on the tests. Be sure to take advantage of these hints to increase your mastery of the skill. You will find additional tests in Part Three, "Applying the Skills."

5 **Use the book as a reference tool.** Following the above sequence, work your way through the book. In Part Two, pay special attention to the section on paper format on pages 185–186. Refer to other sections of Part Two as needed or as your instructor suggests. To help you find your way around the book, use the table of contents at the front, the index at the back, and the correction symbols and page references on the inside front cover.

AN INTRODUCTION TO GRAMMAR: THE PARTS OF SPEECH

Parts of speech are classifications of words according to their meaning and use in a sentence. There are eight parts of speech:

nouns	verbs	adjectives	conjunctions
pronouns	prepositions	adverbs	interjections

Nouns

A **noun** is a word that is used to name something: a person, a place, an object, or an idea. Here are some examples of nouns:

woman	city	pancake	freedom
Oprah Winfrey	alley	leaf	possibility
actor	island	kiss	hope
Brad Pitt	Chicago	Corvette	mystery

Most nouns begin with a lowercase letter and are known as **common nouns**. These nouns name general things. Some nouns, however, begin with a capital letter. They are called **proper nouns**. While a common noun refers to a person or thing in general, a proper noun names someone or something specific. For example, *woman* is a common noun—it doesn't name a particular woman. On the other hand, *Oprah Winfrey* is a proper noun because it names a specific woman.

For more information about nouns, see "Subjects and Verbs," pages 17–20.

Practice 1

Insert any appropriate noun into each of the following blanks.

1.   Someone left a large *package* at our front door.
2.   *Someone* threw the football to me.
3.   Joanne wrote a(n) *essay* on her computer.
4.   During the storm, a(n) *hawk* fell onto the roof.
5.   Give the *remote* to my brother.

Singular and Plural Nouns

Singular nouns name one person, place, object, or idea. **Plural** nouns refer to two or more persons, places, objects, or ideas. Most singular nouns can be made plural by adding an *s*.

Some nouns, like *kiss, city, leaf,* and *woman,* have irregular plurals. You can check the plural of nouns you think may be irregular by looking up the singular form in a dictionary.

Singular:	pancake	alley	freedom	kiss	city	leaf	woman
Plural:	pancakes	alleys	freedoms	kisses	cities	leaves	women

Practice 2

Underline the three nouns in each sentence. Some are singular, and some are plural.

1.   A <u>hawk</u> just perched in a <u>tree</u> in our <u>yard.</u>
2.   By the <u>end of</u> the <u>game,</u> both <u>teams</u> were exhausted.

3.   My <u>sister</u> is a talented <u>dancer</u> who has never taken a <u>class</u>.

4.   The <u>boys</u> decided to <u>work</u> on the <u>car</u> in Mike's <u>garage</u>.

5.   Some <u>workers</u> prefer <u>jobs</u> with flexible <u>hours</u>.

Pronouns

A **pronoun** is a word that stands for a noun. Pronouns eliminate the need for constant repetition. Look at the following sentences:

> After the phone rang eight times, Bill answered the phone.
>
> Lisa met Lisa's friends in the mall bookstore. Lisa meets Lisa's friends there every Saturday.
>
> The server rushed over to the new customers. The new customers asked the server for menus and coffee.

Now look at how much clearer and smoother the sentences sound with pronouns:

> After the phone rang eight times, Bill answered **it**.
> (The pronoun *it* is used to replace the words *the phone*.)
>
> Lisa met **her** friends in the mall bookstore. **She** meets **them** there every Saturday.
> (The pronoun *her* is used to replace the word *Lisa's*. The pronoun *she* replaces *Lisa*. The pronoun *them* replaces the words *Lisa's friends*.)
>
> The server rushed over to the new customers. **They** asked **him** for menus and coffee.
> (The pronoun *they* is used to replace the words *the new customers*. The pronoun *him* replaces the words *the server*.)

The pronouns in the above sentences are **personal pronouns**. They can act in a sentence as subjects, objects, or possessives:

	Subject	*Object*	*Possessive*
Singular:	I	me	my, mine
	you	you	your, yours
	he, she, it	him, her, it	his, hers, its
Plural:	we	us	our, ours
	you	you	your, yours
	they	them	their, theirs

Practice 3

Fill in each blank with an appropriate personal pronoun from the box above.

1.   Allison feeds her parrot every morning. __She__ also feeds __it__ again when she gets home in the afternoon.

2.   *Action News* reporter Teresa Morales interviewed the striking workers. __They__ told __her__ about their demands for higher wages and longer breaks.

3. Our instructor told us, "_They_ plan to return _our_ tests on Monday."

4. The pilot announced that our plane would fly through some rough air pockets. _He_ said that we should be past _them_ soon.

5. Randall left an important message on Sheila's voice mail. But Sheila told _him_ she never heard _his_ message.

There are a number of other types of pronouns. For convenient reference, they are described briefly in the box below.

For more information about pronouns, see "Pronouns," pages, 81–84, and "Pronoun Types," pages 189–193. For information on indefinite pronouns, see also "Subject-Verb Agreement," pages 39–42.

Other Pronoun Types

Relative pronouns refer to someone or something already mentioned in the sentence.

> who, whose, whom, which, that, whoever, whomever, whichever, whatever (These words begin **dependent-word groups**, also known as **relative clauses** or **subordinate clauses**.)

Interrogative pronouns are used to ask questions.

> who, whose, whom, which, what

Demonstrative pronouns are used to point out particular persons or things.

> *Singular:* this, that   *Plural:* these, those

Note Do not use *them* (as in *them* shoes), *this here, that there, these here,* or *those there* to point out persons or things.

Reflexive pronouns are those that end in -*self* or -*selves*. A reflexive pronoun is used as the object of a verb (as in *Cary cut **herself***) or the object of a preposition (as in *Jack sent a birthday card to **himself***) when the subject of the verb is the same as the object.

> *Singular:*   myself, yourself, himself, herself, itself
> *Plural:*   ourselves, yourselves, themselves

Intensive pronouns have exactly the same forms as reflexive pronouns. The difference is in how they are used. Intensive pronouns are used to add emphasis.

> (***I** myself* will need to read the contract before I sign it.)

Indefinite pronouns do not refer to a particular person or thing.

> ***One*** *words:* anyone, someone, everyone, no one, one, none
> ***Body*** *words:* anybody, somebody, everybody, nobody
> ***Thing*** *words:* anything, something, everything, nothing
> *Other indefinite pronouns:* each, either, both, several, any, most, all, some, more, many

Reciprocal pronouns express shared actions or feelings.

> each other, one another

Verbs

Every complete sentence must contain at least one verb. There are two main types of verbs: **action verbs** and **linking verbs.**

For more information about verbs, see "Subjects and Verbs," pages 17–20; "More about Subjects and Verbs," page 203; "More about Verbs," pages 27–32; and "Even More about Verbs," pages 204–207.

Action Verbs

An **action verb** tells what is being done in a sentence. For example, look at the following sentences:

> Mr. Jensen **swatted** at the bee with his hand.
> Rainwater **poured** into the storm sewer.
> The children **chanted** the words to the TV commercial.

In these sentences, the verbs are *swatted, poured,* and *chanted.* These words are all action verbs; they tell what is happening in each sentence.

Note   Action verbs can also be classified as **transitive** and **intransitive**. Transitive verbs have a **direct object**—something that receives the action: The bee **stung** Mr. Jensen. Intransitive verbs do not have a direct object: The sewer **overflowed**.

Practice 4

Insert an appropriate word into each blank. That word will be an action verb; it will tell what is happening in the sentence.

1.   The surgeon _cut_ through the first layer of skin.
2.   My mail carrier _biked_ over twenty miles a day.
3.   An elderly woman on the street _asked_ me for directions.
4.   A boy in our neighborhood _mows_ our lawn every other week.
5.   Our instructor _marks_ our tests over the weekend.

Linking Verbs

Some verbs are **linking verbs.** These verbs link (or join) a noun to something that is said about it (sometimes called the **subject complement**). For example, look at the following sentence:

> The clouds **are** steel gray.

In this sentence, *are* is a linking verb. It joins the noun *clouds* to words that describe it: *steel gray.* Other common linking verbs include *am, is, was, were, will be, appear, become, seem, grow, remain,* and the "sense verbs" *look, feel,* and *sound. Smell* and *taste* can also be used as linking verbs: The stew **smells** good. It **tastes** good, too.

Practice 5

Fill in each blank with one of the following linking verbs: *am, feel, is, look, were.* Use each linking verb **once**.

1.   All the appliances in my parents' kitchen **were** avocado green.
2.   I **am** anxious to get my test back.
3.   The bananas are yellow and spotted; they definitely **look** ripe.
4.   The convenience store **is** open until 11 p.m.
5.   Whenever I **feel** angry, I go off by myself to calm down.

Helping Verbs

Sometimes the verb of a sentence consists of more than one word. In these cases, the main verb will be joined by one or more **helping verbs**. Look at the following sentence:

   The basketball team **will be leaving** for their game at six o'clock.

In this sentence, the main verb is *leaving*. The helping verbs are *will* and *be*.

Other helping verbs include *am, are, is, was, were, being, been, has, have, having, had, do, does, did, can, could, may, might, must, shall, should, will,* and *would*.

Practice 6

Fill in each blank with one of the following helping verbs: *does, must, should, could,* and *has been*. Use each helping verb **once**.

1.   You really **should** start writing your paper this weekend.
2.   The two-year-old already knew the alphabet and **could** count up to 10.
3.   You **must** scrape food off the dishes before you put them in the dishwasher.
4.   My neighbor's house **has been** featured twice on the local evening news.
5.   The express train **does** not stop at every station.

Prepositions

A **preposition** is a word that connects a noun or a pronoun to another word in the sentence. For example, look at the following sentence:

   A man in the bus was snoring loudly.

In is a preposition. It connects the noun *bus* to *man*.

Here is a list of common prepositions:

about	around	beside	for	off	under
above	at	between	from	on, onto	until
across	before	by	in, into	over	up
after	behind	down	inside	through	upon
along	below	during	like	to	with
among	beneath	except	of	toward	without

The noun or pronoun that a preposition connects to another word in the sentence is called the **object** of the preposition. A group of words that begins with a preposition and ends with its object is called a **prepositional phrase**. The words *in the bus,* for example, are a prepositional phrase.

Now read the following sentences and explanations:

An ant was crawling **up the teacher's leg**.

The noun *leg* is the object of the preposition *up. Up* connects *leg* with the word *crawling*. The prepositional phrase *up the teacher's leg* describes *crawling*. It tells just where the ant was crawling.

The man **with the black mustache** left the restaurant quickly.

The noun *mustache* is the object of the preposition *with*. The prepositional phrase *with the black mustache* describes the word *man*. It tells us exactly which man left the restaurant quickly.

The plant **on the windowsill** was a present **from my mother**.

The noun *windowsill* is the object of the preposition *on*. The prepositional phrase *on the windowsill* describes the word *plant*. It describes exactly which plant was a present.

There is a second prepositional phrase in this sentence. The preposition is *from*, and its object is *mother.* The prepositional phrase *from my mother* explains *present*. It tells who gave the present.

For more information about prepositions, see "Subjects and Verbs," pages 18–19, and "Subject-Verb Agreement," page 40.

Practice 7

Fill in each blank with one of the following prepositions: *of, by, with, in,* and *without*. Use each preposition **once**.

1.   The letter from his girlfriend had been sprayed _With_ perfume.

2.   The weed killer quickly killed every dandelion _in_ our lawn.

3. __without__ giving any notice, the tenant moved out of the apartment.

4. Jamal hungrily ate three scoops __of__ ice cream and an order of French fries.

5. The crates __by__ the back door contain glass bottles and old newspapers.

Adjectives

An **adjective** is a word that describes a noun (the name of a person, place, or thing). Look at the following sentence:

The dog lay down on a mat in front of the fireplace.

Now look at this sentence when adjectives have been inserted:

The **shaggy** dog lay down on a **worn** mat in front of the fireplace.

The adjective *shaggy* describes the noun *dog;* the adjective *worn* describes the noun *mat.*

Adjectives add spice to our writing. They also help us to identify particular people, places, and things.

Adjectives can be found in two places:

1 An adjective may come before the word it describes (a **damp** night, the **moldy** bread, a **striped** umbrella).

2 An adjective that describes the subject of a sentence may come after a linking verb. The linking verb may be a form of the verb *be* (he *is* **furious**, I *am* **exhausted**, they *are* **hungry**). Other linking verbs include *feel, look, sound, smell, taste, appear, seem,* and *become* (the soup *tastes* **salty**, your hands *feel* **dry**, the dog *seems* **lost**).

Note   The words *a, an,* and *the* (called **articles**) are generally classified as adjectives.

For more information about adjectives, see "Adjectives and Adverbs," pages 194–196.

Practice 8

Fill in each blank with an appropriate adjective.

1. The __young__ family greedily devoured a(n) __entire__ pizza.

2. Felipe threw away the shirt because it was __old__ and __greasy__.

3. Although the alley is __dark__ and __scary__, Darcy takes it as a shortcut.

4. Don't buy lettuce that is __brown__ or tomatoes that are __rotten__.

5. When I woke up today, I had a(n) __high__ fever and a(n) __sore__ throat.

Adverbs

An **adverb** is a word that describes a verb, an adjective, or another adverb. Many adverbs end in the letters -*ly*. Look at the following sentence:

The canary sang in the pet-store window as the shoppers greeted each other.

Now look at this sentence after adverbs have been inserted:

The canary sang **softly** in the pet-store window as the shoppers **loudly** greeted each other.

The adverbs add details to the sentence; they tell how the canary sang and how the shoppers greeted each other. They also allow the reader to contrast the singing of the canary to the noise the shoppers are making.

Look at the following sentences and the explanations of how adverbs are used in each case:

The chef yelled **angrily** at the new kitchen helper.

The adverb *angrily* describes the verb *yelled*. It tells how the chef yelled.

My mother has an **extremely** busy schedule on Tuesdays.

The adverb *extremely* describes the adjective *busy*. It tells how busy the schedule is.

The sick man spoke **very faintly** to his loyal nurse.

The adverb *very* describes the adverb *faintly*. *Faintly* tells how the sick man spoke; *very* tells how faintly he spoke.

Some adverbs do not end in -*ly*. Examples include *very, often, never, always,* and *well*.

For more information about adverbs, see "Adjectives and Adverbs," pages 194–196.

Practice 9

Fill in each blank with an appropriate adverb.

1.   Food cooks _quickly_ in a microwave.
2.   Carla _slowly_ drove her car through _barely_ moving traffic.
3.   The 911 telephone operator spoke _calmly_ to the young child.
4.   The game-show contestant waved _happily_ to his family in the audience.
5.   Wes _rarely_ studies, so he did _extremely_ poorly on the exam.

Conjunctions

Conjunctions are words that connect. There are three types of conjunctions:

Coordinating Conjunctions (Joining Words)

Coordinating conjunctions join two equal ideas. Look at the following sentence:

Kevin **and** Steve interviewed for the job, **but** their friend Anne got it.

In this sentence, the coordinating conjunction *and* connects the proper nouns *Kevin* and *Steve*. The coordinating conjunction *but* connects the first part of the sentence, *Kevin and Steve interviewed for the job,* to the second part, *their friend Anne got it.*

Following is a list of the seven coordinating conjunctions. (In this book, they are simply called **joining words**.)

for	and	nor	but	or	yet	so

One good way to remember all seven coordinating conjunctions is with a catchword made from their first letters: FANBOYS.

For more information about coordinating conjunctions, see information on joining words in "Sentence Types," page 51; "Run-Ons and Comma Splices," pages 72–74; "Comma," pages 93–94; and "More about the Comma," pages 212–215.

Practice 10

Fill in each blank with one of the following coordinating conjunctions: *and, but, so, or.* Use each conjunction **once**.

1. For dessert, you may choose berries, Jell-O, _ _or_ _ a hot fudge sundae.

2. I expected roses for my birthday, _ _but_ _ I received a vase of plastic tulips from the dollar store.

3. There was nothing good on TV, _ _so_ _ Gary decided to read a book.

4. Marian brought playing cards _ _and_ _ a pan of brownies to the company picnic.

Subordinating Conjunctions (Dependent Words)

Subordinating conjunctions join two ideas of unequal importance. When a subordinating conjunction is added to a word group, the words can no longer stand alone as an independent sentence. They are no longer a complete thought. (Such a word group is also called a **dependent clause** or **subordinate clause**.) For example, look at the following sentence:

Karen fainted in class.

The word group *Karen fainted in class* is a complete thought. It can stand alone as a sentence.

See what happens when a subordinating conjunction is added to a complete thought:

When Karen fainted in class

Now the words cannot stand alone as a sentence. They are dependent on other words—words that *are* a sentence (also called an **independent clause**)—to complete the thought:

When Karen fainted in class, **we put her feet up on some books**.

Below are some subordinating conjunctions. In this book, they are called **dependent words**, and the word groups containing them are called **dependent word groups**.

after	before	if	though	where, wherever
although	even if	in order that	unless	whether
as	even though	since	until	while
because	how	so that	when, whenever	

Here are some more sentences with subordinating conjunctions:

After she finished her last exam, Suki said, "Now I can relax."

After she finished her last exam is not a complete thought. It is dependent on the other part of the sentence, *Suki said, "Now I can relax,"* to be a complete sentence.

Lamont listens to books on tape **while** he drives to work.

While he drives to work cannot stand by itself as a sentence. It depends on the rest of the sentence, *Lamont listens to books on tape,* to make up a complete thought.

Since apples were on sale, we decided to make an apple pie for dessert.

Since apples were on sale is not a complete sentence. It depends on *we decided to make an apple pie for dessert* to complete the thought.

Note   Do not confuse the preposition *like* with the subordinating conjunction *as.* Use *like* before a noun: That coffee tastes **like** mud. Use *as* or *as if* before a subject and verb: That coffee tastes **as if** it could power a diesel engine. Still, nothing wakes me up as quickly **as** coffee does.

For more information about subordinating conjunctions, see information on dependent words in "Sentence Types," page 52; "Fragments," pages 60–61; and "Run-Ons and Comma Splices," pages 73–74.

Practice 11

Fill in each blank with one of the following subordinating conjunctions: *even though, because, until, when,* and *before.* Use each conjunction **once.**

1. Take the roast out of the oven _____ the timer rings.

2. _____ Paula wants to look mysterious, she wears dark sunglasses and a scarf.

3. _____ the store was closing in fifteen minutes, customers walked through the aisles slowly and continued to shop.

4. _____ anyone else could answer it, Carl rushed to the phone and whispered, "It's me."

5. The staff was told not to serve any food _____ the guest of honor arrived.

Correlative Conjunctions

Correlative conjunctions are pairs of words that join two equal items: *either/ or, neither/nor, both/and, not only/but also.* They are often found in compound subjects and in sentences using parallel structure:

> **Neither** the coach **nor** the players could figure out why they had lost the game.
>
> I am allergic **not only** to fish **but also** to shellfish.

For more examples of the use of correlative conjunctions, see "Parallelism," pages 174–176, and "More about Subject-Verb Agreement," pages 208–209.

Practice 12

In each sentence, fill in the blanks with one of the following pairs of correlative conjunctions: *either/or, neither/nor, both/and.* Use each pair of conjunctions **once.**

1. _____ Jimmy _____ Shane must have scored the winning run.

2. When Fran was caught in the rain, her new leather boots became _____ muddy _____ soaked.

3. Sadly, _____ my mother _____ my father lived to be fifty, so they never got to meet their grandchildren.

Interjections

Interjections are words that can stand independently and are used to express emotion. They are often followed by an exclamation point. Examples are *oh, wow, ouch*, and *oops*. These words are usually not found in formal writing.

"**Hey**!" yelled Maggie. "That's my bike."

Oh, we're late for class.

Words That Can Be More Than One Part of Speech

A word may function as more than one part of speech. For example, the word *dust* can be a verb, a noun, or an adjective, depending on its role in the sentence.

I **dust** my bedroom once a month, whether it needs it or not. *(verb)*

The top of my refrigerator is covered with an inch of **dust**. *(noun)*

Tomorrow I'll pick up a **dust** cloth and start cleaning. *(adjective)*

A FINAL WORD

English Brushup has been designed to benefit you as much as possible. Its format is straightforward, its explanations are clear, and its practices and tests will help you learn through doing. *It is a book that has been created to reward effort,* and if you provide that effort, you can make yourself a competent and confident writer.

John Langan

Janet M. Goldstein

Part One

Sixteen Basic Skills

hello

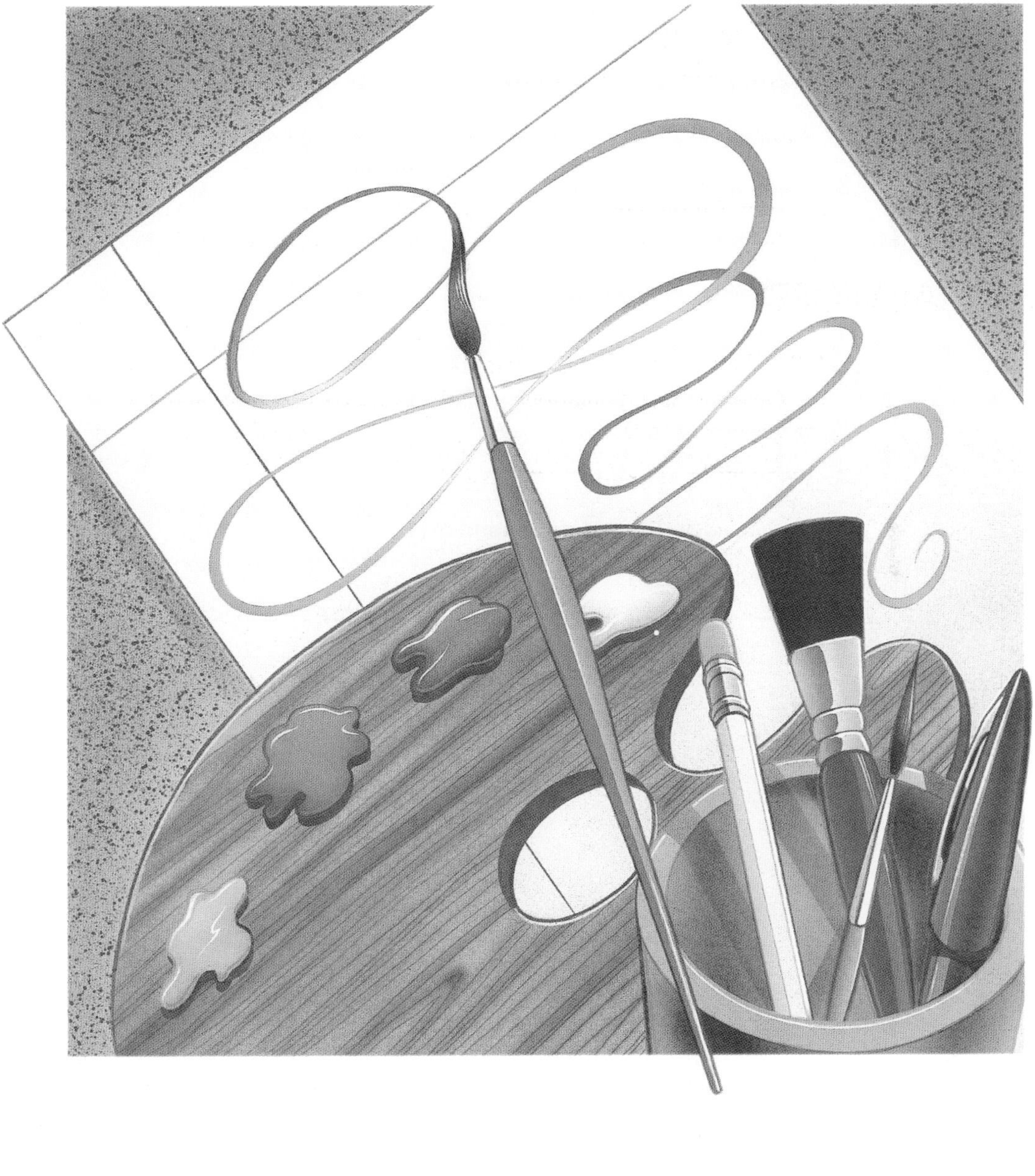

Preview

Part One presents basic information about sixteen key grammar, punctuation, and usage skills:

1 Subjects and Verbs

Seeing What You Know

In each blank, insert a word that seems appropriate. Then read the explanations below.

1. The ___cup___ accidentally ___spilled___ onto the floor.

2. My ___dog___ often ___barks___ at the mail carrier.

3. A ___man___ in the corner ___swore___ loudly to the server.

4. ___You___ should never have ___tried___ to study all night for the test.

Understanding the Answers

If your completed sentences make grammatical sense, the word in the first blank of each sentence will be its **subject**, and the word in the second blank will be the **verb**. Here are some completed versions of the sentences, with the subjects and verbs labeled:

1. The **knife** (*subject*) accidentally **fell** (*verb*) onto the floor.
   The *knife* is what the sentence is about. *Fell* is what the knife did.

2. My **cat** (*subject*) often **meows** (*verb*) at the mail carrier.
   The *cat* is what the sentence is about. *Meows* is what the cat does.

3. A **customer** (*subject*) in the corner **shouted** (*verb*) loudly to the server.
   A *customer* is performing an action. *Shouted* is the action.

4. **Anita** (*subject*) **should** never **have tried** (*verb*) to study all night for the test.
   Anita is the person doing something. *Should [never] have tried* is what the sentence says about her. *Never* is not part of the verb.

Subjects and verbs are the basic parts of sentences. Understanding them will help you with most of the other skills in this book.

FINDING THE SUBJECT

Look at the following sentences:

Eric tripped on the steps.

The brakes on my car squeal.

She owns three motorcycles.

Depression is a common mood disorder.

The **subject** of a sentence is the person, thing, or idea that the sentence is about. To find a sentence's subject, ask yourself, "Who or what is this sentence about?" or "Who or what is doing something in this sentence?"*

Let's look again at the sentences above.

Who is the first one about? *Eric.* (He's the one who tripped.)

What is the second one about? *Brakes.* (They are what squeal.)

Who is the third one about? *She.* (She's the one who owns three motorcycles.)

What is the fourth one about? *Depression.* (It's a common mood disorder.)

So, in the sentences above, the subjects are *Eric, brakes, she,* and *depression.*

Note   Each of these subjects is either a **noun** (the name of a person, place, or thing) or a **pronoun** (a word that stands for a noun). The subject of a sentence will always be either a noun or a pronoun. For more information about nouns and pronouns, see pages 81–84.

The Subject Is Never in a Prepositional Phrase

The subject of a sentence will never be part of a prepositional phrase. A **prepositional phrase**, such as *on my car,* is a group of words that begins with a preposition, ends with a noun or pronoun (the object of the preposition), and answers a question such as "Which one?" "What kind?" "How?" "Where?" or "When?"

Here are some common prepositions:

Prepositions					
about	around	beside	for	off	under
above	at	between	from	on, onto	until
across	before	by	in, into	over	up
after	behind	down	inside	through	upon
along	below	during	like	to	with
among	beneath	except	of	toward	without

---

*In imperative sentences (commands), the subject is understood to be *you:* [You] Come here. [You] Please bring me the check. [You] Stop snoring!

As you look for the subject of a sentence, it is helpful to cross out any prepositional phrases that you find.

The vase ~~on the bedside table~~ belonged to my grandparents. (*Vase* is the subject; *on the bedside table* is a prepositional phrase telling us which vase.)

~~With smiles or frowns~~, students left the exam room. (*Students* is the subject; *with smiles or frowns* is a prepositional phrase describing how they left.)

The noise ~~during the thunderstorm~~ was frightening. (*Noise* is the subject; *during the thunderstorm* is a prepositional phrase telling when it happened.)

FINDING THE VERB

The subject of a sentence is what that sentence is about. The **verb** explains what that sentence says about the subject. Consider the four sentences on the previous page:

What does the first sentence say about Eric? He *tripped*.

What does the second sentence say about the brakes? They *squeal*.

What does the third sentence say about the woman? She *owns* (three motorcycles).

What does the last sentence say about depression? It *is* (a mood disorder).

The verbs in the sentences above are *tripped, squeal, owns,* and *is*.

Here are two other ways to identify a verb:

1   Try putting a pronoun such as *I, you, he, she, it,* or *they* in front of it. If the word is a verb, the resulting sentence will make sense. Notice that in the examples above, *he tripped, they squeal, she owns,* and *it is* all make sense.

2   Look at what the verb tells us. Most verbs show action; they are called **action verbs**. (*Tripped, owns,* and *squeal* are action verbs.) A few verbs, however, are **linking verbs**. They link (join) the subject to something that is said about the subject. In the fourth example, *is* is a linking verb. It connects the subject, *depression,* with an idea about depression (it is a *common mood disorder*). *Am, are, was, were, look, feel, sound, appear, seem, grow, remain,* and *become* are other common linking verbs.

Practice 1

In each of the sentences below, cross out the prepositional phrases. Then underline the subject once and the verb twice. The first one is done for you as an example.

1. <u>Nikki</u> <u><u>waited</u></u> ~~in the supermarket checkout line for nearly half an hour~~.

2. A <u>dog</u> ~~with muddy paws~~ <u><u>padded</u></u> across the ~~clean~~ kitchen floor.

3. <u>One</u> ~~of my cousins~~ <u><u>is</u></u> a tightrope walker ~~in the circus~~.

4. Those <u>kittens</u> ~~at the animal shelter~~ <u><u>need</u></u> a good home.

5. ~~By the end of the month~~, <u>I</u> <u><u>have</u></u> very little <u>money</u> ~~in my wallet~~.

ADDITIONAL FACTS ABOUT VERBS

The hints that follow will further help you find the verb in a sentence.

1   Verbs do not always consist of just one word. Sometimes they consist of a main verb plus one or more **helping verbs**, such as *do, have, may, would, can, could,* or *should.* Here, for example, are some of the forms of the verb *love:*

love	could love	is loving	may have loved
loves	would love	was loving	might have loved
loved	will love	will be loving	must have loved
may love	do love	has loved	should have loved
must love	does love	have loved	could have loved
should love	did love	had loved	would have loved

2   Although words like *not, just, never, only,* and *always* may appear between the main verb and the helping verb, they are never part of the verb.

> Ellen <u>might</u> not <u>make</u> the basketball team this year.
>
> You <u>should</u> always <u>count</u> the change the cashier gives you.
>
> That instructor <u>can</u> never <u>end</u> her class on time.

3   The verb of a sentence never comes after the word *to.*

> Sal <u>chose</u> to live with his parents during college. (Although *live* is a verb, *to live* cannot be the verb of the sentence.)

4   A word ending in *-ing* cannot by itself be the verb of the sentence. It can be part of the verb, but it needs a helping verb before it.

> The strikers <u>were hoping</u> for a quick settlement. (You could not correctly say, "The strikers hoping for a quick settlement.")

Practice 2

In each of the sentences below, cross out the prepositional phrases. Then underline the subject once and the verb twice.

1. <u>Everyone</u> ~~at the plant~~ is <u>working</u> overtime ~~during August.~~

2. A <u>list</u> ~~of award winners~~ will be <u>posted</u> ~~on the school's website.~~

3. ~~Around midnight,~~ a police <u>siren</u> began to <u>wail</u> ~~in the nearby street.~~

4. That <u>shirt</u> should not have been <u>put</u> in the washing machine.

5. ~~On hot days,~~ <u>you</u> must always <u>remember</u> ~~to provide~~ extra <u>water</u> for the <u>dog.</u>

> **Note**   Additional information about subjects and verbs appears on page 203.

Name **Ava Morris**   Section _____ Date _____

Score: (Number right) _____ × 5 = _____ %

■ Subjects and Verbs: Test 1

In each sentence below, cross out the prepositional phrases. Then underline the subject once and the verb twice. Remember to underline all the parts of the verb.

Note   To help in your review of subjects and verbs, use the explanations given for half of the sentences.

1. My <u>brother</u> <u>plays</u> computer games ~~until well past midnight~~.

   Until is a preposition, so *until well past midnight* is a prepositional phrase. The sentence is about my *brother*. *Plays* (computer games) is what he does.

2. ~~With a satisfied grunt,~~ <u>Darnell</u> <u>lifted</u> the hundred-pound barbell ~~over his head.~~

3. ~~Without a doubt,~~ <u>Ramon</u> will <u>win</u> the race.

   Without is a preposition, so *without a doubt* is a prepositional phrase. The sentence is about Ramon. *Will win* (*win* plus the helping verb *will*) is what the sentence says about him.

4. The reality <u>shows</u> ~~on television~~ have <u>been</u> very popular ~~for the past ten years.~~

5. The <u>stars</u> ~~in the cloudless sky~~ <u>seem</u> ~~especially~~ bright tonight.

   In the cloudless sky is a prepositional phrase. The verb *seem* (a linking verb) joins what the sentence is about (*stars*) to a statement describing them (*especially bright*).

6. That freshly baked apple <u>pie</u> ~~on the kitchen counter~~ <u>smells</u> heavenly.

7. The <u>boss's</u> temper <u>tantrums</u> are impossible ~~to ignore~~.

   The sentence is about the boss's temper *tantrums*. The linking verb *are* joins the subject to a statement about the subject (*impossible to ignore*). Since *ignore* has the word *to* in front of it, it cannot be the verb of the sentence.

8. ~~In June,~~ the <u>store</u> is <u>offering</u> to customers a rebate ~~of fifty dollars on every energy-efficient appliance.~~

9. Some <u>people</u> can never <u>forget</u> an insult.

   People are the ones doing something in the sentence. What the sentence says about people is that they *can* never *forget*. The word *never* describes the verb, but it is not part of the verb.

10. ~~For Thanksgiving,~~ <u>we</u> are <u>donating</u> cans of soup, frozen turkeys, and packages of fruit ~~to the neighborhood food bank.~~

Name _____   Section _____   Date _____

Score: (Number right) _____ × 5 = _____ %

■ Subjects and Verbs: Test 2

In each sentence below, cross out the prepositional phrases. Then underline the subject once and the verb twice. Remember to underline all the parts of the verb.

1. The tree ~~in our backyard~~ looks dead.

2. It always relaxes me ~~to walk along the path around the lake.~~

3. My roommate has been sending romantic e-mails ~~to her new boyfriend during computer lab~~.

4. ~~In his entire career,~~ Simon has never missed one day of work.

5. Several shark attacks ~~during the summer~~ alarmed people about swimming ~~in the ocean~~.

6. The last three pages ~~of Elena's term paper~~ vanished ~~from her computer screen.~~

7. The quartz battery ~~in my watch~~ did not need to be replaced ~~for a period of three years~~.

8. Several companies ~~in the city~~ are planning ~~to move to the suburbs to escape the city wage tax~~.

9. ~~From my bedroom window,~~ I can watch all the games ~~on the high school football field~~.

10. ~~After the movie,~~ the six ~~of us~~ decided ~~to have dinner at our favorite~~ Italian ~~restaurant around the corner from the~~ theater.

Name **Ava Morris**   Section _____ Date _____

Score: (Number right) _____ × 5 = _____ %

■ **Subjects and Verbs: Test 3**

Cross out the prepositional phrases. Then, on the lines provided, write the subject and verb of each of the sentences. Remember to find all the parts of the verb.

Note   To help in your review of subjects and verbs, use the explanations given for half of the sentences.

1. The manager ~~of the hospital thrift shop~~ dresses ~~in unusual outfits~~. ~~Today~~ she is wearing a man's tuxedo ~~and a baseball cap.~~

   a.   *Subject:* **manager**   *Verb:* **dresses**
   The sentence is about the *manager. Dresses* is what she does.

   b.   *Subject:* **she**   *Verb:* **wearing**

2. ~~With a shout of delight,~~ the girls leaped into the huge pile of dry leaves. ~~They could not resist the urge~~ to crunch the leaves under their feet.

   a.   *Subject:* **girls**   *Verb:* **leaped**
   The girls are the ones doing something. *Leaped* is what they did.

   b.   *Subject:* **leaves**   *Verb:* **crunch**

3. ~~An enorm~~ous oil truck was racing ~~down the highway~~ at a dangerously high speed. ~~Fortunately,~~ a police car ~~with flashing red lights~~ soon appeared.

   a.   *Subject:* **oil truck**   *Verb:* **racing**
   The sentence is about a *truck. Was racing* is what it did.

   b.   *Subject:* **police car**   *Verb:* **appeared**

4. The young couple stood ~~in front of the jewelry store~~ for a long time. The diamond rings ~~in the window~~ seemed to fascinate them.

   a.   *Subject:* **young couple**   *Verb:* **stood**
   The young *couple* are performing an action. *Stood* is what they did.

   b.   *Subject:* **diamond rings**   *Verb:* **fascinate**

5. The chef ~~at my favorite restaurant~~ surprised me ~~on my birthday~~ with a special dessert. The large bowl must have contained at least four scoops of ice cream, ~~drowning in hot fudge sauce and garnished with raspberries.~~

   a.   *Subject:* **The chef**   *Verb:* **surprised**
   This sentence is about the *chef. Surprised* is what the chef did.

   b.   *Subject:* **large bowl**   *Verb:* **contained**

Name _____   Section _____ Date _____

Score: (Number right) _____ × 5 = _____%

■ Subjects and Verbs: Test 4

Cross out the prepositional phrases. Then, on the lines provided, write the subject and verb of each of the sentences. Remember to find all the parts of the verb.

1. ~~By the 22nd century,~~ everyone could be wearing paper clothing. Also, ~~in the future,~~ people might take food pills ~~instead of eating meals.~~
   a. *Subject:* everyone _____ *Verb:* wearing _____
   b. *Subject:* people _____ *Verb:* ~~~~ take _____

2. The repairs ~~on our van~~ were going to take around five weeks. The insurance company would not provide a loaner vehicle ~~for that length of time.~~
   a. *Subject:* The repairs _____ *Verb:* take _____
   b. *Subject:* insurance company *Verb:* provide _____

3. Walking into ~~the dusty, moldy~~ attic room, Lori began to sneeze violently. ~~After just five minutes,~~ her allergies forced her to leave.
   a. *Subject:* Lori _____ *Verb:* sneeze _____
   b. *Subject:* her allergies _____ *Verb:* forced _____

4. ~~With ice encrusting their leaves,~~ daffodils are poking through ~~the unexpected snow.~~ The unusually cold springtime weather caught both flowers and people off guard.
   a. *Subject:* daffodils _____ *Verb:* poking _____
   b. *Subject:* _____ *Verb:* _____

5. Old-fashioned locomotives seem romantic to us today. But their clouds of black coal smoke damaged the environment.
   a. *Subject:* _____ *Verb:* _____
   b. *Subject:* _____ *Verb:* _____

Name _____   Section _____   Date _____

Score: (Number right) _____ × 5 = _____ %

■ Subjects and Verbs: Test 5

Cross out the prepositional phrases. Then, on the lines provided, write the subject and verb of each of the sentences in the passage. Remember to find all the parts of the verb.

Note To help in your review of subjects and verbs, use the explanations given for five of the sentences.

[1]A delicious smell can make you hungry. [2]Certain perfumes, on the right people, turn your thoughts to romance. [3]Now researchers have discovered even more information about the subject of odors. [4]Pleasant smells seem to raise people's productivity. [5]The effects of fragrance have been studied at several universities. [6]Researchers there rated the productivity of people in boring jobs. [7]Then they gave the workers brief puffs of pleasantly scented air. [8]The workers seemed to do better with peppermint or floral scents in the air. [9]In other studies, pleasant scents helped people to get along better with each other. [10]Maybe peace negotiations should be conducted in rose-scented rooms.

1. *Subject:* _____   *Verb:* _____
   The sentence is about a delicious *smell. Can make* (you hungry) is what it does.

2. *Subject:* _____   *Verb:* _____

3. *Subject:* _____   *Verb:* _____
   About the subject and *of odors* are prepositional phrases. *Researchers* are the ones doing something in the sentence. *Have discovered* (information) is what they have done.

4. *Subject:* _____   *Verb:* _____

5. *Subject:* _____   *Verb:* _____
   Of fragrance and *at several universities* are prepositional phrases. The sentence is about *effects. Have been studied* is what the sentence says about the effects.

6. *Subject:* _____   *Verb:* _____

7. *Subject:* _____   *Verb:* _____
   Of pleasantly scented air is a prepositional phrase. The persons who did something in the sentence are *they* (that is, the researchers); *gave* is what they did.

8. *Subject:* _____   *Verb:* _____

9. *Subject:* _____   *Verb:* _____
   In other studies and *with each other* are prepositional phrases. The sentence is about *scents; helped* (people to get along) is what they did.

10. *Subject:* _____   *Verb:* _____

Name _____ Section _____ Date _____

Score: (Number right) _____ × 5 = _____%

■ Subjects and Verbs: Test 6

Cross out the prepositional phrases. Then, on the lines provided, write the subject and verb of each of the sentences in the passage. Remember to find all the parts of the verb.

¹I will always remember my family's adventures in our blue minivan. ²At the beginning of every summer, we would load our blue Astro minivan with plenty of food, clothing, and games. ³Then we drove two thousand miles across the country to California. ⁴During every trip, something was guaranteed to go wrong. ⁵On one memorable occasion, a swarm of mosquitoes flew into our minivan. ⁶One of them landed on the windshield in front of my mom. ⁷Without a moment's hesitation, Mom squashed the mosquito with her palm. ⁸In doing so, she put a giant crack in the windshield. ⁹Two days later, pebbles from a passing truck struck the windshield with a mighty force, causing it to crack even more. ¹⁰By the end of our trip, the windshield, with all its cracks, was looking like a spider web.

1. *Subject:* _____ *Verb:* _____

2. *Subject:* _____ *Verb:* _____

3. *Subject:* _____ *Verb:* _____

4. *Subject:* _____ *Verb:* _____

5. *Subject:* _____ *Verb:* _____

6. *Subject:* _____ *Verb:* _____

7. *Subject:* _____ *Verb:* _____

8. *Subject:* _____ *Verb:* _____

9. *Subject:* _____ *Verb:* _____

10. *Subject:* _____ *Verb:* _____

2 More about Verbs

Seeing What You Know

For each pair, circle the letter of the sentence that you believe is correct. Then read the explanations that follow.

1. a. I brang the hot dogs to the picnic, but Jerry forgot the rolls.

   b. I brought the hot dogs to the picnic, but Jerry forgot the rolls.

2. a. Many children be afraid of thunder and lightning.

   b. Many children are afraid of thunder and lightning.

3. a. Please phone me as soon as the package arrives.

   b. Please phone me as soon as the package arrive.

4. a. Reba thought her boyfriend was faithful, but then she noticed him holding hands with another woman.

   b. Reba thought her boyfriend was faithful, but then she notices him holding hands with another woman.

Understanding the Answers

1. In the first pair, *b* is correct.
   Bring is an irregular verb; its past tense is *brought,* not *brang.*

2. In the second pair, *b* is correct.
   "Many children *be* afraid" is nonstandard English.

3. In the third pair, *a* is correct.
   Package is singular. In standard English, the verb that goes with it must end in *-s.*

4. In the fourth pair, *a* is correct.
   Since the action in the first part of the sentence is in the past *(thought her boyfriend was faithful),* the other verb in the sentence should be in the past as well *(noticed,* not *notices).*

This chapter covers three areas in which verb mistakes commonly occur: regular and irregular verbs, standard and nonstandard verbs, and shifts in verb tense.

REGULAR AND IRREGULAR VERBS

Verbs have four principal parts: the **basic form** (used to form the present tense), the **past tense**, the **past participle** (used with the helping verbs *have, has, had, is, are, was,* and *were*), and the **present participle** (the basic form of the verb plus *-ing*). All of the verb tenses come from one of the four principal parts of verbs.

Most English verbs are **regular**. That is, they form their past tense and past participle by adding *-d* or *-ed* to the basic form, like this:

Basic Form	Past Tense	Past Participle	Present Participle
ask	asked	asked	asking
drop	dropped	dropped	dropping
raise	raised	raised	raising

Irregular verbs, however, do not follow this pattern. They can have many different forms for the past and past participle. (The present participles, however, are formed in the usual way, by adding *-ing*.) Here are the four principal parts of some common irregular verbs:

Basic Form	Past Tense	Past Participle	Present Participle
become	became	become	becoming
begin	began	begun	beginning
blow	blew	blown	blowing
break	broke	broken	breaking
bring	brought	brought	bringing
catch	caught	caught	catching
choose	chose	chosen	choosing
cut	cut	cut	cutting
drink	drank	drunk	drinking
drive	drove	driven	driving
eat	ate	eaten	eating
fall	fell	fallen	falling
feel	felt	felt	feeling
find	found	found	finding
freeze	froze	frozen	freezing
get	got	got, gotten	getting
go	went	gone	going
hide	hid	hidden	hiding
keep	kept	kept	keeping
know	knew	known	knowing
lay	laid	laid	laying
leave	left	left	leaving

Basic Form	Past Tense	Past Participle	Present Participle
lend	lent	lent	lending
lie	lay	lain	lying
lose	lost	lost	losing
make	made	made	making
read	read	read	reading
ride	rode	ridden	riding
rise	rose	risen	rising
run	ran	run	running
say	said	said	saying
see	saw	seen	seeing
sell	sold	sold	selling
set	set	set	setting
shake	shook	shaken	shaking
sit	sat	sat	sitting
sleep	slept	slept	sleeping
spend	spent	spent	spending
swim	swam	swum	swimming
take	took	taken	taking
teach	taught	taught	teaching
tell	told	told	telling
think	thought	thought	thinking
throw	threw	thrown	throwing
wear	wore	worn	wearing
win	won	won	winning
write	wrote	written	writing

If you think a verb is irregular, and it is not in the list above, look it up in your dictionary. If it is irregular, the principal parts will be listed.

Practice 1

Underline the correct form of the verb in parentheses.

1. We (began, begun) to argue about which route to take to the stadium.

2. The high jumper has just (broke, broken) the world record.

3. After I had (ate, eaten) half of my brother's hot dog and had (drank, drunk) from his water bottle, I worried about catching his cold.

4. After the campers had (drove, driven) away, they looked back and (saw, seen) their dog running after them.

5. Before the writing course ended, students had (read, readed) fifteen essays, had (wrote, written) ten short papers, and had (took, taken) a midterm and a final exam.

STANDARD AND NONSTANDARD VERBS

Some of us are accustomed to using nonstandard English with our families and friends. Like slang, expressions such as *it ain't, we has, I be,* or *he don't* may be part of the rich language of a particular community or group.

However, nonstandard English can hold us back when used outside the home community, in both college and the working world. Standard English helps ensure that we will communicate clearly with other people, especially on the job.

The Differences between Standard and Nonstandard Verb Forms

Study the chart below, which shows both standard and nonstandard forms of the regular verb *like*. Practice using the standard forms in your speech and writing.

Nonstandard Forms		Standard Forms	
Present Tense			
I ~~likes~~	we ~~likes~~	I like	we like
you likes	you likes	you like	you like
~~he,~~ she, it like	they ~~likes~~	he, she, it likes	they like
Past Tense			
I ~~like~~	we ~~like~~	I liked	we liked
you like	you like	you liked	you liked
~~he,~~ she, it like	they ~~like~~	he, she, it liked	they liked

Notes

1 In standard English, always add *-s* or *-es* to a verb in the present tense when the subject is *he, she, it,* or any one person or thing (other than *I* or *you*).

Nonstandard: Aunt Bessie play bingo regularly at her church.
Standard: Aunt Bessie play**s** bingo regularly at her church.

2 Always add the ending *-d* or *-ed* to a regular verb to show it is past tense.

Nonstandard: Last year, Aunt Bessie play bingo 104 times.
Standard: Last year, Aunt Bessie play**ed** bingo 104 times.

Practice 2

Underline the standard form of the verb in parentheses.

1. On April Fools' Day, the principal (dress, dresses) up like a clown.

2. The fans groaned when the receiver (drop, dropped) the pass in the end zone.

3. I (look, looked) all over for my keys and finally found them in my coat pocket.

4. Most people (hate, hates) going to the dentist.

5. Though Kia moved last year, she still (manage, manages) to keep in touch.

Three Problem Verbs

Three irregular verbs that often cause special problems are *be, do,* and *have.* Non-standard English often uses forms such as *I be* (instead of *I am*), *you was* (instead of *you were*), *they has* (instead of *they have*), *he do* (instead of *he does*), and *she done* (instead of *she did*). Here are the correct present- and past-tense forms of these three verbs.

Present Tense		Past Tense	
Be			
I am	we are	I was	we were
you are	you are	you were	you were
he, she, it is	they are	he, she, it was	they were
Do			
I do	we do	I did	we did
you do	you do	you did	you did
he, she, it does	they do	he, she, it did	they did
Have			
I have	we have	I had	we had
you have	you have	you had	you had
he, she, it has	they have	he, she, it had	they had

Practice 3

Underline the standard form of the verb in parentheses.

1. To my surprise, my little sister (did, done) a terrific job of cleaning the house.

2. Jamal (have, has) the best handwriting in our family.

3. You (was, were) wrong to assume that because the instructor gave you a D, he dislikes you.

4. It (doesn't, don't) make sense to sign up for a course and then not go to class.

5. Fran (were, was) halfway to the supermarket when she realized she had no money in her wallet.

SHIFTS IN VERB TENSE

In writing and in conversation, people sometimes shift from one verb tense (the form of the verb that tells us when something happened) to another. Note the tense shifts in the following passage:

> With his oversized T-shirt, the little boy looked even smaller than he was. His skinny arms extend out of the flopping sleeves that reach to his elbows. He needed a haircut; he has to brush his bangs out of his eyes to see. His eyes fail to meet those of the people passing by as he asked them, "Could you give me fifty cents?"

Although the action is in the past, the writer continuously shifts from the past tense *(boy looked . . . he was . . . He needed . . . he asked)* to the present *(arms extend . . . that reach . . . he has . . . eyes fail)*. These tense shifts will confuse a reader, who won't know when the events happened. In the above passage, the verbs should be consistently in the past tense:

> With his oversized T-shirt, the little boy looked even smaller than he was. His skinny arms extended out of the flopping sleeves that reached to his elbows. He needed a haircut; he had to brush his bangs out of his eyes to see. His eyes failed to meet those of the people passing by as he asked them, "Could you give me fifty cents?"

In your own writing, shift tenses only when the time of the action actually changes.

Practice 4

Cross out the one verb in each item that is not in the same tense as the others. Then write the correct form of that verb on the line provided.

_____   1. The mossy green log lay in the shallow water. When it began to move, I realize that it was an alligator.

_____   2. Every time my mother feels like snacking, she brushes her teeth, and the hunger disappeared.

_____   3. I came home early because I felt sick; then I discover I did not have my house key.

_____   4. The children love going to the school library because they can take out any book they wanted, even if they can't read it yet.

_____   5. After the coach yells at him, Gary thought all night about quitting the team, but then he decided to give himself one more chance.

> **Note**   Additional information about verbs appears on pages 204–207.

Name _____ Section _____ Date _____

Score: (Number right) _____ × 10 = _____ %

■ More about Verbs: Test 1

For each sentence below, fill in the correct form of the verb.

Note To help you master the different verb skills in this chapter, directions are given for half of the sentences.

done
did

1. I _____ everything I could to get an *A* in the class, but I still got a *B*.
   Use the past tense of the irregular verb *do*.

stops
stop

2. The student guides on our campus _____ at every building to explain what's inside.

become
became

3. When my son _____ a doctor, he decided to work at a clinic instead of a private practice.
   Use the past test of the irregular verb *become*.

ate
eaten

4. The children have already _____ all the Halloween candy.

starts
started

5. A colorful hot-air balloon drifted over the meadow, and then it _____ a slow descent to the landing area.
   The sentence begins in the past tense, so the past tense of *start* is needed.

forgets
forgot

6. The man began to introduce his boss; then, in his nervousness, he _____ his boss's name.

be
is

7. My brother and I are outgoing, but our sister _____ very shy.
   Use the standard present tense form of the verb.

has
have

8. Some people brag a lot about their money-making schemes, but they never actually _____ very much cash.

ran
run

9. When the girls returned to the locker room after their softball game, they were arguing about who had _____ the bases the fastest.
   Use the past participle of the irregular verb *run*.

wore
worn

10. Martin enjoys wearing his old blue shorts so much that he has practically _____ them out.

Name _____ Section _____ Date _____

Score: (Number right) _____ × 10 = _____ %

■ More about Verbs: Test 2

For each sentence below, fill in the correct form of the verb.

drove
drived

1. To get home in time for her family's Thanksgiving dinner, Eve _____ the whole night without stopping.

are
were

2. Two flavorings that seem to go well with just about everything _____ garlic and lemon juice.

wrote
written

3. So many students had _____ such poor essays that over half the class failed the exam.

was
were

4. In the original *Star Trek* television series, Captain James T. Kirk's middle name _____ Tiberius.

needs
needed

5. The manager of the auto repair shop telephoned a customer with the bad news that his car's transmission _____ replacing.

did
done

6. Sarita was told not to leave the house until she had _____ all her chores.

jams
jam

7. The copying machine always _____ when someone tries to make more than ten copies of anything.

flew
flown

8. Most of the birds have already _____ south for the winter, and it's not even October yet.

serve
served

9. The waiter took our order, disappeared for twenty minutes, and then _____ us the wrong food.

took
taken

10. Delores didn't do very much work on the project, but she has _____ all the credit.

Name _____ Section _____ Date _____

Score: (Number right) _____ × 10 = _____%

■ More about Verbs: Test 3

Each of the items below contains **two** of the types of verb mistakes discussed in this chapter. Find and cross out these two mistakes. Then, in the spaces provided, write the correct forms of the verbs.

Note   To help you master the different verb skills in this chapter, directions are given for one of the mistakes in each group of sentences.

1. The boy ran into the house and angrily throws his books on the kitchen table. "I've spended enough time on school," he shouted. "On Monday I'm quitting and getting a job."

   a. _____   Change the one present tense verb to the
   b. _____   past tense.

2. Even though Rita winned her company's "Employee of the Month" award, she doesn't believe she be doing a good enough job. She worries all the time that she's about to be fired.

   a. _____   Use the past tense of the irregular
   b. _____   verb *win.*

3. I tried to stay interested in the movie, but as it turn more and more boring, I began to feel sleepy. Next thing I knew, my brother had shook me awake. "You slept through the whole second half," he said accusingly.

   a. _____   Use the standard English past tense of
   b. _____   the regular verb *turn.*

4. The dog circled the tree and then barks as if he spotted something. We looked up and seen a raccoon hiding among the leaves.

   a. _____   Other verbs in the passage (*circled,*
   b. _____   *looked,* etc.) are in the past tense.

5. Because he was working part-time while he was in college, Toshio knowed it would take a long time for him to finish his degree. However, he believes that a college degree was worth the time and effort.

   a. _____   Use the past tense of the irregular
   b. _____   verb *know.*

■ More about Verbs: Test 4

Each of the items below contains **two** of the types of verb mistakes discussed in this chapter. Find and cross out these two mistakes. Then, in the spaces provided, write the correct forms of the verbs.

1. "Whatever becomed of the boy I sat next to in our high-school English class?" I asked my best friend. She tells me that he went to Hollywood and was now a well-known screenwriter.

   a. _____

   b. _____

2. Last year my nephew readed *Charlotte's Web,* a story about a spider who made friends with a pig. He liked the story a great deal. In fact, afterward he refuse to eat bacon or kill spiders.

   a. _____

   b. _____

3. The housepainters didn't seem to be very well organized. First, they forgot what day they were supposed to begin work. Then once they finish the job, they leaved a ladder behind.

   a. _____

   b. _____

4. When she was in her twenties, Belle decide to become a registered nurse. For years, she worked during the day, attends classes in the evening, and then came home and cared for her children.

   a. _____

   b. _____

5. Every time Megan placed her new puppy out on the porch for the night, he cries pitifully. After she brought his box into the living room, he were quiet for the rest of the night.

   a. _____

   b. _____

Name _____ Section _____ Date _____

Score: (Number right) _____ × 10 = _____%

■ More about Verbs: Test 5

Each of the sentences in the following passage contains one of the verb problems discussed in this chapter. Underline these errors. Then, in the spaces provided, write the correct forms of the verbs.

Note To help you master the different verb skills in this chapter, directions are given for five of the sentences.

¹When I lived in the jungle of Costa Rica, I encounter many different types of wildlife, some of which did truly weird or scary things. ²One morning we discovered that a monkey had ate some mangoes that we had set on the porch for our breakfast. ³Later, an armadillo in the road jump straight up and hit the underside of our jeep. ⁴Another time an armadillo stay underwater for five minutes. ⁵My roommate, Julia, were surprised to find a scorpion in her bed. ⁶Julia and I seen a cockroach the size of my hand above the refrigerator. ⁷One night, while I was sitting at my desk, a tarantula falled onto my head. ⁸I shook it off and begun screaming as it ran outside. ⁹My neighbor, Diane, nearly trip over a poisonous snake on her porch. ¹⁰Shaking with fear, Diane and I watch as the snake slithered away into the grass.

1. _____   The second verb should match the past tense form of the other verbs.

2. _____

3. _____   Use the standard English form of the regular verb *jump*.

4. _____

5. _____   Use the correct past tense form of the irregular verb *be*.

6. _____

7. _____   Use the correct past tense of the irregular verb *fall*.

8. _____

9. _____   Use the standard English form of the regular verb *trip*.

10. _____

Name _____ Section _____ Date _____

Score: (Number right) _____ × 10 = _____%

■ More about Verbs: Test 6

Each of the sentences in the following passage contains one of the verb problems discussed in this chapter. Underline these errors. Then, in the spaces provided, write the correct forms of the verbs.

[1]Vincent Van Gogh were one of the greatest painters of all time. [2]But during his own lifetime, people consider Van Gogh a failure, even a madman. [3]Only one Van Gogh painting selled while he was alive. [4]Van Gogh was an odd, passionate man with whom few people feeled comfortable. [5]An illness that causes him to behave in violent, self-destructive ways made his life difficult. [6]During one attack of this illness, he remove part of his ear with a razor. [7]Lonely and isolated, Van Gogh throwed himself into his work. [8]He often produce a wonderful painting in just one day. [9]His intense, colorful paintings of sunflowers and wheat fields have became world-famous since his death, and collectors now pay millions of dollars for them. [10]Sadly, Van Gogh ends his own unhappy life when he was only thirty-seven.

1. _____

2. _____

3. _____

4. _____

5. _____

6. _____

7. _____

8. _____

9. _____

10. _____

3 Subject-Verb Agreement

Seeing What You Know

Underline the verb that you think should be used in each of the following sentences. Then read the explanations below.

1. The two gray cats sitting by the trash can (belongs, belong) to a neighbor.

2. Which one of the bikes (is, are) Enrique going to buy?

3. Nobody in my family (carries, carry) a gun.

4. Chicago and Atlanta (has, have) the busiest airports in the United States.

Understanding the Answers

1. The two gray cats sitting by the trash can **belong** to a neighbor.
   The subject, *cats,* is plural, so the verb must be plural as well.

2. Which one of the bikes **is** Enrique **going** to buy?
   The subject, *Enrique,* and the verb, *is going,* are both singular.

3. Nobody in my family **carries** a gun.
   The subject, *nobody,* is a singular indefinite pronoun, so it requires a singular verb.

4. Chicago and Atlanta **have** the busiest airports in the United States.
   Chicago and Atlanta is a compound subject and requires a plural verb.

In a correctly written sentence, the subject and verb **agree** (match) **in number**. Singular subjects have singular verbs; plural subjects have plural verbs.

In a simple sentence of few words, it's not difficult to make the subject (*s*) and verb (*v*) agree:

$$s \qquad v \; (plural) \qquad\qquad\qquad s \qquad v \; (singular)$$

My **parents** **work** at two jobs. My **grandmother** **takes** care of the children.

However, not all sentences are this straightforward. This chapter will present four types of situations that can pose problems in subject-verb agreement: (1) subject and verb separated by a prepositional phrase, (2) verb coming before the subject, (3) indefinite pronoun subject, and (4) compound subjects.

1 SUBJECT AND VERB SEPARATED BY A PREPOSITIONAL PHRASE

In many sentences, the subject is close to the verb, with the subject coming first. But in some sentences, the subject and verb do not appear side by side:

$$s \qquad\qquad\qquad v$$

Most **stores** in the mall **are having** sales this weekend.

Who or what is the sentence about? The answer is *stores* (not *mall*). What are the stores doing? They *are having* (sales). Since the subject *(stores)* is plural, the verb *(are having)* must be plural as well.

In the sentence above, a prepositional phrase, *in the mall,* separates the subject and the verb. (A **prepositional phrase** is a group of words that begins with a preposition and ends with a noun or pronoun. *In, on, for, from, of, to,* and *by* are prepositions; a longer list of prepositions is on page 18.) Remember that the subject of the sentence is never part of a prepositional phrase. To find the subject, cross out prepositional phrases. Then make the verb agree with the subject—not with a word in the prepositional phrase.

Practice 1

Cross out the prepositional phrases in the sentences below. Then underline the subject of each sentence. Finally, double-underline the verb in parentheses that agrees with the subject.

1. The workers behind the counter (likes, like) to joke with their customers.

2. Two women on my bowling team always (scores, score) over 250.

3. The noise in the city streets sometimes (hurts, hurt) my ears.

4. A bag of nonfat potato chips (contains, contain) 440 calories.

5. The instructions for downloading software from the Internet (is, are) confusing for many people.

2 VERB COMING BEFORE THE SUBJECT

In most English sentences, the verb follows the subject. (*I saw an eagle. The knife fell to the floor. A train crashed.*) But in some sentences, the verb comes *before* the subject. These sentences often are questions, or they may begin with prepositional phrases or word groups like *there is* and *here are*. The verb must agree with the subject—even when the verb comes before the subject.

> There **are** many starving **actors** in Hollywood. *(Plural verb, plural subject)*
>
> Here **is** the data **file** for that project. *(Singular verb, singular subject)*
>
> In that box **are** other **supplies**. *(Plural verb, plural subject)*
>
> What **was** the **purpose** of that assignment? *(Singular verb, singular subject)*

If you are not sure of the subject in a sentence, find the verb and then ask "Who?" or "What?" In the first sentence above, for example, you would ask, "What are there in Hollywood?" The answer, "starving *actors,*" is the subject. For the second sentence, the question would be, "What is here?" The answer: "The data *file.*"

Practice 2

Cross out the prepositional phrases in the sentences below. Then underline the subject of each sentence. Finally, double-underline the verb in parentheses that agrees with the subject.

1. Where (is, are) the keys to the minivan?

2. Underneath that big rock (lives, live) hundreds of bugs.

3. There (was, were) seventeen people ahead of me in the bank line today.

4. Why (does, do) dogs always bark the loudest at 2 a.m.?

5. Inside each cardboard carton (is, are) a dozen boxes of Girl Scout cookies.

3 INDEFINITE PRONOUN SUBJECTS

The following **indefinite pronouns** always take singular verbs.

Singular Indefinite Pronouns			
each	anyone	anybody	anything
either	everyone	everybody	everything
neither	someone	somebody	something
one	no one	nobody	nothing

Note the subject-verb relationships in the following sentences with indefinite pronouns:

One of those writing courses **is** still open. *(Singular subject, singular verb)*

Neither of my parents **has** called. *(Singular subject, singular verb)*

Somebody was reading my mail. *(Singular subject, singular verb)*

Everyone loves to get something for nothing. *(Singular subject, singular verb)*

Practice 3

Underline the subject of each sentence. Then double-underline the verb in parentheses that agrees with the subject.

1. Everything on those shelves (is, are) on sale at 50 percent off.

2. Neither of the lights in the basement (works, work).

3. No one in my family (is, are) right-handed.

4. Each of those kittens (deserves, deserve) a good home.

5. Everybody in my apartment building (knows, know) when someone is having a party.

4 COMPOUND SUBJECTS

A **compound subject**—usually two or more subjects joined by *and*—requires a plural verb.

Rent and car insurance **were** my biggest expenses each month.

There **are** canoes and sailboats for rent.

Do the TV and DVD player **provide** stereo sound?

Practice 4

Underline the compound subject of each sentence. Then double-underline the verb in parentheses that agrees with the compound subject.

1. Our cats and dog (stays, stay) at a neighbor's house when we go on vacation.

2. (Is, Are) all the CDs and DVDs in the store included in the sale?

3. My sister and her best friend (drive, drives) to the gym every morning at 5 A.M.

4. The scratches and dents on our new car (was, were) definitely our son's fault.

5. My accounting course and my statistics course (requires, require) long written reports.

Note   Additional information about subject-verb agreement appears on pages 208–209.

Name _____   Section _____   Date _____

■ Subject-Verb Agreement: Test 1

In each sentence, fill in the correct form of the missing verb.

Note   To help you learn subject-verb agreement, explanations are given for five of the sentences.

likes
like

1. Nobody _____ to be laughed at.
   Nobody is an indefinite pronoun that always requires a singular verb.

smells
smell

2. Everything in our attic _____ of mothballs.

is
are

3. Black and white _____ the only colors Jermaine wears.
   Black and white is a compound subject requiring a plural verb.

makes
make

4. Bright yellow daisies and blue morning glories _____ the tiny yard beautiful.

gives
give

5. The lamps on either side of the couch _____ very little light.
   Lamps, the subject, is a plural noun and so needs a plural verb. *On either side* and *of the couch* are prepositional phrases. The subject is never in—or affected by—a prepositional phrase.

needs
need

6. All the suits in my closet except one _____ to get cleaned.

was
were

7. There _____ three accidents on the freeway this morning.
   When a sentence begins with *here* or *there,* the subject will come after the verb. *Accidents,* the subject, is plural, so it requires a plural verb.

is
are

8. Here _____ the names of three doctors you can call.

is
are

9. When _____ the deadline for dropping a course?
   In a question, the subject often follows the verb. The subject, *deadline,* is singular, so it requires a singular verb form.

Does
Do

10. _____ your aunt and uncle know that you wrote an essay about them?

Name _____   Section _____   Date _____

Score: (Number right) _____ × 10 = _____%

■ Subject-Verb Agreement: Test 2

In each sentence, fill in the correct form of the missing verb.

stands
stand

1. Across the street _____ the oldest house in town.

belongs
belong

2. The leather jacket beside the books _____ to our teacher.

remain
remains

3. Mark and Wayne _____ friends even though they disagree on almost everything.

annoys
annoy

4. Junk e-mail and chain letters _____ many Internet users.

Is
Are

5. _____ those parking spaces in front of the administration building reserved for the faculty?

attracts
attract

6. The flowers in my neighbor's garden _____ many butterflies.

is
are

7. Magnolia trees and Spanish moss _____ common in many parts of the South.

was
were

8. Running down the back alley toward the fire _____ several police officers.

seems
seem

9. Three of the boys on the team _____ to be more interested in the cheerleaders than the game.

is
are

10. Every one of my roommates _____ depressed over getting poor grades on the psychology exam.

Name _____   Section _____ Date _____

Score: (Number right) _____ × 10 = _____%

■ Subject-Verb Agreement: Test 3

Each of the following passages contains **two** mistakes in subject-verb agreement. Find and underline the two verbs that do not agree with their subjects. Then write the correct form of each verb in the spaces provided.

Note   To help you learn subject-verb agreement, explanations are given for the first mistake in each passage.

1. Construction of the apartment buildings have been going on for months. The noise from the bulldozers, cranes, and backhoes are deafening. Everyone in the neighborhood wants it to end.

   a. _____   *Of the apartment buildings* is a prepositional phrase. The
   b. _____   subject of the first sentence, *construction,* is singular.

2. It is not true that the skin of snakes are slimy. Also, warts are not caused by touching a toad. Why does reptiles and amphibians have so many false stories told about them?

   a. _____   The subject of the first sentence is *skin; of snakes* is a
   b. _____   prepositional phrase.

3. Neither of the drivers were injured in the accident. However, both cars, a green Jaguar and a cherry-red Corvette, was totaled.

   a. _____   *Neither* is a singular indefinite pronoun that needs a
   b. _____   singular verb.

4. The new employee's quick wit and willingness to work hard pleases her boss very much. She is the kind of person whom everyone in the office enjoy having as a coworker.

   a. _____   The compound subject, *wit and willingness,* requires
   b. _____   a plural verb.

5. "Having a successful marriage is not easy," admitted Neal. "There has been many times I've thought about leaving. However, my commitment to my marriage and my love for my family stops me. Later, I'm always glad that I stayed."

   a. _____   The subject of the second sentence, *times,* is plural.
   b. _____

Name _____ Section _____ Date _____

Score: (Number right) _____ × 10 = _____ %

■ Subject-Verb Agreement: Test 4

Each of the following passages contains **two** mistakes in subject-verb agreement. Find and underline the two verbs that do not agree with their subjects. Then write the correct form of each verb in the spaces provided.

1. My friend Daniel and I was walking to the mall when we saw an injured cat in the parking lot. There was two other people walking behind us who stopped to help, and they volunteered to take the cat to their veterinarian.

   a. _____

   b. _____

2. There are a lot of young women in my office. It seems as if everyone have had a baby recently. All the baby presents costs me a fortune.

   a. _____

   b. _____

3. High on the closet shelf is several brightly wrapped packages—the little girl's birthday presents. The girl knows that they are there. Every day, she and her sister tries for hours to guess what might be inside those mysterious boxes.

   a. _____

   b. _____

4. Cara invited her two sisters to the party, but neither of them are coming. Each sister is busy, one with a work deadline and the other with a school reunion. "Why," Cara complained, "does the only important events in their lives this month have to happen at the same time?"

   a. _____

   b. _____

5. The computers in the office gives me heartburn. Everybody, it seems, have success with them except me. I'm going to take a computer course so I can show them who is boss.

   a. _____

   b. _____

Name _____   Section _____   Date _____

Score: (Number right) _____ × 10 = _____ %

■ Subject-Verb Agreement: Test 5

Each sentence in the following passage contains one mistake in subject-verb agreement. Find and underline the ten verbs that do not agree with their subjects. Then write the correct form of each verb on the lines below.

Note   To help you learn subject-verb agreement, explanations are given for five of the mistakes.

[1]I have never understood why there is so many followers of World Wrestling Entertainment (WWE). [2]At first, I thought the fans who watched wrestling on television was crazy if they believed that the matches were real. [3]One of these fans happen to be engaged to my daughter, so I asked Anthony to explain why WWE is so popular. ([4]From childhood, his friends and he was so caught up in the wrestling frenzy that they would even hold wrestling shows in their backyards. [5]In fact, a few friends, for Anthony's 28th birthday, plans to host a party with a wrestling theme and even some friendly competitions.) [6]According to Anthony, it is the E in WWE that tell the whole story. [7]Fans of wrestling sees spectacular moves and athleticism. [8]They understand there is a scripted storyline (like soap operas), and each of them enjoy learning as much as possible about favorite wrestling superstars. [9]Finally, anybody who watches the matches know that some of the moves are rehearsed, like fight scenes in movies. [10]So I now realize that wrestling fanatics, like Anthony, is not crazy; they're just looking for a good time, an amusing storyline, and a few hours of pure entertainment.

1. _____   The subject is *followers,* not *there. Is,* a singular verb, needs to be replaced by a plural verb.

2. _____

3. _____   *One,* an indefinite pronoun, is singular, and thus needs a singular verb.

4. _____

5. _____   The subject, *friends,* is plural and requires a plural verb.

6. _____

7. _____   The subject is *Fans,* so the singular verb, *sees,* needs to be replaced by a plural verb.

8. _____

9. _____   The subject is *anybody,* a singular pronoun, so a singular verb must be used.

10. _____

Name _____ Section _____ Date _____

Score: (Number right) _____ × 10 = _____%

■ Subject-Verb Agreement: Test 6

Each sentence in the following passage contains one mistake in subject-verb agreement. Find and underline the ten verbs that do not agree with their subjects. Then write the correct form of each verb on the lines below.

¹Millions of tons of trash floats in our oceans. ²There is all kinds of items, including fishing nets and bottles. ³Currents in the ocean carries this debris so that it collects in big areas known as garbage patches. ⁴These areas of garbage has been increasing in size since plastic came to be commonly used, about sixty years ago. ⁵Anything made of plastic materials are very durable and buoyant, so it will float in the ocean for many years. ⁶The biggest one of the garbage patches lie about halfway between Hawaii and San Francisco; it is about the size of Texas and is at least 100 feet deep. ⁷Why is these garbage patches such a problem? ⁸For one thing, birds and fish mistakes the plastic for food and are dying. ⁹In addition, if they eat these fish, animals and people risks harm from the plastic or from poisonous substances in the garbage. ¹⁰Until everyone finally stop making so much trash, there is no point in trying to clean up the garbage patches.

1. _____

2. _____

3. _____

4. _____

5. _____

6. _____

7. _____

8. _____

9. _____

10. _____

4 Sentence Types

Seeing What You Know

A. In each blank, add a word that fits the sentence.

1. The noisy _____ woke the baby.

2. The forest ranger _____ at the campers.

B. In each sentence that follows, insert *and, but,* or *so.* Use each word once.

3. My pencil is broken, _____ my pen is out of ink.

4. The pool is closed, _____ we can't go swimming.

5. I have an envelope, _____ I can't find a stamp.

C. In each sentence that follows, insert *after, although,* or *because.* Use each word once.

6. We called an exterminator _____ we have termites.

7. _____ their big fight, Jessica sent her boyfriend flowers.

8. _____ my closet is full of clothes, I have nothing to wear.

Understanding the Answers

A. Sentence 1 could be completed with a subject such as *party;* the verb is *woke.* Sentence 2 could be completed with a verb such as *waved;* the subject is *ranger.*
Some sentences in English are **simple,** made up of one subject-verb combination expressing a complete thought. Sentences 1 and 2 are examples of simple sentences.

B. You should have inserted *and* in sentence 3, *so* in 4, and *but* in 5.
Other sentences are **compound,** made up of two or more complete thoughts connected by a joining word such as *and, so,* or *but.* Sentences 3–5 are all compound sentences.

C. You should have inserted *because* in sentence 6, *after* in 7, and *although* in 8.
Yet other sentences are **complex,** made up of one complete thought and at least one dependent thought. Dependent thoughts begin with a dependent word such as *because, although,* or *after.* Sentences 6–8 are all complex sentences.

The three most basic kinds of sentences in English are simple, compound, and complex sentences. This chapter explains and provides practice in all three sentence types. It also discusses two types of words you can use to combine ideas into one sentence: (1) joining words (for compound sentences) and (2) dependent words (for complex sentences).

THE SIMPLE SENTENCE

A **simple sentence** has only one subject-verb combination and expresses a complete thought.

> An owl hooted.
>
> The winning contestant could have chosen money or a car.

A simple sentence may have more than one subject:

> Lemons and limes taste sharp and tangy.
>
> (In this sentence, *lemons* and *limes* are the subjects.)

A simple sentence may have more than one verb:

> The puppies nipped and nuzzled one another playfully.
>
> (In this sentence, *nipped* and *nuzzled* are the verbs.)

A simple sentence may even have several subjects and verbs:

> Every New Year's Eve, my parents, aunts, and uncles eat, dance, and welcome the new year together.
>
> (There are three subjects in this sentence: *parents, aunts,* and *uncles.* There are also three verbs: *eat, dance,* and *welcome.*)

Practice 1

Complete the simple sentences below by filling in one or more subjects, one or more verbs, or both.

1. That _____ needs to be washed.

2. A thoughtless driver _____ an empty soda can onto the highway.

3. _____ and _____ make a delicious sandwich combination.

4. Mike and _____ often _____ together in the park.

5. _____ and _____ looked at old family photographs and then _____ dinner on the porch.

THE COMPOUND SENTENCE

A **compound sentence** is made up of two or more complete thoughts. For instance, look at the following simple sentences:

Supper is ready.

The guests have not arrived.

These two simple sentences can be combined to form one compound sentence:

Supper is ready, **but** the guests have not arrived.

The process of joining two ideas of equal importance is known as **coordination.** Put a comma plus a joining word (also known as a **coordinating conjunction**), such as *and, but,* or *so,* between the two complete thoughts. Other joining words— *or, for, nor,* and *yet*—appear on pages 73 and 212–213.

The cover is torn off this book, **and** the last few pages are missing. (**And** means *in addition:* The cover is torn off this book; *in addition,* the last few pages are missing.)

The kittens are darling, **but** we can't have another pet. (**But** means *however:* The kittens are darling; *however,* we can't have another pet.)

Kendra has to get up early tomorrow, **so** she isn't going to the party tonight. (**So** means *as a result:* Kendra has to get up early tomorrow; *as a result,* she isn't going to the party tonight.)

Practice 2

Use a comma and a suitable joining word to combine each pair of simple sentences into a compound sentence. Use each of the following joining words **once.**

and	but	so

1. I turned in my paper two days early.
   It was on the wrong topic.

   _____

   _____

2. All my clothes were dirty this morning.
   I'm wearing my husband's shirt.

   _____

   _____

3. Virginia has learned karate.
   She carries a can of self-defense spray.

   _____

   _____

THE COMPLEX SENTENCE

As you have learned, a compound sentence is made up of two or more complete thoughts. Each thought could stand alone as an independent statement. A **complex sentence**, on the other hand, includes one independent statement and at least one dependent statement, which *cannot* stand alone. Look at the following example:

If it thunders, our dog hides under the bed.

The second statement in this sentence is **independent**. It can stand alone as a simple sentence: *Our dog hides under the bed.* The first statement, however, cannot stand alone. It is **dependent**—it depends on the rest of the sentence to finish the thought *If it thunders.* Dependent statements begin with dependent words (also known as **subordinating conjunctions**), such as *after, although, as, because, when,* and *while.* (A full list is on page 60.) A dependent statement also includes a subject and a verb. (The subject of the dependent statement above is *it;* the verb is *thunders.*)

Punctuation note   Put a comma at the end of a dependent statement that begins a sentence, as in the example above.

Practice 3

Combine each pair of simple sentences into a complex sentence. To change a simple sentence into a dependent statement, add a dependent word to it, as shown in the example. Choose a suitable dependent word from the following:

after   **although**   **as**

Use each word **once**. Put a comma after a dependent statement that starts a sentence.

Example   We ate the pork chops with our hands.
            We were out of clean silverware.
            We ate the pork chops with our hands because we were out of clean silverware.

1. The familiar "Wedding March" played.
   The bride and her father walked down the aisle.

   _____

   _____

2. Jeff broke out in red blotches.
   He walked through a bank of poison ivy.

   _____

   _____

3. The chocolate cake was delicious.
   Everyone at the dinner party was dieting.

   _____

   _____

Name _____   Section _____   Date _____

Score: (Number right) _____ × 20 = _____ %

■ Sentence Types: Test 1

Part A   Use a comma and a suitable joining word to combine the following pairs of simple sentences into compound sentences. Choose from *and, but,* and *so.*

1. One of the concertgoers had fainted in the restroom.
   I ran out to get help.

   _____

   _____

2. My niece is an excellent basketball player.
   She does not plan to try out for the team.

   _____

   _____

Part B   Use a suitable dependent word to combine the following pairs of simple sentences into complex sentences. Choose from *although, because,* and *when.* Use each word **once**. Place a comma after a dependent statement when it starts a sentence.

3. Sandra never rides the Ferris wheel.
   She is afraid of heights.

   _____

   _____

4. I get home after work.
   I'll give you a call.

   _____

   _____

5. Melissa has played the guitar since she was seven years old.
   She does not know how to read music.

   _____

   _____

Name _____   Section _____   Date _____

Score: (Number right) _____ × 20 = _____%

■ Sentence Types: Test 2

Part A   Use a comma and a suitable joining word to combine the following pairs of simple sentences into compound sentences. Choose from *and, but,* and *so.*

1. Neither of us had a car or a bicycle.
   We decided to jog to the library.

   _____

   _____

2. The workers dripped paint on the carpet.
   They stomped through the flower bed.

   _____

   _____

Part B   Use a suitable dependent word to combine the following pairs of simple sentences into complex sentences. Choose from *although, because,* and *when.* Use each word **once**. Place a comma after a dependent statement when it starts a sentence.

3. Strawberries become ripe.
   They must be picked quickly.

   _____

   _____

4. Flora has six brothers and sisters.
   She never talks about her family.

   _____

   _____

5. I was nervous all morning.
   I had to get a tooth extracted in the afternoon.

   _____

   _____

Name _____ Section _____ Date _____

Score: (Number right) _____ × 20 = _____%

■ Sentence Types: Test 3

Combine each group of simple sentences into compound sentences, complex sentences, or both. Write two sentences for item 1 and three sentences for item 2. Use any of the following joining words and dependent words.

Joining words:	**and**	**but**	**so**	
Dependent words:	**after**	**although**	**because**	**when**

Here are two hints about commas: (1) Use a comma between two thoughts joined by *and, but,* or *so.* (2) Place a comma after a dependent statement when it starts a sentence.

1. I was seventeen years old and not very mature.
   I decided to start my own business.
   The business failed after a few months.
   I knew nothing about making sales or managing money.

   _____

   _____

   _____

   _____

   _____

   _____

2. Grandpa never graduated from high school.
   He strongly believes in education.
   He was the first one to take me to a library.
   He has always encouraged me to study hard.
   Grandpa retired from his job at the factory.
   He began studying to get a high-school diploma.

   _____

   _____

   _____

   _____

   _____

   _____

Name _____ Section _____ Date _____

Score: (Number right) _____ × 20 = _____ %

■ Sentence Types: Test 4

Combine each group of simple sentences into compound and/or complex sentences. Write two sentences for item 1 and three sentences for item 2. Use any of the following joining words and dependent words.

Joining words:	**and**	**but**	**so**	
Dependent words:	**after**	**although**	**because**	**when**

Here are two hints about commas: (1) Use a comma between two thoughts joined by *and, but,* or *so.* (2) Place a comma after a dependent statement when it starts a sentence.

1. Robert Louis Stevenson wrote about Dr. Jekyll and Mr. Hyde.
   He heard about a man named William Brodie.
   Brodie was a respected businessman during the day.
   At night he led a gang of robbers.

   _____

   _____

   _____

   _____

   _____

   _____

2. You want to save money in the supermarket.
   You should learn where the bargains are and are not.
   Managers want to sell high-cost items like imported mustard.
   They place those items on eye-level shelves.
   Shoppers are less likely to look on lower shelves.
   Managers put less profitable items there.

   _____

   _____

   _____

   _____

   _____

   _____

Name _____ Section _____ Date _____

Score: (Number right) _____ × 20 = _____ %

■ Sentence Types: Test 5

Combine the five pairs of italicized simple sentences into compound or complex sentences. Write the new sentences on the lines provided, adding commas as needed. Use any of the following joining words and dependent words. (Remember that there is more than one way of revising these sentences.)

Joining words:	**and**	**but**	**so**	
Dependent words:	**although**	**as**	**because**	**while**

Here are two hints about commas: (1) Use a comma between two thoughts joined by *and, but,* or *so.* (2) Place a comma after a dependent statement when it starts a sentence.

Jay's fishing trip with his buddies was not exactly a success. *They drove to the cabin in the mountains. They had a flat tire.* _____

_____

Once they arrived at the cabin, they found the last renters had left the place in terrible condition. *The cabin was full of dirty dishes, empty food containers, food scraps, and newspapers. Jay and his friends had to spend a long time cleaning.*

_____

_____

They did manage to catch a few trout before suppertime. Bad luck soon struck again. _____

_____

Jay was frying fish over the campfire. His flannel shirt burst into flames.

_____

_____

Thinking quickly, Jay jumped into the nearby lake and put the fire out. The guys went to bed early after their unlucky first day. *"Surely tomorrow will be better," thought Jay, climbing into his bunk. He was wrong.* _____

_____

As Jay ran down the stairs the next morning, a step broke under his weight. He spent the rest of the day in a nearby emergency room, having a cast put on his broken ankle.

■ Sentence Types: Test 6

Combine the five pairs of italicized simple sentences into compound or complex sentences. Write the new sentences on the lines provided, adding commas as needed. Use any of the following joining words and dependent words. (Remember that there is more than one way of revising these sentences.)

| *Joining words:* | **and** | **but** | **so** | |
| *Dependent words:* | **although** | **as** | **because** | **before** |

Each year for four days in early August, hundreds of thousands of people shop at the world's longest yard sale. *The sale runs from northern Ohio to Alabama. It includes parts of five states.* _____

_____

_____.

The sale is more than 600 miles long. It runs mostly along US Highway 127.

_____

_____.

The sale began more than twenty years ago to encourage people to exit the highways and explore rural areas in the United States. All sorts of items can be found at the sale. *Residents fill their yards with unwanted items. Professional vendors, such as antiques dealers, also offer merchandise to the shoppers.* _____

_____

_____.

The emphasis is on the yard sale. The route also includes beautiful scenery, national parks, museums, and entertainment. _____

_____

_____

Visitors to the yard sale could not possibly see everything in just four days. They might want to drive a different stretch of the route each year. _____

_____

_____

5 Fragments

Seeing What You Know

Underline the statement in each item that you think is *not* a complete sentence. Then read the explanations below.

1. After the shopping mall opened. Several local stores went out of business.

2. The nursing student poked my arm four times. Trying to take a blood sample. I was beginning to feel like a pincushion.

3. Some young people are learning old-fashioned dances. Such as the waltz, polka, and Lindy.

4. The manager always wears a suit and tie to the office. Then takes off his jacket and tie by ten o'clock.

Understanding the Answers

1. *After the shopping mall opened* is not a complete sentence.
   The writer does not follow through and complete the thought by telling us what happened after the shopping mall opened. Correct the fragment by adding it to the sentence that follows it.

2. *Trying to take a blood sample* is not a complete sentence.
   The word group lacks both a subject and a verb, and it does not express a complete thought. Correct the fragment by adding it to the sentence that precedes it.

3. *Such as the waltz, polka, and Lindy* is not a complete sentence.
   Again, the word group lacks a subject and a verb, and it does not express a complete thought. Correct the fragment by adding it to the sentence that precedes it.

4. *Then takes off his jacket and tie by ten o'clock* is not a complete sentence.
   The word group lacks a subject. Correct the fragment by adding the subject *he*.

To be a complete sentence, a group of words must contain a subject and a verb. It must also express a complete thought—in other words, it must make sense by itself. A **fragment** is *less than a sentence* because it lacks a subject, lacks a verb, or does not express a complete thought.

This chapter describes the most common types of fragments: dependent-word fragments, -*ing* and *to* fragments, added-detail fragments, and missing-subject fragments.

DEPENDENT-WORD FRAGMENTS

Although dependent-word fragments contain a subject and a verb, they do not express a complete thought. To complete the thought, they depend on another statement, usually one that comes after the fragment. For instance, below is a word group that starts with the dependent word *because*. The incomplete thought it expresses is completed in the statement that follows it.

Because there was a mosquito in the room. I could not fall asleep.

The dependent-word group is a fragment because it does not express a complete thought. It leaves the reader expecting something more. The writer must follow through *in the same sentence* and tell what happened because there was a mosquito in the room. In the sentence below, the writer has corrected the fragment by completing the thought in one sentence:

Because there was a mosquito in the room, I could not fall asleep.

Here is a list of some common dependent words:

Dependent Words				
after	even if	since	until	wherever
although	even though	so that	what	whether
as	how	that	when	which
because	if	though	whenever	while
before	in order that	unless	where	who

Whenever you begin a statement with a dependent word, make sure that you complete your thought. Look at the following examples:

Although we had eaten a full meal. We still ordered dessert. The rum cake was irresistible.

Some people are victims of migraine headaches. That force them to lie motionless in bed for many hours. Medications do not offer much relief.

The word groups that begin with the dependent words *although* and *that* are fragments. Neither word group expresses a complete thought. The reader wants to know *what happened* although a full meal had been eaten and *what* forces people to lie motionless in bed for many hours.

A common way to correct a dependent-word fragment is to connect it to the sentence that comes before or after it. For example,

Although we had eaten a full **meal, we** still ordered dessert. The rum cake was irresistible.

Some people are victims of migraine **headaches that** force them to lie motionless in bed for many hours. Medications do not offer much relief.

Punctuation note   Put a comma at the end of a dependent-word group that starts a sentence. (See the first example above.)

Practice 1

Underline the dependent-word fragment in each of the following. Then correct it on the lines provided.

1. When I sat down to answer the exam questions. My mind went completely blank.

   When I sat down to answer the exam
   questions, My mind went completely blank.

2. Because smoke detectors are so important to a family's safety. Their batteries should be checked often.

   Because smoke detectors are so important to a family's
   Safety, their batteries should be checked often.

3. After the children washed the family car. They had a water fight with the wet sponges.

   After the children washed the family car, they
   had a water fight with the wet sponges.

4. Please hang up the damp towel. That you just threw on the floor.

   Please hang up the damp towel that you just
   threw on the floor.

-*ING* AND *TO* FRAGMENTS

When -*ing* or *to* appears at or near the beginning of a word group, a fragment may result. Consider this example:

Cliff sat by the telephone for hours. Hoping that Lisa would call.

The first statement is a complete sentence. However, the second word group is not a complete thought, so it cannot stand on its own as a sentence.

Consider the following example as well:

To balance their checkbooks without making mistakes. Many people use pocket calculators.

The second statement is a complete sentence. But the first word group lacks a subject and verb *and* fails to express a complete thought.

There are two ways to correct *-ing* and *to* fragments:

a Connect an *-ing* or a *to* fragment to the sentence it explains.

Cliff sat by the telephone for **hours, hoping** that Lisa would call.

To balance their checkbooks without making **mistakes, many** people use pocket calculators.

b Create a complete sentence by adding a subject and a verb to the fragment. To do so, revise the material as necessary.

Cliff sat by the telephone for hours. **He hoped** that Lisa would call.

Many people use pocket calculators. **They want** to balance their checkbooks without making mistakes.

Practice 2

Underline the *-ing* or *to* fragment in each of the following. Then correct it on the lines provided, using one of the two methods given above.

1. Police officers stood near the corner. Directing people around the accident.

   Police officers stood near the corner, directing people around the accident.

2. The magician ran a sword through the box. To prove no one was hiding inside.

   The magician ran a sword through the box, ~~hoping~~ proving no one was inside.

3. Sitting quietly on the couch. The dog didn't look as if he'd eaten my sandwich.

   Sitting quietly on the couch, the dog didn't look as if he'd eaten my sandwich.

4. Kaylin walked quickly down the street and up the hill. To meet her boyfriend on time at the restaurant.

   To meet her boyfriend on time at the restaurant, Kaylin walked quickly down the street and up the hill.

ADDED-DETAIL FRAGMENTS

Another common kind of fragment often begins with one of the following words: *like, including, especially, also, for example, for instance, except, without,* or *such as.*

Almost everyone loves ice cream. Especially vanilla.

Many college students experience a great deal of stress. For instance, about money, grades, and personal relationships.

In the above examples, the second word group lacks both a subject and a verb. There are two ways to correct an added-detail fragment:

a Simply add the fragment to the sentence it explains. In most cases, use a comma to set off the fragment from the rest of the sentence.

Almost everyone loves ice **cream, especially** vanilla.

b Create a new sentence by adding a subject and verb to the fragment.

Many college students experience a great deal of stress. For instance, **they worry** about money, grades, and personal relationships.

Practice 3

Underline the added-detail fragment in each of the following. Then correct it on the lines provided, using one of the two methods given above.

1. Television censors watch out for material that viewers might find offensive. Such as sexual or racial jokes.

   Television censors watch out for material that
   viewers might find offensive, such as sexual or
   racial jokes.

2. The children's toys were everywhere. Except in the toy chest.

   The childrens toys were everywhere, except
   in the toy chest.

3. All applicants at that company must take a skills assessment test. Also a personality profile test.

   All applicants at that company must take a
   skills assessment test. They must also take a personality
   profile
   test.

4. The film class saw every Dustin Hoffman film. Including his first one, *The Graduate.*

   The film class saw every Dustin Hoffman film.
   They watched his first one, The Graduate.

MISSING-SUBJECT FRAGMENTS

Some word groups are fragments because, while they do have a verb, they lack a subject. Here are examples:

The telephone caller kept asking questions. But did not identify herself.

The children dug a large hole in the grass. And then tried to fill it with water.

There are two ways to correct a missing-subject fragment:

a   Connect the missing-subject fragment to the sentence it follows.

The telephone caller kept asking **questions but** did not identify herself.

The children dug a large hole in the **grass and** then tried to fill it with water.

b   Create a new sentence by adding a subject to the fragment. Normally, you will add a pronoun standing for the subject of the previous sentence.

The telephone caller kept asking questions. **She** did not identify herself.

The children dug a large hole in the grass. Then **they** tried to fill it with water.

Practice 4

Underline the missing-subject fragment in each of the following items. Then correct it on the lines below, using one of the two methods given above.

1. Our instructor seems strict. But is actually friendly and helpful.

    Our instructor seems strict, but is actually friendly and helpful.

2. A mouse's face popped out of a hole near the sink. Then disappeared quickly.

    A mouse's face popped out of a hole near the sink. Then it disappeared quickly.

3. The nurse brought the patient an extra pillow and a glass of water. But forgot his pain medication.

    The nurse brought the patient an extra pillow and a glass of water, but forgot his pain medication

4. The pot of coffee sat on the burner for hours. And became too strong and bitter to drink.

    The pot of coffee sat on the burner for hours. It became too strong and bitter to drink

Note   Not all word groups beginning with *and, but, so,* or another joining word are fragments. A sentence beginning with a joining word is grammatically complete—and correct—if both a subject and a verb follow the joining word.

Name _____ Section _____ Date _____

Score: (Number right) _____ × 12.5 = _____%

■ Fragments: Test 1

Underline the fragment in each item that follows. Then correct the fragment, using one of the methods described in the chapter.

Note To help you recognize and correct these fragments, directions are given for half of the items.

1. Before the tornado appeared. The air became perfectly still.

   _____

   The first word group begins with the dependent word *Before*. Correct the fragment by adding it to the second word group.

2. Until an American reaches the age of eighteen. He or she cannot vote in a presidential election.

   _____

   _____

3. To let students get home before the storm. The school dismissed classes early.

   _____

   The first word group lacks a subject and verb. Connect it to the complete statement that follows it.

4. To make a long story short. I got the job.

   _____

5. Every single piece of camping equipment got soaked in the rain. Including our sleeping bags.

   _____

   The second word group lacks a subject and verb. Connect it to the complete statement that comes before it.

6. The six-year-old girl already loves to read. Especially books about animals.

   _____

7. Near the end of the race, the runner felt a cramp developing in her leg. But gritted her teeth and continued running.

   _____

   _____

   Add a subject to the second word group to make it a complete thought.

8. The party had barely gotten started. And was already so noisy that the neighbors were complaining.

   _____

   _____

Name _____ Section _____ Date _____

Score: (Number right) _____ × 12.5 = _____ %

■ Fragments: Test 2

Underline the fragment in each item that follows. Then correct the fragment, using one of the methods described in the chapter.

1. After last week's heat and humidity. Today's cold and rainy weather is actually a relief.

   _____

   _____

2. Often barking all night. The neighbor's dog has become a serious nuisance.

   Often barking all night, the neighbors dog has become a serious nuisance.

3. The restaurant specializes in Mexican food. Including burritos, tacos, and refried beans.

   The restaurant specializes in Mexican foods, including burritos, tacos, and refried beans.

4. The moon rose, full and silvery. And cast its magical light over the countryside.

   _____

   _____

5. Hundreds of people called the radio station. Hoping to win the concert tickets.

   Hundreds of people called the radio station. They were hoping to win the concert tickets.

6. All the food in the refrigerator will certainly spoil. Unless the power comes back on soon.

   _____

   _____

7. If you see a penny lying on the sidewalk. Do you leave it there or pick it up?

   _____

   _____

8. The luscious-looking cake was covered with a cherry glaze. And decorated with sugar swans.

   The luscious-looking cake was covered with a cherry glaze, and decorated with sugar swans.

Name __Ava Morris__   Section __3__   Date __March 8th__

Score: (Number right) _____ × 12.5 = _____ %

■ **Fragments: Test 3**

Underline the **two** fragments in each short passage that follows. Then correct the fragments, using one of the methods described in the chapter.

Note   To help you recognize and correct fragments, explanations are given for two of the passages.

1. My phone rang at least ten times this morning. Then was silent the rest of the day. I finally called the telephone company. To see if my phone was out of order.

   ...this morning, then it was silent...
   ...telephone company, to see if my phone...

   The word group beginning with *Then was silent* needs a subject. The word group beginning with *To see* needs a subject and verb. It can be added to the previous sentence.

2. Although hot dogs, french fries, and rich ice cream are not healthy foods. They're still favorites for many Americans. People are determined to enjoy themselves. And don't want to hear about fat and cholesterol.

   ...are not healthy foods, they're still favourites...
   people don't want to hear abt fat and cholesterol,
   they are determined to...

3. Sarita boasts that she can read a book in one evening. But she doesn't read the whole book. For example, a chapter here and a page there. She misses a lot of the book's detail. Because she skips parts that she thinks won't interest her.

   ...in one evening, but she doesn't read...
   For example, she reads a chapter...
   Because she skips the parts...interest her, she misses a lot,

   The word group starting with *For example* needs a subject and verb. The word group starting with *Because*, a dependent word, needs to be added to the sentence it explains.

4. Many people have poor telephone manners. Such as beginning all of their conversations by saying, "Who's this?" Some people don't ask if their call has come at a convenient time. Or identify themselves when calling.

   Many ppl who have poor telephone manners, begin
   conversations by... Some people on the phone don't
   ask if..., or they don't identify...

Name _____ Section _____ Date _____

Score: (Number right) _____ × 12.5 = _____ %

■ Fragments: Test 4

Underline the **two** fragments in each short passage that follows. Then correct the fragments, using one of the methods described in the chapter.

1. Because members of a youth group in Finland once felt that Donald Duck was immoral. They tried to have Donald Duck cartoons banned from their town. They objected to the fact that Donald had been keeping company with Daisy Duck for more than fifty years. Without ever getting married.

   They tried to have... from their town, because members...
   They objected to the fact that... fifty years, without ever...

2. Itching for several days. Mosquito bites are one of the little miseries of summer. The itch is the result of the mosquito's saliva. Which produces a mild allergic reaction in most people.

   ... miseries of summer, itching for several days.
   ...Mosquitos saliva, it produces a mild allergic...

3. Although soccer is much more popular in other countries. It has enjoyed a rebirth in the United States in the past ten years. It has become the second most popular sport. For those between the ages of 12 and 24.

   Although soccer is..., soccer has enjoyed a rebirth...
   Soccer has become..., for those between the ages...

4. In 1891, an English sailor was swallowed by a whale. And lived to tell the story. James Bartley survived for most of a day in the belly of a whale that his ship had been chasing. When the animal was butchered. Bartley was found unconscious but unharmed.

   In 1891, an english..., and he lived to tell...
   James Bartley survived for...
   Bartley was found..., when the animal was butchered

Name _____   Section _____   Date _____

■ Fragments: Test 5

The following passage contains eight fragments. Underline each fragment. Then rewrite it correctly on the lines below.

Note   To help you recognize and correct fragments, explanations are given for half of the items.

The game of Monopoly was created by Charles Darrow. After he had lost his job during the Great Depression. Remembering family vacations at the seashore. He wrote Atlantic City street names on the kitchen oilcloth and added splashes of color to them. Then he typed up title deeds. And cut tiny houses and hotels from scraps of wood. He invented a game that his family played every night. Using buttons for play money. Soon friends were playing, too. And wanted to buy their own games. Darrow made more sets of his game. Which he sold for $2.50 apiece. He presented his game to Parker Brothers, but the company wouldn't buy it. Because the executives didn't think it would be popular. They changed their minds after 5,000 games had been sold. Darrow soon became a millionaire. Today an estimated 250,000,000 Monopoly games have been sold. The game is available in 103 countries. Also in 37 languages.

1. _____

   _____

   After he had lost his job during the Great Depression is a dependent-word fragment. Adding it to the sentence it explains will complete its meaning.

2. _____

   _____

3. _____

   And cut tiny houses and hotels from scraps of wood needs a subject. It can be added to the previous sentence.

4. _____

5. _____

   And wanted to buy their own games needs a subject. It can be added to the previous sentence.

6. _____

7. _____

   _____

   Because the executives didn't think it would be popular is a dependent-word fragment. Adding it to the preceding sentence will complete its meaning.

8. _____

Name _____   Section _____ Date _____

Score: (Number right) _____ × 12.5 = _____%

■ Fragments: Test 6

The following passage contains eight fragments. Underline each fragment. Then rewrite it correctly on the lines below.

When we graduated from college. My best friend Karen and I decided to take a trip to New York City. We managed to gather enough money to spend two weeks exploring the sights. The Big Apple is the home of some of the most important museums in the United States. Like the Museum of Modern Art. Of course, we visited the Metropolitan Museum of Art. To see some of the paintings featured in our art history course. We spent a whole day at the Museum of Natural History. Which houses one of the best dinosaur exhibits in the United States, if not the world. We wanted to see a few Broadway plays, but we did not have enough time to see more than one. Or wait after the show for autographs. Karen is a baseball fan, so we attended a Yankees game. Since we had spent most of our money on plane tickets, hotel costs, food, and admission fees. We had just a little left to do some shopping. While visiting the West Village, we had to stop into at least one boutique. And spend some time in the historic Orchard Street shopping district. We certainly enjoyed our whirlwind two weeks. Taking enough photos to fill three albums and spending all the money we had saved. Our visit was more than just a trip, though; it was an experience that we will never forget.

1. _____

   _____

2. _____

   _____

3. _____

   _____

4. _____

   _____

5. _____

   _____

6. _____

   _____

7. _____

   _____

8. _____

   _____

6 Run-Ons and Comma Splices

Seeing What You Know

Read the following pairs of items and, for each pair, check the item that is punctuated correctly. Then read the explanations below.

1. ____ a. Our math professor has the flu, half the class is sick as well.

   ____ b. Our math professor has the flu, and half the class is sick as well.

2. ____ a. Sue seldom got to play in an actual game. She was tempted to quit the team.

   ____ b. Sue seldom got to play in an actual game she was tempted to quit the team.

3. ____ a. My father had no brothers or sisters, he never learned to share.

   ____ b. Because my father had no brothers or sisters, he never learned to share.

Understanding the Answers

1. Item *b* is punctuated correctly.
   Item *a* is a comma splice. It is made up of two complete statements that are incorrectly connected by only a comma. In item *b*, the two statements are correctly connected—by a comma and a joining word, *and*.

2. Item *a* is punctuated correctly.
   Item *b* is a run-on sentence. It is made up of two complete statements: (1) *Sue seldom got to play in an actual game.* (2) *She was tempted to quit the team.* In item *a*, each of these two complete thoughts is stated in a separate sentence.

3. Item *b* is punctuated correctly.
   Item *a* is a comma splice. It is made up of two complete statements: (1) *My father had no brothers or sisters.* (2) *He never learned to share.* In item *b*, the first statement is subordinated to the second statement with the addition of the dependent word *because*.

Run-on sentences and **comma splices** are the opposite of fragments. They are *more than a sentence* because they combine two complete thoughts without putting appropriate words or punctuation between them. This chapter will show you how to recognize and correct run-ons and comma splices.

RUN-ONS

When there is *no punctuation at all* separating two complete statements, the result is a **run-on**, also called a **fused sentence**. The two statements are simply fused, or run together, into one sentence.

Complete statement 1:	Test anxiety is a very real condition.
Complete statement 2:	Some symptoms are stomach cramps and headaches.
Run-on:	Test anxiety is a very real condition some symptoms are stomach cramps and headaches.
Complete statement 1:	Computer skills are useful in college.
Complete statement 2:	They will help you in the job market as well.
Run-on:	Computer skills are useful in college they will help you in the job market as well.

A good way to prevent run-ons is to read your work aloud. You will naturally tend to pause between complete thoughts. Also look within the sentence for words like *I, you, he, she, it, we, they, there, this, that, now, then,* and *next.* Such words often signal the beginning of a second complete thought. (See page 211 for other words that can lead to run-ons.)

Correcting Run-Ons

Here are three methods of correcting a run-on:

1   Divide the run-on into two sentences.

Run-on:	Test anxiety is a very real condition some symptoms are stomach cramps and headaches.
Corrected:	Test anxiety is a very real condition. Some symptoms are stomach cramps and headaches.

2   Put a comma plus a joining word (such as *and, but,* or *so*) between the two complete statements.

Run-on:	Computer skills are useful in college they will help you in the job market as well.
Corrected:	Computer skills are useful in college, **and** they will help you in the job market as well.
Run-on:	I'd love to go out to eat tonight I'm short of money right now.
Corrected:	I'd love to go out to eat tonight, **but** I'm short of money right now.

Run-on: Carmen has a broken foot she won't do any hiking this fall.

Corrected: Carmen has a broken foot, **so** she won't do any hiking this fall.

Note 1   Be sure to use a logical joining word. In the first example, *and* is appropriate because it means *in addition.* (Computer skills are useful in college; *in addition,* they will help you in the job market as well.) In the second example, *but* is appropriate because it means *however.* (I'd love to go out to eat tonight; *however,* I'm short of money right now.) In the third example, *so* means *as a result.* (Carmen has a broken foot; *as a result,* she won't do any hiking this fall.)

Note 2   The comma always goes *before* the joining word—not after it.

Note 3   Other joining words are *for* (which means *because*), *or, nor,* and *yet* (which means *however*). (For information on when to use these words, see pages 212–213.)

3   Use subordination to make one of the complete thoughts dependent on the other one.

To subordinate a complete thought, change it from a statement that can stand alone as a sentence to one that cannot stand by itself. To do so, begin the thought with an appropriate dependent word, such as *because, when, if, before, since, until, unless, while, as, although,* and *after.* (Additional dependent words appear on page 60.)

Run-on: Carmen has a broken foot she won't do any hiking this fall.

Corrected: **Because** Carmen has a broken foot, she won't do any hiking this fall.

Important punctuation note   Be sure to put a comma at the end of a dependent-word group that begins a sentence.

Practice 1

Draw a slash (/) between the two complete thoughts in each of the fused sentences that follow. Then correct each fused sentence, using one of the methods described above. Use a different method for each sentence.

1. It's easy to begin smoking / it's much harder to quit.

   It's easy to begin smoking, so its much harder to quit.

2. Some people at the office have gotten raises / the other workers are jealous.

   Since some people at the office have gotten raises, the other workers are jealous.

3. That color isn't right for you / the style is wrong as well.

   That color isn't right for you, and the style is wrong as well.

COMMA SPLICES

When a comma alone separates two complete thoughts, the result is called a **comma splice**. A comma alone is not enough to mark the break between complete statements. Something stronger is needed.

Complete statement 1: Kevin was always nervous about tests.

Complete statement 2: His grades were usually the highest in the class.

Comma splice: Kevin was always nervous about tests, his grades were usually the highest in the class.

Correcting Comma Splices

A comma splice can be corrected by using one of the same three methods suggested for correcting a run-on:

1 Divide the comma splice into two sentences: Kevin was always nervous about tests. **H**is grades were usually the highest in the class.

2 Connect the two complete thoughts by placing a joining word (such as *and, but,* or *so*) after the comma: Kevin was always nervous about tests**, but** his grades were usually the highest in the class.

3 Use subordination (add a dependent word to one of the complete thoughts): Kevin was always nervous about tests **although** his grades were usually the highest in the class.

Practice 2

Correct each of the comma splices that follow, using one of the methods described above. Use a different method for each sentence.

1. Hakim was talking on the phone, he was switching TV channels with his remote control at the same time.
   even though
   Hakim was talking on the phone, he was switching TV channels with his remote control at the same time

2. I chose the shortest checkout line at the supermarket, then the one customer in front of me pulled out dozens of coupons.
   I chose the shortest checkout line at the supermarket, but then the one customer in front of me pulled out dozens of coupon

3. The electricity at Jasmin's house went out, she had to write her paper by candlelight.
   The electricity at Jasmin's house went out. She had to write her paper by candlelight.

Note Additional information about run-ons and comma splices appears on pages 210–211.

Name _____ Section _____ Date _____

Score: (Number right) _____ × 12.5 = _____%

■ Run-Ons and Comma Splices: Test 1

Put a slash (/) between the two complete thoughts in each of the following run-on sentences or comma splices. Then rewrite the sentences, using (1) a period and capital letter, (2) a comma and a joining word, or (3) a dependent word. Be sure to use all three methods.

Note   To help you correct the errors, explanations are given for half of the sentences.

Splice 1. My alarm clock rang like a fire bell / I slowly rolled out of bed.

My alarm clock ran like a fire bell, and I slowly rolled out of bed.

My alarm clock rang like a fire bell is a complete thought. *I slowly rolled out of bed* is also a complete thought. Use the subordinating word *when* before the first thought.

run on 2. Rosa got a parking ticket / she decided to fight it in traffic court.

Rosa got a parking ticket, so she decided to fight it in traffic court.

run on 3. One student made a lasting impression at his interview / he arrived an hour late.

One student made a lasting impression at his interview, where he arrived an hour late.

The word group *he arrived an hour late* is a second complete thought. Put each complete thought into its own sentence.

run on 4. Tyrone got lost driving to the wedding / he refused to stop to ask for directions.

Tyrone got lost driving to the wedding. He refused to stop to ask for directions.

5. The salad included shredded carrots / chopped peanuts were sprinkled on top.

The salad included shredded carrots, and chopped peanuts were sprinkled on top.

Use a comma and the joining word *and* to connect the two complete thoughts.

Splice 6. Prices were high at the concession stand / the lines were long as well.

Prices were high at the concession stand. The lines were long as well.

Splice 7. Sharon glanced down at her feet / then she realized her socks didn't match.

Sharon glanced down at her feet, but then she realized her socks didn't match.

Put each complete thought into its own sentence.

8. Bicycles may be the world's best method of transportation / they require little maintenance and don't pollute.

Bicycles may be the worlds best method of transportation, as they require little maintenance and dont pollute

Name _____   Section _____   Date _____

Score: (Number right) _____ × 12.5 = _____%

■ Run-Ons and Comma Splices: Test 2

Put a slash (/) between the two complete thoughts in each of the following run-on sentences or comma splices. Then rewrite the sentences, using (1) a period and capital letter, (2) a comma and a joining word, or (3) a dependent word. Be sure to use all three methods.

1. Whoever is knocking on the door will have to wait I am in the bathtub.

   _____

2. David tried to appear calm his trembling hands gave him away.

   _____

   _____

3. The customer waited impatiently the clerk seemed to be filling his grocery bags in slow motion.

   _____

   _____

4. I have worked for the company for three years my boss still doesn't know my name.

   _____

   _____

5. The boy in the old story "The Boy Who Cried Wolf" was finally telling the truth, nobody believed him.

   _____

   _____

6. I cannot find my car keys anywhere, I'm going to take the bus.

   _____

   _____

7. The flashlight was very bright even its beams could not reach the back of the deep cave.

   _____

   _____

8. Many people never buy hardcover books, they prefer to wait for the paperback versions.

   _____

   _____

Name _____ Section _____ Date _____

Score: (Number right) _____ × 12.5 = _____%

■ Run-Ons and Comma Splices: Test 3

Each passage contains **one** run-on and **one** comma splice.
Correct the two errors by using (1) a period and capital letter, (2) a comma and a joining word, or (3) a dependent word. Be sure to use all three methods.

Note   To help you correct the errors, explanations are given for two of the passages.

1. The female panda was thought to be pregnant the zookeepers watched her closely for signs of the coming birth. However, many months went by with no baby panda, the keepers finally gave up hope.

    _____

    _____

    _____

    Correct the first run-on by adding the dependent word *When* before the first complete thought. Correct the second run-on by adding the joining word *so* between the two complete thoughts.

2. My sister stops by the second-hand clothing store every day she claims that there is always new merchandise for sale. I visit about once a month, I see the same things that were there the month before.

    _____

    _____

    _____

3. Many of us have heard warnings about swimming on a full stomach the truth is that we are better off swimming when full. Muscles are starved for energy in a hungry body, they cannot work efficiently and may cramp.

    _____

    _____

    _____

    Correct the first run-on by using a period and a capital letter. Correct the second run-on by adding *Because* before the first complete thought.

4. The most popular song in the world was composed in 1893, it was written by two sisters in Kentucky. Mildred and Patty Hill's song was first titled "Good Morning to You" later the sisters changed the words to "Happy Birthday to You."

    _____

    _____

    _____

Name _____   Section _____   Date _____

Score: (Number right) _____ × 12.5 = _____%

■ Run-Ons and Comma Splices: Test 4

Each passage contains **one** run-on and **one** comma splice.
Correct the two errors by using (1) a period and capital letter, (2) a comma and a joining word, or (3) a dependent word. Be sure to use all three methods.

1. June is a month of nice weather that doesn't explain why it is the most popular month for weddings. The month is named after Juno, the Roman goddess of marriage. People believed that Juno would bless couples married during her month, we've now forgotten about Juno but still prefer June weddings.

    _____

    _____

    _____

2. Teenagers often have a strong need to show their independence this desire often brings them into conflict with their parents. Some teens rebel in harmless ways, others show their independence in more dangerous fashion, such as by drinking and driving.

    _____

    _____

    _____

3. On their first date, Alicia and Mark went to a movie. The story was very sad Alicia tried to keep from crying. She glanced over at Mark, she was surprised to see a tear running down his cheek. Alicia was glad that she didn't have to hide her feelings from Mark.

    _____

    _____

    _____

4. Everyone has a cure for hiccups, there's holding your breath, breathing into a paper bag, or having someone scare you. These methods do not work for me the only home remedy that really helps is sugar. Swallowing a teaspoon of white granulated sugar always stops my hiccups.

    _____

    _____

    _____

Name _____   Section _____ Date _____

■ **Run-Ons and Comma Splices: Test 5**

The following passage contains ten run-ons and comma splices. Correct each error in the space provided by using (1) a period and capital letter, (2) a comma and a joining word, or (3) a dependent word. Be sure to use all three methods.

Note   To help you correct the errors, explanations are given for half of the sentences.

¹Terry is a lively talker, her listening skills are underdeveloped. ²She calls herself a caring person the truth is, however, that she never really listens to anyone. ³Terry is thinking about what to say next, she only *seems* to be listening. ⁴Her friends know she doesn't listen to them, they don't discuss important things with her. ⁵One friend learned the hard way he told Terry that his mother had cancer. ⁶Terry was full of sympathy, she kept saying, "I'm so glad you told me." ⁷She sounded very supportive, the friend felt better. ⁸His mother died, Terry asked, "Why didn't you tell me your mother wasn't well?" ⁹Terry thinks she is a kind and loyal friend she doesn't realize the truth. ¹⁰She isn't a real friend at all, her only real friend is herself.

1. _____

   Correct the comma splice by inserting *but* between the two complete thoughts.

2. _____

   _____

3. _____

   Correct the comma splice by inserting *since* before the first complete thought.

4. _____

   _____

5. _____

   Correct the run-on by inserting *when* before *he told Terry that his mother had cancer.*

6. _____

7. _____

   Correct the comma splice by inserting *so* before *the friend felt better.*

8. _____

   _____

9. _____

   Correct the run-on by putting a period and capital after *kind and loyal friend.*

10. _____

Name _____ Section _____ Date _____

Score: (Number right) _____ × 10 = _____%

■ Run-Ons and Comma Splices: Test 6

The following passage contains ten run-ons and comma splices. Correct each error in the space provided by using (1) a period and capital letter, (2) a comma and a joining word, or (3) a dependent word. Be sure to use all three methods.

The three sons of legendary quarterback Archie Manning also became talented football players. Peyton Manning began playing quarterback for the Indianapolis Colts in 1998, he holds many team records. Peyton's younger brother, Eli, began playing quarterback for the New York Giants in 2004. Peyton led the Colts to a Super Bowl victory over the Chicago Bears in 2006, two years later, Eli led the Giants to a Super Bowl victory over the New England Patriots. The oldest Manning brother is Cooper he is less well-known than Peyton and Eli. In high school, Cooper wasn't satisfied being a third-string quarterback he became a wide receiver. His father helped him perfect his receiving skills, Cooper didn't drop a single pass his entire junior year! As a senior, Cooper played wide receiver, younger brother Peyton was the team's quarterback. The two Manning brothers led their team to a state championship Cooper was named the team's most valuable player. Many colleges wanted Cooper to play for them his bright future in football seemed assured. He developed spinal stenosis, this painful condition kept him from playing any more football. Cooper Manning is happy for his brothers' football success he is not bitter that his own football career ended at age eighteen.

1. _____

_____

2. _____

_____

3. _____

_____

4. _____

_____

5. _____

_____

6. _____

_____

7. _____

_____

8. _____

_____

9. _____

_____

10. _____

_____

7 Pronouns

Seeing What You Know

Cross out the pronoun mistake in each of the following sentences, and write the corrections above the mistakes. Then read the explanations below.

1. Each of my sons required two chances to pass their driver's test.

2. If there are stains on any hotel towels, they should be removed immediately.

3. I don't shop at that supermarket because they are so slow at the checkout counters.

4. People go to the local diner because you can get low-priced meals there all day.

Understanding the Answers

1. Each of my sons required two chances to pass **his** driver's test.
   Each is singular. It needs a singular pronoun, *his,* to refer to it.

2. If there are stains on any hotel towels, **the towels** should be removed immediately.
   Which does the writer want us to remove—the stains or the towels? The pronoun *they* could refer to either one. Replacing *they* with *the towels* makes the meaning of the sentence clear.

3. I don't shop at that supermarket because **the clerks** are so slow at the checkout counters.
   Who are *they*? The word *they* doesn't refer to anything specific. The sentence should be clarified by replacing *they* with what it is meant to represent.

4. People go to the local diner because **they** can get low-priced meals there all day.
   People requires a third-person pronoun, *they.* Sentences that begin in the third person should not suddenly shift their point of view to the second person, *you.*

Pronouns are words that stand for nouns (names of persons, places, or things). Personal pronouns are *I, me, my, mine, you, your, yours, he, him, his, she, her, hers, it, its, we, us, our, ours, they, them, their,* and *theirs.*

> Freddy is a wrestler. **He** weighs 270 pounds. (*He* stands for *Freddy.*)
>
> Rita always writes **her** letters in purple ink. (*Her* stands for *Rita's.*)
>
> "If **my** kids talk back, **I** let **them** know **they** are asking for trouble," Jeff said. (*My* stands for *Jeff's; I* stands for *Jeff. Them* and *they* stand for *kids.*)

This chapter shows you how to avoid the three most frequent kinds of pronoun mistakes: in pronoun agreement, in pronoun reference, and in pronoun point of view. (Additional information about pronouns appears on pages 4–5 and 189–193.)

PRONOUN AGREEMENT

A pronoun must agree in number with the word it refers to (sometimes called the pronoun's **antecedent**). Singular words require singular pronouns; plural words require plural pronouns.

> The book Henry lent me is missing **its** cover. (*Its,* a singular pronoun, refers to *book,* a singular noun.)
>
> If your cousins don't get here soon, **they** will miss the movie. (*They,* a plural pronoun, refers to *cousins,* a plural noun.)

The indefinite pronouns listed below are always singular. (See also page 41.)

Singular Indefinite Pronouns			
each	anyone	anybody	anything
either	everyone	everybody	everything
neither	someone	somebody	something
one	no one	nobody	nothing

> Each of the wild horses raced for **its** freedom.
>
> Neither of my sisters ever feels like cleaning **her** room.
>
> No one in the class wanted to read **his** (or **her**) paper out loud.

Note   In the last example, choose a pronoun that fits the situation. If all the members of the class are male, use *his.* If they all are female, use *her.* If the class includes both men and women, use *his or her:*

> No one in the class wanted to read **his or her** paper out loud.

Or avoid the extra words by rewriting the sentence in the plural:

> No **students** in the class wanted to read **their papers** out loud.

Practice 1

Underline the correct word or words in the parentheses in the sentences below.

1. Each of the actresses who auditioned believes (she / they) should be chosen for the starring role.

2. Many high schools now require (its / their) students to take a computer course.

3. If anybody here has a cell phone, (they / he or she) should turn it off now so that it doesn't ring during the performance.

4. Either exercise is fine, but (it / they) must be done regularly to do any good.

5. Somebody in the men's locker room hid Paco's clothes, and Paco would love to get back at (him / them).

PRONOUN REFERENCE

A pronoun must also refer *clearly* to the word it stands for. If the meaning of a pronoun is uncertain, the sentence will be confusing. For example,

> Gloria told Renée that she had gotten an A on her paper. (Who got the A—Gloria or Renée? The words *she* and *her* could refer to either one.)

> I wanted a ham and cheese sandwich, but they were all out of cheese. (Who was all out of cheese? The word *they* has no one to refer to.)

> There were no questions after the lecture, which was regrettable. (What was regrettable—the lecture or the lack of questions? Be careful how you use the pronouns *which* and *this*. They must clearly refer to *one* thing or situation.)

> Both of Ben's parents are accountants, but this doesn't interest Ben. (What doesn't interest Ben? The pronoun *this* doesn't refer to anything in the sentence.)

To avoid mistakes like these, simply write what you mean by the pronoun.

> Gloria told Renee, "**You** got an A on **your** paper."

> *Or:* Gloria told Renee, "**I** got an A on **my** paper."

> I wanted a ham and cheese sandwich, but **the deli** was all out of cheese.

> There were no questions after the lecture. **Not having questions** was regrettable.

> Both of Ben's parents are accountants, but **accounting** doesn't interest Ben.

Practice 2

Underline the correct word or words in the parentheses in the sentences below.

1. When Roy told his father about the surprise party, (he / his father) grinned.

2. Students complain that (they / the maintenance people) keep the library too hot.

3. While Eric was adding sugar to his coffee, he spilled (it / the sugar) all over the table.

4. Someone offered to show me a copy of next week's history test, but I said that I didn't believe in (this / cheating).

5. Many older people shop at the mall because (they / the stores) give a 15 percent discount to senior citizens.

PRONOUN POINT OF VIEW

Pronouns are either **first person** (referring to the speaker), **second person** (referring to the one spoken to), or **third person** (referring to everyone else):

	First person	*Second person*	*Third person*
Singular	I, me, my, mine	you, your, yours	he, him, his; she, her, hers; it, its
Plural	we, us, our, ours	you, your, yours	they, them, their, theirs

When you write, your pronoun point of view must stay the same. Do not shift unnecessarily from one point of view to another, as in the following sentences:

What **I** like best about vacations is that **you** don't have to set an alarm.

The **workers** here have to take a break at 10:30 whether **we** want to or not.

Instead, write the entire sentence in the same person:

What **I** like best about vacations is that **I** don't have to set an alarm.

The **workers** here have to take a break at 10:30 whether **they** want to or not.

Practice 3

Underline the correct pronoun in the parentheses in the sentences below.

1. I know spring is really here when (I / you) see neighborhood kids playing softball.

2. My father says he prefers to drive at night because then the sun won't get in (his / your) eyes.

3. First-year students at this school are required to take a math course. (You / They) must also take a computer course.

4. Although Sharon and I were good friends, (we / you) could tell that we would not be good roommates.

5. If you want to advance in this company, (we / you) must be willing to work overtime and to move to a new location every couple of years.

Note   Additional information about pronouns appears on pages 4–5 and 189–193.

Name _____   Section _____   Date _____

Score: (Number right) _____ × 10 = _____%

■ Pronouns: Test 1

Underline the correct word or words in the parentheses in the sentences below.

Note   To help you recognize and correct pronoun mistakes, explanations are given for half of the items.

1. Neither of the sisters likes to do (her / their) chores.

   Neither, an indefinite pronoun, is singular. The second pronoun must agree with it in number.

2. Everyone in the class was told to bring (his or her / their) laptop to class on Wednesday.

3. My mother told my girlfriend (she looked marvelous. / , "You look marvelous.")

   The pronoun *she* could refer to either *my mother* or *my girlfriend.*

4. Mrs. Owen told her daughter (that she couldn't babysit Friday night. / , "I can't babysit Friday night.")

5. When you drive from New York to South Carolina, (you / one) should plan to stay overnight at a motel on the way.

   The sentence begins in the second person (*you*). Do not shift the pronoun point of view.

6. We don't want the local clinic to close because then (you / we) would have to drive all the way to the city for medical treatment.

7. Both travel agents thought that (she / they) had won the free trip to Hawaii.

   Agents is plural. The second pronoun must agree in number.

8. For Halloween, Dave and Scott both dressed up in (his / their) sisters' cheer-leading uniforms.

9. When Lian learned that her new sister-in-law was a Navy pilot, she became interested in (it / a Navy career) too.

   For the sentence to be clear, the writer must state what Lian is interested in.

10. Many people enjoy hiking and camping, but I'm not interested in (them / those activities).

■ Pronouns: Test 2

Underline the pronoun mistake in each of the sentences that follow. Then correct the mistake by rewriting the sentence in the space provided.

1. Mario told the manager that he needed to hire more help.

   _____

   _____

2. Each of the quarterbacks wanted their chance to lead the team.

   _____

   _____

3. I won't go to the concert tonight because there's no way you could get a ticket.

   _____

   _____

4. Maria enjoys reading to her little girl even though she sometimes gets sleepy during the stories.

   _____

   _____

5. Any basketball player who fails a course will lose their scholarship.

   _____

   _____

6. Every time Barb paints her nails, I have to leave the room because the smell of it makes me sick.

   _____

   _____

7. Many people love trying foreign restaurants where you can experience a whole new way of cooking.

   _____

   _____

8. When I was stopped for speeding, he said I'd been going fifteen miles over the limit.

   _____

   _____

Name _____ Section _____ Date _____

Score: (Number right) _____ × 10 = _____%

■ Pronouns: Test 3

Each of the following passages contains **two** pronoun mistakes. Find and underline these two mistakes. Then write the corrections in the spaces provided.

Note To help you recognize and correct pronoun mistakes, explanations are given for the first error in each passage.

1. My friend wanted to lose weight, but she was convinced you would have to starve to do so. Then she joined an online dieting site, where they encourage each other. She ended up losing twenty pounds.

   a. _____   *You* is a shift in pronoun point

   b. _____   of view.

2. I wear disposable contact lenses instead of glasses because I find them more comfortable. However, it's easy for you to forget to change the lenses every week.

   a. _____   *Them* could refer to either the lenses

   b. _____   or the glasses.

3. In the department store, women often block the aisles and spray perfume samples on the shoppers. This annoys many people, so you have to avoid that part of the store.

   a. _____   *This* could refer to either blocking

   b. _____   the aisles or spraying the perfume.

4. Although every person has the right to their own opinion, heckling a speaker is not the way to express a view. Instead, one should picket a speech or write a letter to their local newspaper.

   a. _____   *Every person* is singular and

   b. _____   requires a singular pronoun.

5. Bob told Luis that he needed a new car. Bob went on to say, "I still like my old Corvette, but the car spends more time in the garage than on the road." Luis agreed that anybody who had to pay for so many repairs to their car should buy a new one.

   a. _____   *He* could refer to either Bob

   b. _____   or Luis.

■ Pronouns: Test 4

Each of the following passages contains **two** pronoun mistakes. Find and underline these two mistakes. Then write the corrections in the spaces provided.

1. The thing that customers like about shopping at McRay's Hardware is that you get a great deal of assistance from the clerks there. He must spend a lot of time training people after he hires them.

   a. _____

   b. _____

2. Everyone in my family was late to their job on Tuesday. A storm had knocked down power lines during the night. The utility plant got all of their workers to restore power, but most people's alarm clocks fell behind by two hours during the outage.

   a. _____

   b. _____

3. Denise was so tired last night that she went to bed without washing her face. When she woke up this morning, most of her makeup had worn off her face, and it was all over the pillow. "This is disgusting," she thought.

   a. _____

   b. _____

4. A well-known columnist advises us not to respond to e-mail messages from strangers. Somebody who tries to start a relationship by e-mail could be lying about their age, marital status, or even gender. Or the writer could be tempting us to go to a Web site where your password or credit card number will be stolen.

   a. _____

   b. _____

5. As we watched, two movers carried the piano out to their double-parked van, then left it in the middle of the street while they went for coffee. Fifteen minutes later, the movers had still not come back, and you could see cars backed up for several blocks.

   a. _____

   b. _____

Name _____   Section _____   Date _____

Score: (Number right) _____ × 10 = _____%

■ **Pronouns: Test 5**

Each sentence in the following passage contains one pronoun mistake. Find and underline these ten mistakes. Then write the corrections on the lines below.

Note   To help you recognize and correct pronoun mistakes, explanations are given for five of the errors.

¹Two of my friends, Alyssa and Marla, and I decided they wanted to go to Lollapalooza, one of the oldest and largest annual music festivals in the United States. ²Alyssa suggested to Marla that since the festival site was so close, she should drive. ³It was going to be a sellout, so the three of us would have to reserve rooms in a nearby motel in advance. ⁴Unfortunately, by the time we finalized our plans, they were unavailable, so we decided to stay at a local campground. ⁵When we got there, the camp host told us that you had to make a reservation, but he would let us put up a tent in one of the few vacant sites. ⁶When Marla complained that she wasn't happy about sleeping on the ground or showering in public, we reminded her that this was much cheaper than a motel. ⁷Unfortunately, nobody had wanted to pitch their tent in one of the small, rocky and noisy campsites behind the restroom building, so that's where we had to stay. ⁸Although we had hot dogs and hamburgers in our cooler, you couldn't cook them because no barbecue grill was available. ⁹Alyssa and Marla had volunteered to bring snacks and drinks, but she forgot to pack them. ¹⁰We didn't sleep or eat much that weekend, and things hadn't gone as we had planned, but everyone enjoyed themselves because this trip was always about the music.

1. _____

I is a first-person pronoun. *They* is a shift to the third-person point of view.

2. _____

3. _____

It does not refer to anything in the sentence.

4. _____

5. _____

We is a first-person pronoun. *You* is a shift to the second-person point of view.

6. _____

7. _____

Nobody is an indefinite pronoun, so it is singular.

8. _____

9. _____

The pronoun *she* is singular and cannot refer to the plural *Alyssa and Marla*.

10. _____

Name _____   Section _____   Date _____

Score: (Number right) _____ × 10 = _____ %

■ Pronouns: Test 6

Each sentence in the following passage contains one pronoun mistake. Find and underline these ten mistakes. Then write the corrections on the lines below.

[1]Anyone who is involved in an auto accident may have to decide whether to drive their car afterward or have it towed to a repair shop. [2]Drivers usually consider expense and convenience, but you should also know about another important factor: safety. [3]Obviously, some cars are so badly wrecked in an accident that driving it is impossible. [4]After a less serious accident, many drivers reluctantly pay high repair bills for their cars, saying they must not have been very well made in the first place if a little accident could cause all this harm. [5]However, some people with damaged cars say they would rather keep driving the car as it is. [6]If people knew more about a car's frame, they might look at this differently. [7]Many people do not realize that his or her car's frame is designed to protect them by absorbing the impact of a collision. [8]The frame may crumple, sustaining damage that is far from the point of impact; some of it may not even be visible to the naked eye. [9]Everyone should keep in mind that their car frame is designed to absorb the impact of only *one* crash. [10]A bent car frame cannot properly protect against another collision, and they risk serious injury by riding in a damaged car.

1. _____

2. _____

3. _____

4. _____

5. _____

6. _____

7. _____

8. _____

9. _____

10. _____

8 Comma

Seeing What You Know

Insert commas where needed in the following sentences. Then read the explanations below.

1. The restaurant dessert tray featured carrot cake, coconut cream pie, and something called Death by Chocolate.

2. Because I was three hours short of graduation requirements, I had to take a course during the summer.

3. The weather according to last night's forecast, will improve by Saturday.

4. Students hurried to the campus store to buy their fall textbooks, but several of the books were already out of stock.

5. My sister asked, "Are you going to be on the phone much longer?"

Understanding the Answers

1. The restaurant dessert tray featured carrot cake, coconut cream pie, and something called Death by Chocolate.
   Commas are needed to separate the items in a series.

2. Because I was three hours short of graduation requirements, I had to take a course during the summer.
   The comma separates the introductory words from the rest of the sentence.

3. The weather, according to last night's forecast, will improve by Saturday.
   The words *according to last night's forecast* interrupt the flow of the rest of the sentence, so they are set off by commas.

4. Students hurried to the campus store to buy their fall textbooks, but several of the books were already out of stock.
   The comma separates two complete thoughts connected by the joining word *but*.

5. My sister asked, "Are you going to be on the phone much longer?"
   The comma separates a direct quotation from the rest of the sentence.

This chapter explains five main uses of the comma.

1 BETWEEN ITEMS IN A SERIES

Commas are used to separate three or more items in a series.

> Bears, chipmunks, raccoons, and groundhogs all hibernate during the winter.
>
> Felipe groaned when he learned that his exams in biology, economics, and sociology were scheduled for the same day.
>
> The mechanic started the engine, fiddled with the fan belt, and announced that the problem was solved.

But   Do not use a comma when the series contains only two items.
The mechanic started the engine and fiddled with the fan belt.

Practice 1

In the following sentences, insert commas between items in a series.

1. My community recycles newspapers, cardboard, glass, aluminum, and plastic.

2. Walking, bicycling, and swimming are all good aerobic exercises.

3. We collected the kids, loaded the van, and set off for the amusement park.

4. Signs of burnout include insomnia, inability to concentrate, and depression.

2 AFTER INTRODUCTORY MATERIAL

A comma is used to separate introductory material from the rest of the sentence. (If you were reading the sentence aloud, you would probably pause slightly at the end of the introductory material, where the comma belongs.)

> Although the county issues a large number of jury-duty notices, many people find reasons not to serve.
>
> Pushing and laughing, the second-graders spilled onto the playground.
>
> In the middle of the thunderstorm, all the lights on our street went out.

Practice 2

Insert a comma after the introductory material in each of the following sentences.

1. During the first-aid course, one student accidentally broke her finger.

2. When the power went back on, all the digital clocks in the house began to blink.

3. Pausing in the doorway, the actress smiled warmly at the photographers.

4. After waiting in line for two hours, the students were told that the registrar's office was closing for lunch.

3 AROUND WORDS THAT INTERRUPT THE FLOW OF A SENTENCE

Sentences sometimes contain words (often called **parenthetical expressions**) that interrupt the flow of thought. Such words and word groups should be set off from the rest of the sentence by commas. For example,

Someone's car, a blue Ford, was blocking the store entrance.

If you read this sentence out loud, you can hear that the words *a blue Ford* interrupt the flow of thought. (This type of interrupter, a noun that means the same as the noun before it, is called an **appositive**.) Such interrupters often contain information that is less important to the sentence.

Here are some other examples of sentences with interrupters:

The owner of the blue Ford, *grumbling angrily,* came out to move his car.

Our house, *which was built in 1975,* needs a new roof and extra insulation.

The house's storm windows, *though,* are in fairly good shape.

Note   Some interrupters, however, are needed to make the sentence clear. Information about punctuating these word groups appears on page 212.

Practice 3

Insert commas around the interrupting words in each of the following sentences.

1. The Beatles, who originally called themselves the Quarrymen, released twenty-nine single records in their first year.

2. Frozen yogurt, a dessert that is relatively low in calories, is as delicious to many people as ice cream.

3. Some dieters, on the other hand, would rather give up desserts completely.

4. The new office building, forty stories high, provides a fine view of the parkway.

4 BETWEEN COMPLETE THOUGHTS CONNECTED BY A JOINING WORD

When two complete thoughts are combined into one sentence by a joining word like *and, but,* or *so,* a comma is used before the joining word.

They were five strangers stuck in an elevator, **so** they told each other jokes to ease the tension.

Each part of the sentence is a complete thought: *They were five strangers stuck in an elevator. They told each other jokes to ease the tension.* The parts are combined into one sentence by the joining word *so.*

Here are more sentences with complete thoughts connected by joining words:

Money may not buy happiness, **but** it makes misery a lot more comfortable.

Ved has a restaurant job this summer, **and** his sister has an office position.

Punctuation note   Don't add a comma just because a sentence contains the word *and, but,* or *so.* Use a comma only when the joining word comes between two complete thoughts. Each of those thoughts must have its own subject and verb.

> *Comma:* Lois spent two hours in the *gym,* **and then she went** to class. (Each complete thought has a subject and a verb: *Lois spent* and *she went.*)

> *No comma:* Lois spent two hours in the **gym and then went** to class. (The second thought isn't complete because it doesn't have its own subject.)

Practice 4

Insert a comma before the joining words in the following sentences.

1. The horror-movie heroine screamed for help, but nobody heard her.

2. Melba wasn't wearing her glasses, so she couldn't read the fine print in the ad.

3. I used to be able to type very quickly, but now I'm out of practice.

4. Frequent TV watchers spend less time interacting with friends and family, and their reading is often limited to magazines such as *TV Guide.*

5 WITH DIRECT QUOTATIONS

A comma is used to separate directly quoted material from the rest of the sentence.

> Someone shouted, "Look out below!"

> The customer grumbled to the waiter, "This coffee tastes like mud."

> "To learn more about lions," the zookeeper told the visiting children, "you should read the book *Born Free.*"

Punctuation note   When the comma is placed at the end of a quotation, it is included within the quotation marks.

Practice 5

Insert commas to set off quoted material in the following sentences.

1. When the bank robber Willie Sutton was asked why he robbed banks, he replied, "Because that's where the money is."

2. "Only fifteen more minutes until this class ends", Sharon whispered.

3. "Let me explain to you", said the math instructor, "why I want you to prepare your answer sheet in this way."

4. "When you hear the beep, you know what to do", says the message on my friend's answering machine.

> **Note**   Additional information about the comma appears on pages 212–215.

Name _____   Section _____ Date _____

Score: (Number right) _____ × 10 = _____ %

■ Comma: Test 1

On the lines provided, write the word or words in each sentence that need to be followed by a comma. Be sure to include each comma.

Note   To help you master the comma, explanations are given for five of the sentences.

1. The kids' Halloween bags were full of quarters, peanuts, gum, and candy bars.

   _____   Commas separate items in a series.

2. Opal has evening classes on Mondays, Wednesdays, and Thursdays.

   _____

3. Carrying her popcorn, Sylvia looked for an empty seat in the theater.

   ___popcorn___   Use a comma after introductory material.

4. After she read the Harry Potter books, Yoko began calling her younger brothers and sisters "Muggles."

   ___books___

5. That pizza, the one with broccoli and mushrooms, is the best I've ever eaten.

   ___pizza___   Place commas around interrupting words in a sentence.

6. I ate Rocky Road ice cream, which is not on my diet for dinner last night.

   ___cream___

7. My father wanted to attend college, but his family didn't have the money.

   ___college___   A comma is needed before the word that joins two complete thoughts.

8. Bad weather destroyed much of last season's orange crop, so the price of orange juice is high this year.

   ___crop___

9. "It's hard for me to believe that you are almost 90 years old, when you don't have one wrinkle on your face," I told my grandmother.

   ___face___   The comma separates a direct quotation from the rest of the sentence.

10. "All I want," said Jeff wearily, "is to crawl into bed and stay there for a week."

    _____

Name _____   Section _____   Date _____

Score: (Number right) _____ × 10 = _____ %

■ Comma: Test 2

In the space provided, write the letter of the one comma rule that applies to each of the following sentences. Then insert one or more commas where they belong in each sentence.

a	Between items in a series
b	After introductory material
c	Around interrupting words
d	Before a word that joins two complete thoughts
e	With direct quotations

_C_ 1. The caged panther, which kept striding from one side of its enclosure to the other, looked both magnificent and pitiful.

_B_ 2. When I first picked up the telephone, I didn't recognize Roger's voice.

_A_ 3. You'll know my uncle immediately—he has a walrus mustache, an eye patch, and a wooden leg.

_D_ 4. Michael lives in a section of the city that isn't very safe, so he installed three locks on both his front and back doors.

_E_ 5. "I'll go to the party," said Vicky, "if you promise to be there."

_C_ 6. Many parents, although they dearly love their children, sometimes dream about being young and free again.

_D_ 7. Being educated doesn't mean having a head full of facts, but it does mean knowing how and where to find the facts.

_E_ 8. The insensitive TV reporter shouted to his camera crew, "Make sure you get some close-ups of the accident victims!"

_A_ 9. When my mother opened my refrigerator, she saw only a bottle of water, two eggs, and a package of cream cheese covered with blue mold.

_B_ 10. On the other hand, the freezer was well stocked with frozen dinners and ice cream.

Name *Ava*   Section 3   Date *March 1*

Score: (Number right) _____ × 10 = _____ %

■ Comma: Test 3

On the lines provided, write out the parts of each passage that need commas. Be sure to include the commas.

Note   To help you master the comma, explanations are given for half of the corrections.

1. "I'm not going to help you anymore" she told her brother "because it's time that you help yourself." Although it would be very difficult she was ready to let him do just that.

   a. *"I'm not going to help you anymore," she told her brother,*
   A comma is needed to separate quoted words from the rest of the sentence.

   b. *she told her brother, "because its time that you help you self,*

2. My psychology class is very practical. We've learned about causes of stress everyday defense mechanisms and coping skills. In addition, I now understand a good deal about the anger I have toward my parents.

   a. *My psychology class is very practical, we've learned*
   Commas are needed to separate the items in a series.

   b. *We've learned about stress, everday defense mechanisms, and coping skills*

3. A fire siren outside woke Kim at 5:30 so she got dressed and went for an early morning run. "You're up bright and early" a neighbor called to her.

   a. *went for an early morning run and a veighbour called to her, "you're up"*
   Put a comma before the word that joins two complete thoughts.

   b. *woke Kim at 5:30, so she got dressed*

4. Alvin who weighs 260 pounds works as a bouncer in a nightclub. When he tells people it's time to leave few of them argue with Alvin.

   a. *Alvin, who weighs 260 pounds, works as a*
   Commas are needed around the words that interrupt the first sentence.

   b. *its time to leave, few of them argue*

5. Home from his first day at kindergarten the little boy stumbled into the house. He dropped his brightly colored book bag on the floor collapsed on the couch and promptly fell asleep.

   a. *first day at kindergarten, the little boy stumbled*
   Put a comma after the introductory words.

   b. *book bag on the floor, collapsed on the couch, and promptly*

Name _____   Section _____ Date _____

Score: (Number right) _____ × 10 = _____ %

■ Comma: Test 4

On the lines provided, write out the parts of each passage that need commas. Be sure to include the commas.

1. The trees especially the newly planted maples were badly damaged by the construction trucks. Broken branches oozing bark and wilted leaves were all signs that the trees might die.

   a. _____

   b. _____

2. "I just hate what's happened to the Sunday paper" Mel said. "The comics section my favorite part is now in small print and hidden inside the TV listings."

   a. _____

   b. _____

3. My eighteen-year-old brother's dream is an apartment of his own a new Corvette with racing stripes and a beautiful girlfriend with a good job. Although I think he's hopelessly unrealistic I don't want to be the one to discourage him.

   a. _____

   b. _____

4. P. T. Barnum the master showman once hitched an elephant to a plow in order to promote his circus. As a result it is still a crime in North Carolina to plow a field with an elephant.

   a. _____

   b. _____

5. Although the gap between men's and women's wages has narrowed a bit in the past ten years it remains a problem that must be solved. This gap causes women, throughout their lifetime, to earn far less even with the same education and the same job than men.

   a. _____

   b. _____

Name _____ Section _____ Date _____

Score: (Number right) _____ × 10 = _____ %

■ Comma: Test 5

On the lines provided, write the word or words in each sentence that need to be followed by a comma. Be sure to include the commas. One comma rule applies in each sentence.

Note To help you master the comma, explanations are given for five of the sentences.

[1]Most of us probably think that "reality television", which features ordinary people in unscripted situations, is a 21st-century phenomenon. [2]The truth is, that this kind of programming is not new, for it actually began more than sixty years ago. [3]Today's reality TV programs can be traced back to the hidden-camera programs, game shows, and talent competitions of the 1940s and 1950s. [4]Allen Funt, the creator and original host of *Candid Camera*, would set up unusual situations and film people without their knowledge. [5]Then he would say, "Smile! You're on *Candid Camera*." [6]*Candid Camera*, originally broadcast in 1948, is considered the first reality TV show and the ancestor of recent programs like *Punk'd*. [7]Thanks to the 1950s game show *Beat the Clock*, we now have such "elimination" shows as *The Amazing Race* and *Survivor*. [8]Beginning with *American Idol* in 2002, talent competitions have become quite popular. [9]Few people today remember *Ted Mack's Original Amateur Hour* or *Arthur Godfrey's Talent Scouts*, but both of these 1948 shows also had amateur contestants and audience voting. [10]Because reality shows have been popular for such a long time, we will probably see even more of them in future seasons.

c 1. _around interrupting words (c)_
Use commas around interrupting words in a sentence.

b 2. _After introductory Material (b)_

a 3. _Between items in a series (a)_
Use commas to separate items in a series.

c 4. _Around interrupting words (c)_

e 5. _with direct quotations (e)_
Use a comma to separate quoted words from the rest of the sentence.

c 6. _before a word that joins two complex thoughts (d)_

b 7. _After introductory Material (b)_
Use a comma after introductory material.

b 8. _After introductory Material (b)_

d 9. _before a word that joins two complete thoughts (d)_
Use a comma before a word that joins two complete thoughts.

b 10. _After introductory Material (b)_

hello hello hello hello hel

■ ∞

Name _____ Section _____ Date _____

Score: (Number right) _____ × 10 = _____%

■ Comma: Test 6

On the lines provided, write the word or words in each sentence that need to be followed by a comma. Be sure to include the commas. One comma rule applies in each sentence.

[1]I love old-fashioned horror films that feature vampires werewolves mummies and zombies. [2]The monster movie I love best of all is *Frankenstein* but it was only recently that I read the original book by that name. [3]I was surprised to learn that its author Mary Shelley was very young. [4]The daughter of scholars Mary was an intelligent and talented young woman. [5]She eloped at seventeen with Percy Shelley a well-known poet and traveled to Switzerland. [6]In Switzerland, their party included Mary her husband another poet (Lord Byron) and Byron's physician. [7]Someone in the group said "Let's each write a story about the supernatural." [8]Mary's contribution a story about a living creature made from dead bodies was *Frankenstein*. [9]The story published when Mary was twenty-one years old became an instant classic. [10]Because of its wide appeal it has been the subject of many movies—and nightmares.

1. _____

2. _____

3. _____

4. _____

5. _____

6. _____

7. _____

8. _____

9. _____

10. _____

9 Apostrophe

Seeing What You Know

Insert apostrophes where needed in the four sentences below. Then read the explanations that follow.

1. Its impossible for water to run uphill.

2. The prosecutor cant try any new cases until next month.

3. No one likes the registrars new procedures for dropping a course.

4. The omelets at the Greens diner are the best in town. Mrs. Green is the chef, and her husband is the host.

Understanding the Answers

1. **It's** impossible for water to run uphill.
   It's is the contraction of the words *it is.* The apostrophe takes the place of the letter *i,* which has been left out.

2. The prosecutor **can't** try any new cases until next month.
   Can't is the contraction of the words *can not.* The apostrophe shows that two letters, *n* and *o,* have been left out.

3. No one likes the **registrar's** new procedures for dropping a course.
   The apostrophe plus *s* shows that the new procedures belong to the registrar. The apostrophe goes after the last letter of *registrar. Likes* does not get an apostrophe; it is a verb. *Procedures* also does not get an apostrophe, because it is not possessive. It is a plural word meaning "more than one procedure."

4. The omelets at the **Greens'** diner are the best in town. Mrs. Green is the chef, and her husband is the host.
   The apostrophe after the *s* shows that the Greens own the diner. With possessive plural words ending in *s,* the apostrophe alone shows possession. *Omelets* does not need an apostrophe, because it is simply a plural word meaning "more than one omelet."

The apostrophe is a punctuation mark with two main purposes. It is used in a **contraction** to show that one or more letters have been left out of a word. The apostrophe is also used to show **possession**—that is, to show that something belongs to someone or something.

APOSTROPHE IN CONTRACTIONS

A contraction is formed when two words are combined to make a new word. The apostrophe takes the place of the letter or letters omitted in forming the contraction. It goes where the missing letters used to be.

Here are a few common contractions:

I + am = **I'm** (the letter *a* in *am* has been left out)

it + is = **it's** (the *i* in *is* has been left out)

does + not = **doesn't** (the *o* in *not* has been left out)

do + not = **don't** (the *o* in *not* has been left out)

she + will = **she'll** (the *wi* in *will* has been left out)

you + would = **you'd** (the *woul* in *would* has been left out)

will + not = **won't** (*o* takes the place of *ill;* the *o* in *not* has been left out)

Contractions are commonly used in everyday speech and writing, as seen in this passage:

Let's go to the movies tonight. *There's* a film *I've* been wanting to see, but it *hasn't* been in town until now. *Didn't* you say *you've* been wanting to see it too? *Shouldn't* we ask Michael and Ana to go with us? *They're* always ready to see a good film. And they *don't* have anything to do this evening.

Practice 1

In the spaces provided, write the contractions of the words in parentheses.

1. *(What is)* _____ the best reality show *(that is)* _____ on TV this season?

2. When the timer goes off, *(you will)* _____ know *(it is)* _____ time to take the potatoes out of the microwave.

3. *(I would)* _____ like to speak to the person *(who is)* _____ in charge of the shoe department.

4. Many teenagers *(are not)* _____ able to find jobs in the summer, so it *(is not)* _____ easy for them to save money for college tuition.

5. The game show contestants *(did not)* _____ win the trip to Hawaii, but *(they are)* _____ getting a box of pineapples as a consolation prize.

Four Confusing Pairs

Four contractions that can cause problems are **they're** (meaning *they are*), **it's** (meaning *it is* or *it has*), **you're** (meaning *you are*), and **who's** (meaning *who is*). They are easily confused with the possessive forms **their** (meaning *belonging to them*), **its** (meaning *belonging to it*), **your** (meaning *belonging to you*), and **whose** (meaning *belonging to whom*). Notice how each of these words is used in the sentences below:

> **They're** *(they are)* very angry about the damage done to **their** new mailbox *(the new mailbox belonging to them)*.

> **It's** *(it is)* a shame that your car has blown **its** engine *(the engine belonging to it)*.

> **Your** parents *(the parents belonging to you)* said that **you're** *(you are)* supposed to be home by midnight.

> **Who's** *(who is)* the person **whose** car *(the car belonging to whom)* is taking up two parking spaces?

Practice 2

Underline the correct word in each set of parentheses.

1. (It's, Its) too late now to give the dog (it's, its) bath.

2. (They're, Their) not real friends if they can't keep a secret or mind (they're, their) own business.

3. (Who's, Whose) going to tell me (who's, whose) drink this is?

4. I think that (you're, your) best quality is (you're, your) sense of humor.

5. (It's, Its) revealing that only four pieces of United States currency have had women's pictures on (they're, their) front or back sides. The women (who's, whose) faces have been on US money are Martha Washington, Pocahontas, Susan B. Anthony, and Sacajawea. What's (your, you're) guess as to why these four women were chosen?

THE APOSTROPHE TO SHOW POSSESSION

To show that something belongs to someone or something, we could say, for example, *the truck owned by Sally, the radial tires belonging to the car,* or *the Great Dane of the neighbor.* But it's much simpler to say the following:

> *Sally's* truck

> *the car's* radial tires

> *the neighbor's* Great Dane

To make a singular word (or a plural word not ending in *s*) possessive, add an apostrophe plus an *s.* To decide *what* to make possessive, ask yourself the following:

1   Who or what is owned?

2   Who or what owns something?

Then put the apostrophe plus an *s* after the name of the owner.
    For example, look at the following word group:

    the truck owned by Sally

First ask yourself, "What is owned?" The answer is *the truck.* Then ask, "Who is the owner?" The answer is *Sally.* So add an apostrophe plus *s* after the name of the owner: *Sally's truck.* The apostrophe plus *s* shows that the truck belongs to Sally.
    Here is another example:

    the toys belonging to the children

Again, ask yourself, "What is owned?" The answer is *toys.* Then ask, "Who is the owner?" The answer is *the children.* So add an apostrophe plus *s* after the name of the owner: *the children's toys.* The apostrophe plus *s* shows that the toys belong to the children.

Notes

1   An apostrophe plus *s* is used to show possession, even with a singular word that already ends in *s:*

Tess**'s** purse (the purse belonging to Tess)

the boss**'s** car (the car owned by the boss)

2   But an apostrophe alone is used to show possession with a plural word that ends in *s:*

several students**'** complaints (the complaints of several students)

the two teams**'** agreement (the agreement of the two teams)

Practice 3

Two apostrophes are needed to show possession in each sentence below. In each space provided, write the word or words that need the apostrophe (the owner) as well as what is owned. The first sentence is done for you as an example.

1. The spiders web glistened with moisture from last nights rain.

    _____*spider's web*_____   _____*last night's rain*_____

2. The mail carriers job is not made any easier by that mans vicious dog.

    _____   _____

3. Everyones assignment is to prepare a two-minute speech for Mondays class.

    _____   _____

4. Ben Franklins inventions were often a combination of other peoples ideas.

_____   _____

5. Doriss grades are better than both of her brothers grades ever were.

_____   _____

When Not to Use an Apostrophe: In Plurals and Verbs

People sometimes confuse possessive and plural forms of words. Remember that a plural is formed simply by adding an *s* to a word; no apostrophe is used. Look at the sentence below to see which words are plural and which are possessive:

Tina's new boots have silver buckles.

The words *boots* and *buckles* are plurals—there is more than one boot, and there is more than one buckle. But *Tina's,* the word with the apostrophe plus *s,* is possessive. Tina owns the boots.

Also, many verbs end with just an *s*—for example, the word *owns* in the sentence "Tina owns the boots." Do not put an apostrophe in a verb.

Practice 4

In the spaces provided under each sentence, add the one apostrophe needed and explain why the other words ending in *s* do not get apostrophes.

Example The little boys daily temper tantrum seems to last for hours.

boys: *boy's, meaning "belonging to the little boy"*

seems: *verb*

hours: *plural meaning "more than one hour"*

1. Lucys boyfriend texts her before and after every class.

Lucys: _____

texts: _____

2. That old storefronts grimy window has not been cleaned in many years.

storefronts: _____

years: _____

3. The managers mood is much better after she gives out the assignments for the day.

managers: _____

gives: _____

assignments: _____

4. This years new television shows are much worse than the programs of past seasons.

years: _____

shows: _____

programs: _____

seasons: _____

5. The motor of our sons old car coughs and wheezes whenever it starts.

sons: _____

coughs: _____

wheezes: _____

starts: _____

6. One of Theos failings is jumping to conclusions.

Theos: _____

failings: _____

conclusions: _____

7. Dieters should drink eight glasses of water a day because of waters ability to make the stomach feel more full.

Dieters: _____

glasses: _____

waters: _____

8. On the game reserve, dozens of elephants crowded around the two water holes edges.

dozens: _____

elephants: _____

water holes: _____

edges: _____

Note   Additional information about the apostrophe appears on page 216.

Name _____ Section _____ Date _____

Score: (Number right) _____ × 10 = _____ %

■ Apostrophe: Test 1

Each of the sentences below contains one word that needs an apostrophe. Write each word, with its apostrophe, in the space provided.

Note   To help you master the apostrophe, explanations are given for half of the sentences.

1. The teachers broken leg kept her out of class for two weeks.

   _____   The broken leg belongs to the teacher.
   Weeks is plural.

2. Most of my friends have their own cars, but many of them cant afford gas or insurance.

   _____

3. Im taking extra courses so I can graduate one semester early.

   _____   An apostrophe should take the place of the missing *a* in the contraction.

4. The instructors policies state clearly that students are not permitted to use cell phones once her class has begun.

   _____

5. The huge green frogs sticky tongue soon captured several flies.

   _____   The frog owns the sticky tongue. *Flies* is a simple plural.

6. Endorphins, the bodys natural painkillers, are released when people exercise.

   _____

7. A sign in front of the store entrance says, "Dont even *think* of parking here!"

   _____   *Don't* is a contraction of *do not,* with the *o* in *not* left out. *Says* is a verb.

8. Its supposed to rain for the next three days, so we can skip watering the lawn.

   _____

9. A tornado destroyed the barns roof, but no animals were killed.

   _____   The roof belongs to the barn. *Animals* is a simple plural.

10. Even though they live a thousand miles apart, the two brothers relationship has remained strong through the years.

    _____

■ Apostrophe: Test 2

Each of the sentences below contains one word that needs an apostrophe. Write each word, with its apostrophe, in the space provided.

1. Because I had a lot of e-mails to answer, I didnt get to sleep until 2 a.m.

   _____

2. According to many scientists, the shrinking of Earths ozone layer will result in rising temperatures.

   _____

3. When the ballparks gates opened, hundreds of fans were already waiting outside.

   _____

4. Many of the streets residents have lived there for at least twenty years.

   _____

5. If the canary hasnt eaten its food by morning, you should take the canary to the veterinarian.

   _____

6. Babysitters dont usually agree to take care of those twins a second time.

   _____

7. More than one-fourth of the librarys books are missing from the shelves.

   _____

8. My sisters husband got lost while hiking, but rescuers found him two miles from where he had parked his car.

   _____

9. Because the company made more money than expected, its rewarding the hard-working employees with generous bonuses.

   _____

10. Ramona couldnt start either of her cars, so she had to call a tow truck.

   _____

Name _____   Section _____ Date _____

Score: (Number right) _____ × 10 = _____ %

■ Apostrophe: Test 3

Each of the short passages below contains two words that need apostrophes. Underline the words that need apostrophes. Then write each word, with its apostrophe, in the space provided.

Note   To help you master the apostrophe, explanations are given for the first sentence in each passage.

1. Dianas sisters helped her study for her vet school finals. Theyve been her study partners since high school.

   a. _____   The sisters belong to Diana.

   b. _____

2. Whos the person in charge of repairs around here? The copy machines red light is flashing again.

   a. _____   An apostrophe should take the place of the

   b. _____   missing *i* in the contraction.

3. "Im surprised that you take my grades so seriously," said Ned to his father. "Grades are no measure of a persons true worth."

   a. _____   An apostrophe should take the place of the

   b. _____   missing *a* in the contraction.

4. Kates tights began to slip down to her knees as she walked back from the school stage. She couldnt do anything about it, so she kept her head down and hoped nobody would notice.

   a. _____   The tights belong to Kate.

   b. _____

5. A tiny crack appeared in the fish tanks corner. The goldfish looked unconcerned, but their owner didnt feel as calm.

   a. _____   The corner belongs to the fish tank.

   b. _____

Name _____ Section _____ Date _____

Score: (Number right) _____ × 10 = _____%

■ Apostrophe: Test 4

Each of the short passages below contains two words that need apostrophes. Underline the words that need apostrophes. Then write each word, with its apostrophe, in the space provided.

1. Just as I finished typing my paper, my computers hard drive crashed. Fortunately, I had backed up the papers previous draft on a flash drive.

    a. _____

    b. _____

2. The books cover shows a beautiful woman and a handsome man in each others arms. That is odd, because the book is not a love story at all.

    a. _____

    b. _____

3. "Ricks sneakers are in the middle of the kitchen floor," his father said. "So hes sure to be around here somewhere."

    a. _____

    b. _____

4. Some peoples lack of consideration is beyond belief. Our neighbors, for example, have parties every Saturday night where they sing and play loud music until dawn. And they havent invited us to a single one.

    a. _____

    b. _____

5. "Youre not thinking of asking me for my car keys again, are you?" Ivan said to his sixteen-year-old daughter. "Getting a drivers license does not mean you automatically get a car to go with it."

    a. _____

    b. _____

Name _____   Section _____   Date _____

Score: (Number right) _____ × 10 = _____ %

■ Apostrophe: Test 5

Each sentence in the following passage contains a word that requires an apostrophe. Underline the ten words. Then, on the lines following the passage, write the corrected form of each word.

Note   To help you master the apostrophe, explanations are given for five of the sentences.

[1]In this paragraph youre likely to learn something new about President Barack Obama. [2]As a six-year-old child in Indonesia, he ate grasshopper, dog meat, and snake meat, which are not among Indonesias main dishes. [3]His classmates nickname for him, which he used until college, was "Barry." [4]His familys pets included birds, a dog, two baby crocodiles, and an ape named Tata. [5]At age ten, Barack moved back to Hawaii to live with his grandparents and attended Honolulus prestigious Punahou School. [6]Ever since working at Baskin-Robbins as a teenager, he hasnt liked ice cream. [7]In 2006, Obama won a Grammy Award for a voice recording of his first book, *Dreams from My Father,* which is about Obamas search for his identity. [8]Obama plays basketball, and soon after the election, he said that hed install a basketball court on the White House grounds. [9]During his presidential campaign, he watched sports regularly but didnt watch the news very much. [10]Barack Obama has become one of the worlds most respected figures since being elected the first African American president of the United States.

1. _____   The contraction of *you are* needs an apostrophe.

2. _____

3. _____   The nickname was used by his classmates, so the plural possessive is needed.

4. _____

5. _____   Punahou School belongs to the city of Honolulu.

6. _____

7. _____   The search belonged to Obama.

8. _____

9. _____   The contraction of *did not* needs an apostrophe.

10. _____

Name _____ Section _____ Date _____

Score: (Number right) _____ × 10 = _____ %

■ Apostrophe: Test 6

Each sentence in the following passage contains a word that requires an apostrophe. Underline the ten words. Then, on the lines following the passage, write the corrected form of each word.

[1]One of historys most fascinating figures is Cleopatra, a queen of ancient Egypt. [2]She was born in the year 69 B.C., and in keeping with one of the ancient Egyptian traditions, she became her brothers wife when she was made queen. [3]Her brother soon drove her from Egypts throne, however, and she began making plans to go to war against him. [4]When Cleopatras beauty and charm caught the eye of the Roman general Julius Caesar, they became lovers. [5]Caesars feelings for Cleopatra were so strong that he went to war for her, killing her brother. [6]She became queen again, marrying a younger brother, but it wasnt long before she poisoned her new husband. [7]Later on, Caesar was murdered, and Cleopatra became the mistress of one of Romes most powerful military figures, Mark Antony. [8]But when Antonys soldiers were defeated in battle, Cleopatra agreed to join the plot of an enemy, Octavian, by pretending to commit suicide. [9]Antony didnt want to live without her, so he killed himself. [10]When she couldnt persuade Octavian to become her lover and ally, Cleopatra put an end to her own violent life.

1. _____

2. _____

3. _____

4. _____

5. _____

6. _____

7. _____

8. _____

9. _____

10. _____

10 Quotation Marks

Seeing What You Know

Insert quotation marks or underlines as needed in the following sentences. One sentence does not need quotation marks. Then read the explanations below.

1. The mechanic said, Your car needs more than a tune-up.

2. To tell you the truth, said my husband, I'm thinking of quitting my job.

3. My sister called to say that she needed heart surgery.

4. According to The Book of Answers, the most widely sung song in the English-speaking world is Happy Birthday to You.

Understanding the Answers

1. The mechanic said, "Your car needs more than a tune-up."
   The words *Your car needs more than a tune-up* need quotation marks. These are the exact words that the mechanic said. Since *Your* is the first word of a quoted sentence, it is capitalized.

2. "To tell you the truth," said my husband, "I'm thinking of quitting my job."
   Each of the two word groups spoken by the husband, since they are his exact words, needs a set of quotation marks.

3. My sister called to say that she needed heart surgery.
   The words *that she needed heart surgery* are not the speaker's exact words. (Her exact words would have been "I need heart surgery.") In such an indirect quotation, no quotation marks are used.

4. According to <u>The Book of Answers</u>, the most widely sung song in the English-speaking world is "Happy Birthday to You."
   Titles of short works, such as songs, are put in quotation marks. Titles of longer works, such as books, are either italicized or underlined.

Quotation marks enclose the exact words of a speaker or writer. Quotation marks also set off the title of a short work.

QUOTATION MARKS TO SET OFF THE WORDS OF A SPEAKER OR WRITER

Use quotation marks to set off the exact words of a speaker or writer.

> After the bombing of Pearl Harbor, President Franklin Roosevelt described the day as "a date which will live in infamy."
> (President Roosevelt's exact words are enclosed in quotation marks.)

> "When we're done with the dishes," said Terry, "we'll be ready to go."
> (Terry's exact words are set off by two sets of quotation marks. The words *said Terry* are not included in the quotation marks since they were not spoken by him.)

> Opal told her uncle, "We'll serve dinner at seven o'clock. If you can't make it then, stop in later for dessert."
> (Because the two sentences give Opal's words without interruption, they require just one set of quotation marks.)

> "Experience," wrote Vernon Law, "is a hard teacher because she gives the test first, the lesson afterward."
> (The exact words that Law wrote are enclosed in quotation marks.)

Punctuation note   Quoted material is usually set off from the rest of the sentence by a comma. When the comma comes at the end of quoted material, it is included inside the quotation marks. The same is true for a period, exclamation point, or question mark that ends quoted material:

Incorrect:	"If it rains", said Connie, "the ball game will be canceled".
Correct:	"If it rains," said Connie, "the ball game will be canceled."

Notice, too, that a quoted sentence begins with a capital letter, even when it is preceded by other words.

Incorrect:	Marco said, "let's go to the fair tonight."
Correct:	Marco said, "Let's go to the fair tonight."

Practice 1

Insert quotation marks where needed.

1. My throat is so sore I can't talk, Larry whispered.

2. Wilson Mizner once said, Life's a tough proposition, and the first hundred years are the hardest.

3. Don't go in that door! the audience shouted to the actor on the movie screen.

4. If you can't help me, I'll have to find someone else who can, my sister yelled as she slammed my bedroom door behind her.

5. If at first you don't succeed, my wife joked, you should read the directions.

Direct and Indirect Quotations

Often we communicate someone's spoken or written thoughts without repeating the exact words used. We quote indirectly by putting the message into our own words. Such **indirect quotations** do not require quotation marks. The word *that* often signals an indirect quotation.

The following example shows how the same material could be handled as either a direct or an indirect quotation.

Direct Quotation

Keshia said, "If I pass all my exams, I will graduate this June."
(These are Keshia's exact words, so they are put in quotation marks.)

Indirect Quotation

Keshia said that if she passes all her exams, she will graduate this June.
(These are *not* Keshia's exact words. No quotation marks are used.)

Practice 2

Turn each of the following indirect quotations into a direct quotation. You will have to change some of the words as well as add quotation marks. The first one is done for you as an example.

1. Emmet asked if he could borrow my dictionary.

   Emmet asked, "Could I borrow your dictionary?"

2. Coach Hodges told Lori that she had played an outstanding game.

   _____

3. Manuel insisted that his new glasses haven't improved his vision one bit.

   _____

4. The detective exclaimed that he knew the murderer's identity.

   _____

5. Our instructor told us to study well because we couldn't use the book or our notes on the test.

   _____

QUOTATION MARKS TO SET OFF THE TITLES OF SHORT WORKS

The titles of short works are set off in quotation marks. Short works include short stories, newspaper and magazine articles, song titles, poems, episodes of television shows, and chapters of books.

Note   The titles of longer works, such as books, newspapers, magazines, plays, movies, television series, and albums, should be underlined when written. (When longer works are mentioned in printed material or in a paper prepared on a computer, their titles are usually set in *italic type*.)

> "The Body," a short story by Stephen King, was later made into the movie Stand By Me.

> I remember memorizing Robert Frost's poem "Stopping by Woods on a Snowy Evening" when I was in eighth grade.

> "Jimmy's World," an article in the Washington Times about a drug-addicted child, won a Pulitzer Prize, but the story was later proved to be a fake.

> Bing Crosby's recording of the song "White Christmas" is still one of the biggest sellers of all time.

Practice 3

Insert quotation marks or underlines where needed in the sentences below.

1. I bought a copy of the cookbook titled The Good Food Book because I wanted to read the chapter called How to Eat More and Weigh Less.

2. One of my favorite poems is the one by William Carlos Williams called The Red Wheelbarrow.

3. Whenever Gina sees the movie The Sound of Music, the song near the end, Climb Every Mountain, makes her cry.

4. Randy couldn't remember whether he had read the article All Gamblers Lose in Newsweek or in Time.

5. An article called Will the Circle Be Unbroken? in The Atlantic Monthly includes interviews with four people about death and dying.

Note   Additional information about quotation marks appears on pages 217–218.

Name _____   Section _____   Date _____

■ **Quotation Marks: Test 1**

On the lines provided, rewrite the following sentences, adding quotation marks as needed. Two of the sentences do not need quotation marks.

Note   To help you master quotation marks, explanations are given for half of the sentences.

1. Beverly said, I'm too tired to stay up any longer.

   _____

   Beverly's words and the period at the end of the sentence should be included within quotation marks.

2. Don't laugh so loud—you'll wake the children, Chris whispered.

   _____

3. I'm furious, shouted Kareem, about your constant lies!

   _____

   Each of the two parts of Kareem's statement requires a set of quotation marks. The words *shouted Kareem* do not get quotation marks because they are not part of his statement.

4. On your way out, called my mother, please put out the kitchen trash.

   _____

5. Carole said that she was staying home for the weekend.

   _____

   Carole's message is communicated indirectly.

6. The student explained that he'd fallen asleep during class.

   _____

7. Is that a wig? Can I touch it? the little girl asked her uncle.

   _____

   The little girl's two questions are uninterrupted, so they are included within one set of quotation marks.

8. You're right! It is snowing! exclaimed Raymond.

   _____

Name _____   Section _____   Date _____

Score: (Number right) _____ × 10 = _____%

■ Quotation Marks: Test 2

On the lines provided, rewrite the part or parts of each sentence that need quotation marks. One of the ten items does not need quotation marks.

1. The firefighter asked the neighbors, Is anyone else still in the building?

   _____

2. The food machines in the lunchroom should offer healthier choices, suggested Tran.

   _____

3. Those shoes, the salesclerk assured me, will never go out of style.

   _____

4. The bookstore manager told us that he couldn't buy back books with writing in them.

   _____

5. My sixteen-year-old niece asked if she could have her own car. Not until you have your own money, her mother said.

   _____

6. Can't I stay up a little longer? the little boy asked the babysitter.

   _____

7. Did you read the funny article called What People Really Want for Christmas in today's newspaper?

   _____

8. I'm afraid of only one thing, the Scarecrow told Dorothy. That's a lighted match.

   _____

9. The Black Cat and The Tell-Tale Heart are two of Edgar Allan Poe's most chilling stories.

   _____

10. My next-door neighbor shouted, Please try to control your dog. She's ruining all my flower beds.

    _____

Name _____ Section _____ Date _____

Score: (Number right) _____ × 10 = _____ %

■ **Quotation Marks: Test 3**

Place quotation marks where needed in the short passages that follow. Each passage needs **two** sets of quotation marks.

Note   To help you master quotation marks, explanations are given for one set of quotation marks in each passage.

1. May I ask you a personal question? asked my nosy neighbor, as if she needed my permission. You may ask it, but I probably won't answer it, I replied.

   The neighbor's question should be set off with one set of quotation marks.

2. Benjamin Franklin is famous for his witty sayings. Many of them give advice on how to behave; others are comments on human nature. For instance, he once wrote, To lengthen thy life, lessen thy meals. He also commented, Three may keep a secret, if two of them are dead.

   Franklin's advice on behavior should be set off with one set of quotation marks.

3. When Mr. Benton asked to withdraw some money from his account, the bank teller said, I'm sorry, but your account is overdrawn. Mr. Benton answered, Nonsense, I must still have money in my account. See, I have lots of checks left.

   The teller's words should be set off with quotation marks.

4. Last week, one of my best friends told me, You need to have more self-confidence. You are smart, beautiful, and everyone's best friend. I responded, I wish I could believe you, but I think you're a bit biased.

   The best friend's exact words should be set off with one set of quotation marks.

5. This article titled How to Find Your Perfect Mate in *Cosmopolitan* is the dumbest thing I've ever read. It actually suggests that before you go on a first date, you ask your date, Please fill out this questionnaire on your likes and dislikes.

   The title of an article is put in quotation marks.

■ Quotation Marks: Test 4

Place quotation marks where needed in the short passages that follow. Each passage needs **two** sets of quotation marks.

1. When the squirrel began to climb up to the bird feeder, my mother yelled, You are not going to steal my birds' food again! Get out of here! The squirrel kept climbing, paying no attention to my frustrated mother. Mom, I really don't think the squirrel understands what you're trying to tell it, I said with a straight face.

2. An angry-looking woman marched up to the customer service desk and slammed a large box on the counter. You sold me this juicer, and now I want my money back, she told the clerk. Every time I turn it on, it spits carrot pieces all over my kitchen table.

3. The interviewer poked her head out of the office door and called out, Please come in, Mr. Ortiz. She asked him a few questions about his education and job history. Then she said, You're the twentieth applicant for this position. Please tell me why I should hire you instead of any of the others.

4. Hey, you, called the homeless man sitting on the sidewalk. A well-dressed young man paused. Are you talking to me? he asked.

5. You bet I am. How would you like to trade places with me? said the homeless man. The young man smiled nervously and then said that he would prefer not to. The older man nodded. I don't blame you, he said and lay back down on the pavement.

Name _____   Section _____ Date _____
                                           Score: (Number right) _____ × 10 = _____ %

■ Quotation Marks: Test 5

Ten of the sentences in the passage below require a set of quotation marks. Insert the quotation marks where needed. On the lines provided at the bottom, write the numbers of the sentences to which you have added quotation marks.

Note   To help you master quotation marks, five of the sentences that need quotation marks are identified for you.

¹Last summer I went with my husband Lenny to his ten-year high school reunion. ²He kept telling me, Oh, boy, are you going to love my old gang. ³I'd heard a lot about the old gang, and I wondered about that. ⁴Not only are we going to have a great time, but I'm going to be master of ceremonies, he announced.

⁵On the big night, we'd barely driven into the parking lot when we were surrounded by a crowd of apparently grown men shouting, Li-zard! Li-zard! Lenny the Lizard has arrived! ⁶I turned and looked at my husband. ⁷Lenny the Lizard? I asked. ⁸He didn't have time to answer. ⁹Party time! he roared, leaping out of the car and disappearing into the building.

¹⁰When I caught up with him, he was being hugged and kissed by a good-looking redhead. ¹¹Ooooohhhh, she said, looking me over. ¹²You sure don't look like the type that Lenny would have married!

¹³After a year or so we sat down to dinner. ¹⁴There, people kept saying things like Do you remember the time Jock dissected the frog and gave its heart to Diane on Valentine's Day? ¹⁵Everybody at the table would break up laughing at that point, while I was still waiting to hear what had happened.

¹⁶Finally it was time for Lenny to get up and speak. ¹⁷He actually did a pretty good job, and he finished his remarks by asking the class members to introduce their spouses. ¹⁸To get things started, he had me stand as he said, And this is my wonderful wife, Betty. ¹⁹Unfortunately, my name is Linda.

²⁰When it's time for Lenny's twentieth, I'm going to stay home and write an article called Surviving Your Spouse's Reunion.

1. Sentence __2__   6. Sentence ____
2. Sentence ____   7. Sentence __12__
3. Sentence __5__   8. Sentence ____
4. Sentence ____   9. Sentence __18__
5. Sentence __9__   10. Sentence ____

■ Quotation Marks: Test 6

Ten of the sentences in the passage below require a set of quotation marks. Insert the quotation marks where needed. On the lines provided at the bottom, write the numbers of the sentences to which you have added quotation marks.

[1]Last summer, I went on a road trip with my best friend, Lindsay. [2]Since we had read an article titled The Majesty of the Grand Canyon, we were both eager to see this natural wonder. [3]We left from Indiana and drove out west, stopping in Colorado to visit some friends from college. [4]You're going to love Colorado in the summer! our friend Jamie kept telling us before we arrived. [5]We planned on staying there for two days before continuing on our trip.

[6]Two weeks later, we were still in Colorado. [7]I have a free pass for white water rafting, Jamie said. [8]I'll take you horseback riding, our friend Brian told us. [9]Would you like to go hiking on the trails behind our house? Bethany asked. [10]When Jamie told us that she could get us tickets to a concert, we decided we would never leave. [11]Everyone was so nice, and there were so many enjoyable things to do.

[12]Eventually, we found ourselves driving out of Colorado and then through Utah. [13]As we drove through the Utah deserts, Lindsay commented, I can't believe how different it is out here. [14]We stared in awe at the gigantic red rocks all around us. [15]Just wait until you see the Grand Canyon! I replied.

[16]Several hours later, we were driving at night. [17]Wow! Lindsay said. [18]What is *that*? [19]I looked ahead and saw a massive row of twinkling lights over the dark horizon. [20]I think it's Las Vegas, I said as I realized we had taken a wrong turn and had missed Arizona. [21]We drove into Las Vegas, deciding to visit the Grand Canyon on another trip.

1. *Sentence* ____   6. *Sentence* ____

2. *Sentence* ____   7. *Sentence* ____

3. *Sentence* ____   8. *Sentence* ____

4. *Sentence* ____   9. *Sentence* ____

5. *Sentence* ____   10. *Sentence* ____

11 Other Punctuation Marks

Seeing What You Know

Add a period, a question mark, or an exclamation mark to each sentence that follows. Use a different end mark in each sentence. Then read the explanations below.

1. Half of all the people in America live in just eight of the fifty states

2. Are you going to the high school reunion

3. Stop that noise before I go crazy

Insert a colon, a semicolon, and parentheses where needed in the following sentences.

4. Rocky Road my favorite ice cream flavor contains marshmallows and nuts.

5. The bearded man looked around the quiet bank then he passed the teller a folded note. Two emotions showed on the teller's face surprise and terror.

Insert a hyphen and dashes where needed in the following sentence.

6. Nobody not even her attorney believed the woman's odd sounding alibi.

Understanding the Answers

1. states.   2. reunion?   3. crazy!
   Sentence 1 makes a statement, so a period is needed. Sentence 2 asks a question and so must end with a question mark. Sentence 3 expresses strong feeling, so an exclamation point is appropriate.

4. (my favorite ice cream flavor)
   The parentheses set off information that is not essential to the rest of the sentence.

5. bank; then . . . face: surprise
   The semicolon connects two complete thoughts, each with its own subject and verb. The colon introduces an explanation of the idea stated just before the colon.

6. Nobody—not even her attorney—believed . . . odd-sounding alibi.
   Dashes emphasize the words *not even her attorney*. A hyphen joins the two words that act together to describe the noun *alibi*.

This chapter first describes three marks of punctuation that are used to end a sentence: the period (.), the question mark (?), and the exclamation point (!). The chapter then describes five additional marks of punctuation: the colon (:), semicolon (;), hyphen (-), dash (—), and parentheses ( ).

PERIOD (.)

Use a period at the end of a statement, a mild command, or an indirect question.

> Only the female mosquito drinks blood.
>
> Go let the dog out.
>
> I wonder if it's going to rain.

The period is also used at the end of most abbreviations.

> Dr. Breslin   Mr. and Mrs. Liu   Ms. Barsky   M. A. degree

QUESTION MARK (?)

The question mark follows a direct question, as in the following examples.

> What's that green stuff in your hair?
>
> Have you seen the new Will Smith movie?
>
> "What did you put in this stew?" Grandpa asked.

Indirect questions, those that tell the reader about a question rather than ask it directly, do not require question marks. They end with periods.

> Please ask the bus driver if we can get off at Spruce Street.
>
> I wonder if I'll ever see Ali again.
>
> Gina asked Stan to jump-start her car.

EXCLAMATION POINT (!)

The exclamation point shows that a word or statement expresses excitement or another strong feeling.

> Look out for that car!
>
> I've won the lottery!
>
> If you insult my dog again, I'll let go of the leash!

Note   Exclamation points lose their power if they are used too frequently. When they are used occasionally and for good reason, they add drama to a paragraph.

Practice 1

Place a period, question mark, or exclamation point at the end of each of the following sentences.

1. When does the library close

2. I wonder if my grades are coming in the mail today

3. Hurry up if you want to see the cat giving birth

4. Although I followed the directions closely, the computer program didn't run

5. Please put all cans and glass bottles in the recycling bins

COLON (:)

The colon says, in essence, "Keep reading. Here comes something important." It has three uses:

1. **To introduce a list.** The bag lady's possessions were few**:** a shopping cart, a sleeping bag, and two or three ragged garments.

2. **To introduce a long or literary quotation.** Charles Dickens begins his classic novel *A Tale of Two Cities* with these well-known words**:** "It was the best of times, it was the worst of times, it was the age of wisdom, it was the age of foolishness. . . ."

3. **To introduce a final fact or explanation.** There's only one explanation for Maude's behavior**:** she's jealous.

Note   Use a colon only where a period would also be appropriate.

SEMICOLON (;)

Unlike the colon, which indicates "Go on," the semicolon says "Pause here." Semicolons are used between two complete thoughts in two ways:

1. **To join two complete thoughts not connected by a joining word.** Barry cleans the house and cooks**;** Lana does the laundry and the grocery shopping.

2. **To join two complete statements with a transitional word.** I've never liked my father-in-law**;** furthermore, he knows it.

Note   Other transitional words that may come after a semicolon include *however, moreover, therefore, thus, also, consequently, otherwise, nevertheless, then, now, in addition, in fact,* and *as a result.* (A longer list appears on page 210.)

Punctuation note   Put a comma after such transitional words.

HYPHEN (-)

The hyphen is used in two ways:

1. **To join two or more words that act together to describe a noun.** We found an excuse to walk away from the fast-talking salesman. (The hyphen shows that *fast* and *talking,* combined, describe the salesman; he talks fast.)

2. To divide a word at the end of a line of writing. If you ever visit California, I hope you'll come see me.

Note   Always divide a word between syllables, and never divide a word of only one syllable. Your dictionary will show you where syllable divisions occur.

DASH (—)

The dash indicates a dramatic pause. By using it, the writer is giving special emphasis to the words that the dash separates from the rest of the sentence.

> CPR sometimes—but not always—succeeds in reviving heart attack victims.
>
> Randy spotted his blind date sitting in the restaurant. He straightened his tie, waved confidently to her, swaggered into the room—and tripped and fell full-length onto the carpet.

Note   To type a dash, type two hyphens. Do not add space before or after a dash.

PARENTHESES ( )

Parentheses show that the information inside them is less important than the other material presented.

> Professor Rodriguez (one of my favorite teachers) is going to retire this year.
>
> The assignments that follow (Exercises 1, 2, and 3) will help sharpen your understanding of everyday defense mechanisms.

Practice 2

Insert a colon, semicolon, hyphen, a dash or dashes, or parentheses where needed in each of the sentences below. Use only one kind of mark in each sentence.

1. The little red haired girl started flirting with my young nephew.

2. My mother's college roommate I think I've mentioned her to you before has invited us to visit her in Florida.

3. As Snow White learned, apples aren't so good for you after all if they're poisoned.

4. The Swiss Army knife came with many attachments a screwdriver, tweezers, magnifying glass, toothpick, and four knife blades.

5. Many people find it very hard to stay on a diet ads tempt them constantly with images of forbidden foods.

Note   Additional information about punctuation marks appears on pages 219–220.

Name _____ Section _____ Date _____

Score: (Number right) _____ × 12.5 = _____ %

■ **Other Punctuation Marks: Test 1**

Each of the following sentences needs one of the kinds of punctuation marks shown in the box below. In the space provided, write the letter of the mark needed. Then add that mark to the sentence. Each sentence requires a different punctuation mark.

Note   To help you master these punctuation marks, explanations are given for half of the sentences.

a	Period .	**e**	Semicolon ;
b	Question mark ?	**f**	Hyphen -
c	Exclamation point !	**g**	Dash or dashes —
d	Colon :	**h**	Parentheses ( )

_____ 1. Three languages are spoken in Switzerland German, French, and Italian.
German, French, and Italian is a list of items.

_____ 2. Which of these offices is the one that processes student loans

_____ 3. My usually soft spoken father began to shout angrily.
The words *soft* and *spoken* need to be joined into one descriptive unit.

_____ 4. Monica barely needed to study in high school however, she's finding college more difficult.

_____ 5. If you ever and I mean ever forget our anniversary again, you'd better start looking for a lawyer.
The phrase *and I mean ever* needs to be set off. It is being emphasized dramatically.

_____ 6. My sister's chemistry textbook it must weigh ten pounds was the most expensive book she had to buy this semester.

_____ 7. Don't pick up that hot plate
The statement is a strong one, which would probably be shouted.

_____ 8. Warren spoke to the restaurant manager and asked if the air conditioning couldn't be turned down just a little

Name _____ Section _____ Date _____

Score: (Number right) _____ × 10 = _____ %

■ Other Punctuation Marks: Test 2

Each of the following sentences needs one of the kinds of punctuation marks shown in the box below. In the space provided, write the letter of the mark needed. Then insert the punctuation into the sentence. Each punctuation mark is used at least once.

a	Period .	**e**	Semicolon ;
b	Question mark ?	**f**	Hyphen -
c	Exclamation point !	**g**	Dash or dashes —
d	Colon :	**h**	Parentheses ( )

_____ 1. Did you know that a slow moving car can cause an accident?

_____ 2. Dozens of birds flocked around the birdfeeder a gray cat crept quietly toward them in the bushes below.

_____ 3. "DE . . . FENSE " screamed the fans as the visiting team passed the basketball back and forth.

_____ 4. I need to get a dress for the wedding however, it has to be an inexpensive one that I can wear again.

_____ 5. The little girl looked very sad as she pulled her test out of her notebook then burst out laughing when her mother saw the A+ on it.

_____ 6. The novel *Beloved* by Toni Morrison who also wrote *The Bluest Eye* is a powerful story about the painful legacy of slavery.

_____ 7. There are two kinds of moviegoers that drive me crazy those who talk constantly and those who blurt out what is going to happen next.

_____ 8. "Hating people," wrote Harry Emerson Fosdick, "is like burning down your own house to get rid of a rat"

_____ 9. The supervisor wondered out loud, "Does Sam ever admit that he made a mistake "

_____ 10. Henry Thompson was a respected businessman, Sunday school teacher, Scout leader and occasional bank robber.

Name _____   Section _____   Date _____

Score: (Number right) _____ × 10 = _____ %

■ **Other Punctuation Marks: Test 3**

Each of the following passages requires **two** of the punctuation marks shown in the box below. In the spaces provided, write the letters of the **two** marks needed in each passage. Then insert the correct punctuation into the sentence. Each punctuation mark is used at least once.

Note   To help you master these punctuation marks, explanations are provided for half of the corrections.

a	Period .	**e**	Semicolon ;
b	Question mark ?	**f**	Hyphen -
c	Exclamation point !	**g**	Dash or dashes —
d	Colon :	**h**	Parentheses ( )

____ ____   1. I watched my sister searching through the drawers. Finally I asked her what she was looking for "Why do you have to know" she asked angrily.

I asked her what she was looking for is an indirect question.

____ ____   2. Jerry's mother once worked for the Peace Corps. She traveled to several countries Thailand, India, Nepal, and Malaysia. She often told me I visited their home many times that Nepal was the most beautiful country in the world.

Thailand, India, Nepal, and Malaysia is a list of items.

____ ____   3. The door-to-door salesman seemed like such a shy, kind person that we invited him in for coffee. It was several hours later when he was probably in the next state that we discovered he had robbed us

The words *when he was probably in the next state* should be emphasized.

____ ____   4. When I came downstairs, the kitchen was deserted. A single half eaten doughnut was all that remained in the box. I stared at the box I couldn't believe my eyes and shouted, "Who ate all the doughnuts?"

Half and *eaten* are acting together to describe a noun, *doughnut.*

____ ____   5. Ron glanced out the diner window onto the parking lot then he jumped to his feet. "They're towing away my truck" he exclaimed as he ran out the door.

The word group beginning with *Ron glanced* is actually two complete thoughts that have been run together with no mark of punctuation between them.

Name _____ Section _____ Date _____

Score: (Number right) _____ × 10 = _____ %

■ Other Punctuation Marks: Test 4

Each of the following passages requires **two** of the punctuation marks shown in the box below. In the spaces provided, write the letters of the **two** marks needed in each passage. Then insert the correct punctuation into the sentence. Each punctuation mark is used at least once.

a	Period .	**e**	Semicolon ;
b	Question mark ?	**f**	Hyphen -
c	Exclamation point !	**g**	Dash or dashes —
d	Colon :	**h**	Parentheses ( )

____ ____   1. Ann's husband can sometimes be very thoughtful, but his half hearted efforts at helping her clean the house are annoying. The other day she left a list of things that he needed to do when he got home from work dump the overflowing trash cans in all the rooms, unload the dishwasher, and dust the electronic equipment in the family room.

____ ____   2. I helped my brother clean his house otherwise, he never would have gotten it done in time. I swept under the radiators a job he usually forgets and dusted the furniture.

____ ____   3. Raoul dressed carefully for his big date He wore his gray suit, new shoes, and a handsome shirt and tie. Just before he went out the door, he glanced in the mirror to admire himself and noticed he had forgotten to shave.

____ ____   4. During the tourist season June through August the population of the seaside town nearly doubles. Tourists come to enjoy cool sea breezes, fresh caught seafood, and, best of all, splashing in the Atlantic.

____ ____   5. "I can't stand it when people keep taking my pencils" Sandy screamed. "Don't they realize I occasionally need to write something down"

Name _____   Section _____ Date _____

Score: (Number right) _____ × 10 = _____%

■ Other Punctuation Marks: Test 5

Each of the ten sentences in the passage below requires punctuation: a colon, semicolon, hyphen, dash or dashes, or parentheses. In each sentence, underline the place where punctuation is needed. Then write the corrections on the lines provided. When you write each correction, include the words before and after the punctuation mark.

Note   To help you master these punctuation marks, directions are given for half of the corrections.

[1]Everyone has a bad dream at times moreover, people often have the same nightmare repeatedly. [2]My friend Carla I've known her since kindergarten frequently dreams she is falling off a cliff. [3]"It's always a slow motion fall," she says, adding, "I have lots of time to be terrified, but I never hit bottom." [4]My roommate Cassie's nightmare is of a huge red boulder always exactly the same size and color rolling down a hill toward her. [5]My father's dream has been the same for years a black cat is sitting on his chest, suffocating him. [6]In my most frequent nightmare, I'm trying to walk somewhere my shoes are terribly slippery. [7]I can see my destination often an exam room on campus, but I just can't get there. [8]My sense of ever increasing frustration stays with me long after I wake up. [9]Psychologists say that nightmares especially the recurring kind tell us a great deal about our inner fears. [10]My particular fear seems obvious it's the fear that I'm incapable of reaching my goals.

1. _____   Add a semicolon.

2. _____

3. _____   Add a hyphen.

4. _____

5. _____   Add a colon.

6. _____

7. _____   Add parentheses.

8. _____

9. _____   Add two dashes.

10. _____

■ Other Punctuation Marks: Test 6

Each of the ten sentences in the passage below requires punctuation: a colon, semicolon, hyphen, dash or dashes, or parentheses. In each sentence, underline the place where punctuation is needed. Then write the corrections on the lines provided. When you write each correction, include the words before and after the punctuation mark.

[1]The late Theodor Seuss Geisel better known as Dr. Seuss was one of the most influential children's authors of the twentieth century. [2]Before starting to write children's books, he worked in advertising for fifteen years, drawing large, weird looking bugs in ads for an insecticide called Flit. [3]During World War II, he helped the war effort in several ways drawing political cartoons, writing and producing documentaries, and creating animated training films with rhymed scripts. [4]His first children's book was rejected by more than twenty different publishers however, Geisel continued to write. [5]Eventually he became a successful, award winning author. [6]His children's books have sold more than 200,000,000 copies and have been translated into more than 15 languages Latin and Hebrew, to name just two. [7]Geisel's work earned him a variety of awards three Academy Awards, an Emmy, a Pulitzer Prize, and three Caldecott Honor Awards for children's book illustration. [8]Some of Geisel's books specifically the later ones deal with contemporary issues. [9]*The Lorax* expresses Geisel's concern for the environment *The Butter Battle Book* shows the danger of the arms race. [10]Dr. Seuss revolutionized reading instruction by teaching a valuable lesson to both children and adults reading can be fun.

1. _____

2. _____

3. _____

4. _____

5. _____

6. _____

7. _____

8. _____

9. _____

10. _____

12 Capital Letters

Seeing What You Know

Place capital letters on the words that need them in the following sentences. Then check your answers by reading the explanations below.

1. the coach growled, "if i see you drop one more pass, ed, you're off the team."

2. At bronx community college in new york, students can take night courses in hispanic literature and asian cooking as well as english.

3. Did you know that thanksgiving is always the fourth thursday in november?

4. At breakfast I often read the latest issue of *people* while eating wheaties sprinkled with raisins and toast spread with skippy peanut butter.

Understanding the Answers

1. **T**he coach growled, "**I**f **I** see you drop one more pass, **E**d, you're off the team."
   The first word of a sentence, the first word of a quoted sentence, the pronoun *I*, and people's names are capitalized. *Coach* and *team,* which are general terms (not specific names), are not capitalized.

2. At **B**ronx **C**ommunity **C**ollege in **N**ew **Y**ork, students can take night courses in **H**ispanic literature and **A**sian cooking as well as **E**nglish.
   Capital letters are used for names of specific places. Names of races, nationalities, and languages are also capitalized. *Students, night courses, literature,* and *cooking* are general terms that are not capitalized.

3. Did you know that **T**hanksgiving is always the fourth **T**hursday in **N**ovember?
   The names of holidays, days of the week, and months are always capitalized.

4. At breakfast I often read the latest issue of *People* while eating **W**heaties sprinkled with raisins and toast spread with **S**kippy peanut butter.
   Titles of magazines and brand names of products are capitalized. General words like *raisins, toast,* and *peanut butter* are not capitalized.

133

Capital letters have many uses, the most common of which appear in this chapter.

THE FIRST WORD IN A SENTENCE OR DIRECT QUOTATION

Sentences begin with capital letters. The first word of a quoted sentence is also capitalized.

My sister said, "Don't forget Nick's surprise party. It's Friday at 8 P.M."

"Let's hope," I replied, "that nobody tells Nick about it."

In the second sentence, the word *that* is not capitalized because it does not start a sentence. It is part of the sentence that begins with the words *Let's hope*.

THE WORD "I" AND PEOPLE'S NAMES

"Today I got a call from an old high school friend, Dick Hess," Sandy said.

Note   A title that comes before someone's name is treated as part of the name.

Next week Uncle Dave and Aunt Gloria are seeing Dr. Mendell for checkups.

But: My uncle and aunt go to the best doctor in town.

NAMES OF SPECIFIC PLACES AND LANGUAGES

In general, if something is on a map (including a street map), capitalize it.

Frankie graduated from Kennedy High School on Main Street, left her home in Altoona, Pennsylvania, moved to New York, and took a job as a waitress in a Greenwich Village restaurant.

Note   Places that are not specifically named do not require capital letters.

Frankie graduated from high school, left her home in a small town, moved to the big city, and took a job as a waitress in a neighborhood restaurant.

The names of languages come from place names, so languages are also capitalized.

Inez, who was born in Spain, speaks fluent Spanish as well as English.

NAMES OF SPECIFIC GROUPS (RACES, RELIGIONS, NATIONALITIES, COMPANIES, CLUBS, AND OTHER ORGANIZATIONS)

Although Barbara is Lutheran and Mark is Jewish, and she is his boss at the local Home Depot store, their marriage seems to work very well.

The robbery suspect is a six-foot-tall Caucasian male with a German accent. The American Civil Liberties Union supports the Ku Klux Klan's right to demonstrate.

Practice 1

Place capital letters on the words that need them in the sentences below.

1. as we watched the movie, doug leaned over and whispered, "don't you think this is pretty boring?"

2. st. mary's seminary in baltimore, maryland, has trained catholic priests for more than two hundred years.

3. we decided to hold the retirement dinner for professor henderson at the florentine, the new italian restaurant on lake street.

4. some of the most expensive shops in the world are found along rodeo drive in beverly hills, california.

5. "when I was a kid," the comedian rodney dangerfield told his audience, "my parents moved a lot—but i always found them."

CALENDAR ITEMS

Basically, everything on a calendar—including names of days of the week, months, and holidays—should be capitalized. The only exceptions are the names of the seasons (*spring, summer, fall, winter*), which are not capitalized.

Since Joy was born on **D**ecember 26, her family celebrates her birthday on **C**hristmas **D**ay.

Next **M**onday, which is **L**abor **D**ay, all government offices will be closed.

Stan watches baseball on television in the spring and summer, football in the fall, and basketball in the winter.

PRODUCT NAMES

Capitalize the copyrighted brand name of a product, but not the kind of product it names.

Pilar won't buy presweetened cereals for her children. She prefers less sugary brands such as **C**heerios and **W**heat **C**hex.

Our cats have refused to eat any more **F**riskies or **N**ine **L**ives cat food. They insist on eating **S**tarkist tuna—right off our plates.

TITLES

The titles of books, television or stage shows, songs, magazines, movies, articles, poems, stories, papers, and so forth are capitalized.

The book *Shoeless Joe* was made into the movie *Field of Dreams.*

I'd much rather read *Newsweek* than the *New York Times.*

Professor Martin praised Aisha's term paper, "**T**he **S**ocial **I**mpact of the **I**ndustrial **R**evolution," but he suggested that she revise one section.

Note   The words *the, of, a, an, and,* and other short, unstressed words are not capitalized when they appear in the middle of a title.

FAMILY WORDS THAT SUBSTITUTE FOR NAMES

When I was a little girl, **G**randma was my favorite baby-sitter.

I'll ask **D**ad if he'd like to go to the movie with us.

Capitalize a word such as *grandma* or *dad* only if it is being used as a substitute for that person's name. Do not capitalize words showing family relationships when they are preceded by possessive words such as *my, her,* or *our.*

Did you know that my grandmother goes to the racetrack every week?

SPECIFIC SCHOOL COURSES

Capitalize the names of specific courses, including those containing a number.

To graduate, I need to take **A**dvanced **B**iology, **S**peech 102, and **L**iterature of **O**ther **C**ultures.

But the names of general subject areas are not capitalized.

To graduate, I still need to take a biology course, a speech course, and a literature course.

Practice 2

Place capital letters on the words that need them in the sentences below.

1. Our student body is about 50 percent caucasian, 30 percent african american, and 10 percent each hispanic and asian.

2. Elvis Presley's hit song "all shook up" was inspired by a bottle of pepsi.

3. Rashid heard that introduction to statistics was impossible to pass, so he signed up for a psychology course instead.

4. The second monday in october is celebrated as columbus day.

5. "But, mommy, it *hurts!*" the boy whimpered as his mother dabbed solarcaine lotion on his sunburn.

Note   Additional information about capital letters appears on pages 221–222.

Name _____ Section _____ Date _____

Score: (Number right) _____ × 4 = _____ %

■ Capital Letters: Test 1

Underline the words that need to be capitalized. Then write the words correctly in the spaces provided. The number of spaces shows how many capital letters are missing in each sentence.

Note   To help you master capitalization, explanations are given for half of the sentences.

1. My uncle, dr. lopez, works at southside clinic.

   _____   _____   _____   _____

   Capitalize people's names, titles that come before names, and names of specific places.

2. A story about my disabled boss, ted, once appeared in *sports illustrated*.

   _____   _____   _____

3. when dad shouted, "don't move!" I froze in fear.

   _____   _____   _____

   Capitalize the first word of a sentence and of a direct quotation. Also capitalize a word used instead of a person's name.

4. The speaker at parkside college's graduation was senator holland.

   _____   _____   _____   _____

5. Every january, renee's grandparents travel to florida for a winter vacation.

   _____   _____   _____

   Capitalize the name of a month, of a particular person, and of a particular place.

6. When the door opened, aunt sarah whispered, "bring in the birthday cake now; then start singing."

   _____   _____   _____

7. Most british people who attend church belong to the church of england.

   _____   _____   _____

   Capitalize names of nationalities. Also capitalize names of religions. Short, unstressed words in the middle of a name are not capitalized.

8. The television show *60 minutes* is Fran's favorite; she's writing a paper about one of its stories for sociology 101.

   _____   _____

Name _____   Section _____ Date _____

Score: (Number right) _____ × 2.5 = _____%

■ Capital Letters: Test 2

Underline the words that need to be capitalized. Then write the words correctly in the spaces provided. The number of spaces shows how many capital letters are missing in each sentence.

1. Twenty years ago, while attending college, mark and i were roommates living in a small apartment on barclay avenue.

   _____   _____   _____   _____

2. The city of new orleans is famous for its celebration of the holiday mardi gras.

   _____   _____   _____   _____

3. In one of his best-remembered speeches, president john kennedy said, "ask not what your country can do for you; ask what you can do for your country."

   _____   _____   _____   _____

4. Since you're going to the supermarket, could you get me a carton of tropicana orange juice, a box of tide, and a can of maxwell house coffee?

   _____   _____   _____   _____

5. *Interview with the vampire,* a book by anne rice, is about a vampire named louis.

   _____   _____   _____   _____

6. The teenagers cruised down grant drive and then headed over to concord mall.

   _____   _____   _____   _____

7. Many years ago, people in hollywood told arnold schwarzenegger he would never succeed as an actor because of his austrian accent.

   _____   _____   _____   _____

8. I last saw grandpa and aunt rhoda at my cousin's wedding in march.

   _____   _____   _____   _____

9. The high-school choir performed some african american spirituals as well as a piece by franz schubert.

   _____   _____   _____   _____

10. A popular ad campaign for chevrolet featured the song "the heartbeat of america."

   _____   _____   _____   _____

Name _____ Section _____ Date _____

Score: (Number right) _____ × 10 = _____ %

■ Capital Letters: Test 3

Underline the **two** words that require capital letters in each group of sentences below. Then write the words (with capital letters) in the spaces provided.

Note   To help you master capitalization, explanations are given for one item in each sentence.

1. I don't know my way around chicago well. If I get too far away from the downtown area known as the loop, I become hopelessly lost. All the streets look the same to me.

   a. _____   Names of specific places are capitalized.

   b. _____

2. Winter is my favorite season. However, my brother says, "what moron likes to be cold and wet all the time? Warm, beautiful june, the beginning of summer, is the best time of year."

   a. _____   Capitalize the first word of a quoted sentence.

   b. _____

3. Lillian, who is Methodist, had never visited a catholic church before. She went with her friend Henry to attend an easter service there. Afterward they stayed for a meal in the church's fellowship hall.

   a. _____   Names of religions are capitalized.

   b. _____

4. On fridays, my girlfriend and I like to eat at a nice place, so we try some of the restaurants that have been reviewed in our local paper. Last week, we tried a new restaurant called gardenia, which specializes in farm-to-table organic meals.

   a. _____   Days of the week are capitalized.

   b. _____

5. My cousin is studying to be a teacher. For a course called Introduction to teaching, she was asked to read a book by Jonathan Kozol called *Savage inequalities,* which criticizes public schools. She now wants to be a public school teacher and help inner-city children get the best education possible.

   a. _____   Names of specific school courses are capitalized.

   b. _____

■ Capital Letters: Test 4

Underline the **two** words that require capital letters in each group of sentences below. Then write the words (with capital letters) in the spaces provided.

1. Karen stayed after class to talk over her grade with professor Hartzler. Although she enjoyed her french classes, she wasn't doing very well. Her professor suggested that Karen get some extra tutoring in the language.

   a. _____

   b. _____

2. Is your uncle going to come to the party? I'd like him to meet aunt Lydia. They're both single and active in the democratic party. Maybe they would like each other.

   a. _____

   b. _____

3. Although grandpa lives in New England for most of the year, he travels to a warmer climate for the winter. He says, "when the snow flies, so do I."

   a. _____

   b. _____

4. Amanda visited New mexico last summer. She was fascinated by the mix of Native American and spanish cultures there. She is reading everything she can find about this region and hopes to go back again someday.

   a. _____

   b. _____

5. Now that Betsy has small children to take along, she no longer enjoys trips to the mall. It's easier for her to buy from catalogs or online. Last week, she ordered clothing from the coldwater creek catalog and computer supplies from two different Web sites.

   a. _____

   b. _____

Name _____   Section _____   Date _____

Score: (Number right) _____ × 4 = _____ %

■ Capital Letters: Test 5

Each sentence in the passage below contains one or more words that require capitalization. Underline these words; then write the words (with capital letters) on the lines below. The number of spaces shows how many capital letters are needed in each sentence.

Note To help you master capitalization, explanations are given for half of the sentences.

¹last summer my husband jerry and i decided to take a vacation. ²As we discussed where we should go, I jokingly said, "you know, we never got to niagara falls on our honeymoon." ³Next thing we knew, we had a house full of road maps and literature from the niagara chamber of commerce. ⁴On the second monday in july, we hopped into our car and headed for the canadian border. ⁵It was a long drive, so we took turns driving and passed some time singing old songs like "home on the range." ⁶When jerry drove, I often read the recent issues of *time* that I'd brought along to catch up on the news. ⁷finally we arrived at our destination, a hotel full of interesting people, including lots of japanese tourists. ⁸There was also a lively convention of people belonging to the american association of retired persons. ⁹That very night, after sending picture postcards to mom and dad, we went out to get our first look at the falls in the dark. ¹⁰Although I'd grown up looking at pictures of the falls on boxes of nabisco cereals, nothing could have prepared me for the majestic beauty of the real thing.

1. _____   _____   _____
   Capitalize the first word of a sentence, people's names, and the word *I*. Names of seasons are not capitalized.

2. _____   _____   _____

3. _____   _____   _____
   Names of particular organizations are capitalized.

4. _____   _____   _____

5. _____   _____
   Capitalize song titles. Do not capitalize short, unstressed words in the middles of titles.

6. _____   _____

7. _____   _____
   Capitalize the first word of a sentence and the names of nationalities.

8. _____   _____   _____   _____

9. _____   _____
   Capitalize names of relatives used in place of their actual names. The word *falls* is used here as a general term, so it is not capitalized.

10. _____

Name _____   Section _____   Date _____

Score: (Number right) _____ × 4 = _____%

■ Capital Letters: Test 6

Each sentence in the passage below contains one or more words that require capitalization. Underline these words; then write the words (with capital letters) on the lines below. The number of spaces shows how many capital letters are needed in each sentence.

[1]Perhaps you have heard of the book, play, or movie called *meet me in st. louis.* [2]The story is set in 1904 during a fair officially called the louisiana purchase exposition. [3]This fair was huge, spanning more than 1200 acres and including much of forest park and washington university. [4]In addition to states and territories of the united states, more than fifty foreign countries participated in the fair. [5]For their headquarters, many states and countries built structures that duplicated important buildings; for example, virginia's pavilion was a replica of thomas jefferson's home. [6]Visitors to the fair saw things they had never seen before—automobiles, airplanes, motion pictures, buildings lit by electricity, entire villages of natives from the philippine islands. [7]The fair's emphasis was on processes; at an exhibit sponsored by the brown shoe company, for instance, people could see shoes being made. [8]More than 20,000,000 people visited the fair between april 30 and december 1. [9]Even the olympics—the first ones to award medals—were part of this remarkable fair. [10]souvenirs and memorabilia from this fair are now scattered throughout the world.

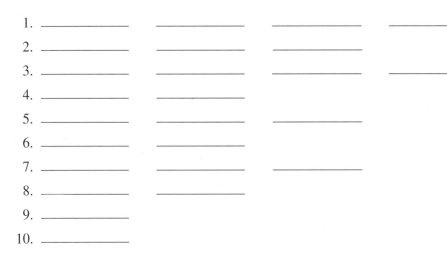

1. _____   _____   _____   _____

2. _____   _____   _____

3. _____   _____   _____   _____

4. _____   _____

5. _____   _____   _____

6. _____   _____

7. _____   _____   _____

8. _____   _____

9. _____

10. _____

13 Homonyms

Seeing What You Know

In the following sentences, underline each correct word in parentheses. Then read the explanations below.

1. (You're, Your) the only student (who's, whose) always (hear, here) on time.

2. (Its, It's) difficult to (break, brake) the habit of smoking.

3. I never (knew, new) that (there, they're) could be such a problem as having (too, to) little money to get through the month.

4. The Fergusons found that (their, there) dog had eaten the (hole, whole) ham.

5. The (plane, plain) had (two, too) engines, and one of them caught on fire.

Understanding the Answers

1. **You're** the only student **who's** always **here** on time.
   You're is the contraction of the words *you* and *are*. *Who's* is the contraction of the words *who is*. *Here* means "in this place."

2. **It's** difficult to **break** the habit of smoking.
   It's is the contraction of the words *it* and *is*. *Break* means "end."

3. I never **knew** that **there** could be such a problem as having **too** little money to get through the month.
   Knew is the past tense of *know*. *There* is used with forms of the verb *to be—is, are, was, were,* and so on. *Too* means "extremely."

4. The Fergusons found that **their** dog had eaten the **whole** ham.
   Their means "belonging to them." *Whole* means "entire."

5. The **plane** had **two** engines, and one of them caught on fire.
   Plane means "airplane." *Two* is the spelling of the number 2.

This chapter looks at a number of words that are mistaken for one another because they are **homonyms**: words that are pronounced the same (or almost the same) but are spelled differently and are different in meaning.

THE BIG FOUR

Of all frequently confused homonyms, the following four groups cause writers the most trouble:

its   *belonging to it*
it's   contraction of *it is*

> If the house doesn't get **its** roof repaired soon, **it's** going to be full of water. (If the house doesn't get the roof *belonging to it* repaired, *it is* going to be full of water.)

> **It's** a shame that the new restaurant lost **its** license. (*It is* a shame that the new restaurant lost the license *belonging to it.*)

their   *belonging to them*
there   (1) *in that place;* (2) used with *is, are, was, were,* and other forms of the verb *to be*
they're   contraction of *they are*

> The coach told the players that **there** was no excuse for **their** unprofessional behavior; **they're** going to run extra laps as punishment. (The coach told the players *there was* [form of *to be*] no excuse for the unprofessional behavior *belonging to them; they are* going to run extra laps as punishment.)

> **They're** showing all the *Star Trek* movies in order at **their** science fiction convention; I'm going to get **there** early. (*They are* showing all the *Star Trek* movies in order at the science fiction convention *belonging to them;* I'm going to get *to that place* early.)

to   (1) used before a verb, as in *to say;* (2) *toward*
too   (1) *overly* or *extremely;* (2) *also*
two   *the number 2*

> It would be **too** confusing **to** name the baby Lucy; her mother and **two** of her cousins are named Lucy **too**. (It would be *overly* confusing *to name* [verb] the baby Lucy; her mother and *2* of her cousins are named Lucy *also.*)

> Let's go **to** the mall **to** look for clothes, unless you are **too** tired. (Let's go *toward* the mall *to look* [verb] for clothes, unless you are *overly* tired.)

your   *belonging to you*
you're   contraction of *you are*

> If **you're** going out in this downpour, take **your** umbrella. (If *you are* going out in this downpour, take the umbrella *belonging to you.*)

Do you think **your** family will be upset when they learn **you're** moving to Alaska? (Do you think the family *belonging to you* will be upset when they learn *you are* moving to Alaska?)

Practice

Underline the correct homonym in each group.

1. (Its, It's) a shame (its, it's) going to rain today; we won't be able to give the front porch (its, it's) second coat of paint.

2. "(There, Their, They're) you go again," Jason said to me, "judging (there, their, they're) intentions even though you don't know what (there, their, they're) going to do."

3. Having (to, too, two) read and take notes on (to, too, two) chapters a night is simply (to, too, two) much work.

4. (Your, You're) not serious when you say (your, you're) planning to sell (your, you're) house and live in a tent in the woods, are you?

OTHER COMMON HOMONYMS

brake (1) *to slow* or *to stop;* (2) *mechanism that stops a moving vehicle*
break (1) *to cause to come apart;* (2) *to bring to an end*

If you don't **brake** your sled as you go down the icy hill, you could easily **break** a leg.

hear (1) *to take in by ear;* (2) *to be informed*
here *in this place*

The music **here** near the band is so loud that I can't **hear** you.

hole *empty or hollow spot*
whole *complete* or *entire*

The mechanic examined the **whole** surface of the flat tire before finding a tiny **hole** near the rim.

knew (past tense of *know*) (1) *understood;* (2) *was or were aware of*
new (1) *not old;* (2) *recently arrived*

Jay **knew** he needed a **new** bike when his old one broke down again yesterday.

know (1) *to understand;* (2) *to be aware of*
no (1) *not any;* (2) *opposite of yes*

I have **no** idea how much other people **know** about my divorce.

passed   (past tense of *pass*) (1) *handed to;* (2) *went by;* (3) *completed successfully*
past   (1) *time before the present;* (2) *by*

As Ben walked **past** Sharon's desk, he **passed** her a Valentine and pleaded, "Let's forget about the **past** and be friends again."

peace   *calmness* or *quiet*
piece   *portion of something*

The usual **peace** of the house was disturbed when my brother discovered that someone had eaten a **piece** of the cake he had baked for his girlfriend's birthday.

plain   (1) *not fancy;* (2) *obvious;* (3) *straightforward*
plane   shortened form of *airplane*

It was **plain** to see that a **plane** had recently landed in the muddy field.

right   (1) *correct;* (2) *opposite of left*
write   *to form letters and words*

I can **write** clearly using my **right** hand; when I use my left, my writing is illegible.

than   word used in comparisons
then   (1) *at that time;* (2) *next;* (3) *as a consequence* (with *if*)

First Aaron realized he was driving faster **than** the speed limit; **then** he saw the police car behind him.

threw   (past tense of *throw*) *tossed*
through   (1) *into and out of;* (2) *finished*

Yesterday I went **through** my old letters and **threw** most of them away.

wear   *to put on* (as with clothing)
where   *in what place* or *to what place*

Because Samantha was not told **where** her friends were taking her for her birthday, she had trouble deciding what to **wear**.

weather   *outside conditions* (rain, wind, temperature, etc.)
whether   *if*

The **weather** won't spoil my vacation; **whether** it rains or not, my days will be spent on the beach.

who's   contraction of *who is* or *who has*
whose   *belonging to whom*

The boss yelled, "**Who's** responsible for this mistake? **Whose** fault is it?"

Note   Additional information about homonyms and other confusing words appears on pages 223–225.

Name _____   Section _____   Date _____

■ **Homonyms: Test 1**

In the ten sentences below, underline the correct word in each group of homonyms.

Note   To help you review some of the homonyms in this chapter, use the definitions given in half of the sentences.

1. Did you (here, hear) the old legend about a famous Native American chief who is buried (here, hear)?

   Did you *take in by ear* the old legend about a famous Native American chief who is buried *in this place*?

2. The extra-credit questions that the professor added (to, two, too) the final exam were just (to, two, too) difficult, so very few students attempted to answer them.

3. The stray dog can't make up (it's, its) mind whether to trust me or not, so (it's, its) still sitting in the driveway watching me.

   The stray dog can't make up *the mind belonging to it* whether to trust me or not, so *it is* still sitting in the driveway watching me.

4. There were a lot of rules that Elaine had to (know, no) for the driver's test, but when I asked her if I could help, she said (know, no), she had to learn them on her own.

5. (Their, There, They're) too afraid of spiders to appreciate (their, there, they're) remarkable beauty.

   They are too afraid of spiders to appreciate the remarkable beauty *belonging to them.*

6. My young niece is crying because she just (threw, through) her soccer ball (threw, through) our neighbors' kitchen window.

7. The loud whistling call of a blue jay about to feed on a (peace, piece) of bread was the only sound to be heard amid the (peace, piece) and quiet.

   The loud whistling call of a blue jay about to feed on a *portion* of bread was the only sound to be heard amid the *calmness* and quiet.

8. Pointing to the chunk of cheese on the table, the little boy said, "Couldn't you afford cheese that was (hole, whole)?" He didn't know that Swiss cheese always has (holes, wholes) in it.

9. The (knew, new) student in Spanish class (knew, new) how to speak the language better than anyone else.

   The *recently arrived* student in Spanish class *understood* how to speak the language better than anyone else.

10. (Your, You're) not supposed to dial 911 unless, in (your, you're) opinion, there's a life-threatening emergency.

Name _____ Section _____ Date _____

Score: (Number right) _____ × 5 = _____ %

■ Homonyms: Test 2

Underline the correct word in each group of homonyms.

1. I know you are angry about seeing me at Elaine's house, but (their, there, they're) was a good reason for me to go (their, there, they're).

2. If you don't (brake, break) before you go over the speed bump, you're going to (brake, break) the shock absorbers.

3. A large paperback bookstore is opening right (hear, here) on campus, and I (hear, here) it plans to sell computer supplies as well as books.

4. Since you (knew, new) that Suki's car was (knew, new), you should have been especially careful with it.

5. The bird injured (its, it's) wing, so (its, it's) having trouble flying.

6. On the celebrity tour, we drove (passed, past) several movie stars' homes; we also (passed, past) the restaurant where many Hollywood people have lunch.

7. The two brothers have not had any (peace, piece) ever since they began arguing over a small (peace, piece) of property their father left them.

8. (Whose, Who's) shoes are these in the middle of the floor, and (whose, who's) been messy enough to leave crumbs all over the table?

9. The teacher told Richard to (right, write) the assignment on the (right, write) side of the blackboard.

10. (Where, Wear) is the blouse that you borrowed? I want to (where, wear) it tonight.

Name _____   Section _____   Date _____

Score: (Number right) _____ × 10 = _____ %

■ Homonyms: Test 3

Each short paragraph below contains **two** homonym errors. Find these errors and underline them. Then write the correct words in the spaces provided.

Note   To help you review some of the homonyms in this chapter, use the hints given for half of the homonyms.

1. If its sunny tomorrow, our English class will meet outside. Unfortunately, we can't know in advance what the whether will be. Even if we meet inside, though, our teacher has promised us an unusual class.

    a. _____   If *it is* sunny tomorrow

    b. _____

2. It's important to provide an adequate and safe supply of drinking water. Not having enough water to drink is more dangerous then having to little food. Humans will die of thirst long before they die of hunger.

    a. _____   Not having water to drink is *being*

    b. _____   *compared with* not having food to eat.

3. There are to many interesting courses being offered this year. It's difficult to choose which ones to take. Should I sign up for something I enjoy, like psychology, or should I take computer science and try to learn a new skill? Their both good choices.

    a. _____   *Overly* many courses

    b. _____

4. After experiencing a tragedy in her life, my aunt began to talk to a counselor. "I can't change the passed," she said, "but it's plane to me that talking can help me cope with it better."

    a. _____   She can't change what happened in

    b. _____   the *time before the present.*

5. Most people no the importance of getting a good night's sleep. However, knew research has shown that any deep sleep, including an afternoon nap, will help us to think better and work more effectively.

    a. _____   Most people *are aware of* the

    b. _____   importance of getting a good night's sleep.

■ Homonyms: Test 4

Each short paragraph below contains **two** homonym errors. Find these errors and underline them. Then write the correct words in the spaces provided.

1. Because my family is so large, the hole family rarely drives anywhere together. Usually four of the children will drive with one parent and five with the other. There are always arguments among the youngest children about who's turn it is to ride in the front seats.

   a. _____

   b. _____

2. The doctor spoke sternly to Donald at his last checkup. "Your overweight, and you almost never exercise," the doctor warned. "I'm telling you in plane language that you're asking for a heart attack."

   a. _____

   b. _____

3. Some parents try to limit the amount of television their children watch. They believe that more then an hour a day of television interferes with schoolwork. They also don't like much of the language that kids here on TV shows.

   a. _____

   b. _____

4. Medical researchers have found that if your often in a bad mood, its more likely you will die of a stress-related disease such as high blood pressure, heart disease, or stroke. To live longer, they advise, take the steps needed to achieve inner peace.

   a. _____

   b. _____

5. The legend of the vampire Dracula is based on the story of a real-life Romanian prince named Vlad, who lived more than five hundred years ago. Vlad was a bloodthirsty madman who may have killed as many as 100,000 people during his six years in power. His favorite method of killing was two run a stake threw his victims. Vlad was finally killed in 1476.

   a. _____

   b. _____

Name _____   Section _____ Date _____

Score: (Number right) _____ × 10 = _____ %

■ Homonyms: Test 5

Underline the correct homonym in each of the following sentences. Then, in the spaces provided, write an explanation for the answer you chose.

Note   To help you review some of the homonyms in this chapter, use the hints given for half of the homonyms.

[1]Selecting your career is one of the most important decisions you will make in your (hole, whole) life. [2]You are likely to spend more than 80,000 hours working at (your, you're) job. [3]Having an occupation that is well suited to you can help to make your working hours fulfilling rather (than, then) frustrating. [4]But how do you (know, no) which career to pursue? [5]Answering (to, too, two) questions can help you identify your expertise and your ambition. [6]First, what activities have been a source of satisfaction for you (threw, through) your life? [7]If, for example, you have enjoyed building things in the (passed, past), you are likely to enjoy a career in construction or architecture. [8]Second, what would you attempt if you (knew, new) you could not fail at it? [9]What you really *want* to do becomes (plane, plain) when you answer this question. [10]If you can realistically say that you would be able to earn a living doing an activity you love, you have probably identified a career that would be (right, write) for you.

1. _____   The sentence is talking about your *entire* life.

2. _____

3. _____   Working hours that are fulfilling are *being compared with* those that are frustrating.

4. _____

5. _____   "First" and "Second" indicate that 2 questions are being asked.

6. _____

7. _____   The sentence refers to an *earlier* time in your life.

8. _____

9. _____   What you want becomes *obvious* when you answer the question.

10. _____

Name _____ Section _____ Date _____

Score: (Number right) _____ × 10 = _____%

■ Homonyms: Test 6

Underline the correct homonym in each of the following sentences. Then, in the spaces provided, write an explanation for the answer you chose.

[1]"(Who's, Whose) résumé is this?" asked the career counselor. [2]Jamila raised her hand, wondering (weather, whether) the counselor thought her résumé was especially good or especially bad. [3]"Let's go (threw, through) this with the class as we discuss what makes a résumé work," said the counselor.

[4]"The biggest problem is that Jamila's entries are (to, too, two) brief," he said. [5]"(Hear, Here), for instance, it says she was a secretary for three years. [6]Surely that doesn't tell the (hole, whole) story of what she did on the job. [7]I'd like to see Jamila (right, write) down every responsibility she had. [8]If she wrote her boss's letters, used a computer, supervised another employee, or planned business meetings, her résumé should let us (know, no) that. [9]Remember this: Employers only glance at most résumés as they decide if an applicant is the best person for (their, there, they're) position. [10](Your, You're) résumé must quickly provide specific information about what you are qualified to do."

1. _____

2. _____

3. _____

4. _____

5. _____

6. _____

7. _____

8. _____

9. _____

10. _____

14 Word Choice

Seeing What You Know

Imagine that the following sentences appeared in a business or school report. Check the sentence in each pair that is worded more appropriately. Then read the explanations below.

1. ____ At this point in time we have not yet scheduled the date of the exam.

   ____ We have not yet scheduled the exam.

2. ____ Fred wishes the office manager would get off his case.

   ____ Fred wishes the office manager would stop criticizing him.

3. ____ The first-grade children have been busy as bees all day, but they still seem fresh as daisies.

   ____ The first-grade children have been active all day, but they still seem energetic.

Understanding the Answers

1. The second sentence is more direct.
   The first sentence is longer than necessary because of the wordy expressions *at this point in time* and *scheduled the date*.

2. The second sentence is more businesslike.
   The slang expression *get off his case* in the first sentence is too informal for school or business writing.

3. The second sentence is less stale.
   The first sentence is weakened by the clichés *busy as bees* and *fresh as daisies*.

153

Not all writing problems involve grammar. A sentence may be grammatically correct yet fail to communicate effectively because of the words that the writer has chosen. Wordiness, slang, and clichés are three enemies of effective communication.

WORDINESS

Which of these signs would help the campus cafeteria run more smoothly?

_____ Due to the fact that our plates and our silverware are in short supply, the management kindly requests all patrons of this cafeteria, when they have finished their meals, to place all used plates and silverware on a cart before leaving the cafeteria so that they may be washed.

_____ Please put your used plates and silverware on a cart.

Wordy writing is writing that—like the first sign above—uses more words than necessary to get a message across. Such writing both confuses and irritates the reader, who resents having to wade through extra words.

To avoid wordiness, edit your writing carefully. Remove words that have the same meaning as other words in the sentence.

Wordy: In my opinion, I think that job quotas in the workplace are unfair.

Revised: I think that job quotas are unfair.

In general, work to express your thoughts in the fewest words possible that are still complete and clear. Notice, for example, how easily the following wordy expressions can be replaced by single words:

Wordy Expression	Single Word
a large number of	many
at this point in time	now
came into the possession of	obtained
despite the fact that	although
due to the fact that	because
during the time that	while
each and every day	daily
few in number	few
in order to	to
in the event that	if
in the near future	soon
in this day and age	now
is of the opinion that	believes
made the decision to	decided
on account of	because
postponed until later	postponed
small in size	small

Practice 1

Cross out the wordy expressions and unnecessary words in the sentences that follow. Then rewrite each sentence as clearly and concisely as possible.

1. Due to the fact that the judge's hair is prematurely gray at an earlier age than most women, people think she is much older than her thirty-eight years of age.

   _____

   _____

2. At this point in time, the company is taking a large number of steps to reduce actions that pollute the environment that is all around us.

   _____

   _____

3. In the event of weather that is problematic, officials will make the decision to postpone the baseball game until a later point in time.

   _____

   _____

SLANG

Which of the following would be appropriate to print in a newspaper?

_____ The police just captured a local criminal who posed as a utility service-man and stole from several trusting senior citizens.

_____ The police just busted a local criminal who posed as a utility serviceman and ripped off several trusting senior citizens.

Slang expressions (like *busted* and *ripped off*) are part of our everyday language. They are lively and fun to use. But while slang may be appropriate in casual conversation, it generally does not belong in formal writing. Slang, by nature, is informal.

Even in less formal writing, slang is often inappropriate because not all readers understand it. Slang is frequently used by limited social groups, and it changes rapidly. When we read slang expressions from the 1960s like *groovy* or *far out*, they sound out-of-date or meaningless. Your use of slang might have the same effect on someone older (or younger) than you. For example, when you write about someone who seems confused or not very bright, "The lights are on, but nobody's home," you may know exactly what you mean. Your reader may not.

Use slang only when you have a specific purpose in mind, such as being humorous or communicating the flavor of an informal conversation.

Practice 2

Rewrite the two slang expressions (printed in *italics*) in each sentence.

1. Nate is always *yapping* about what a *geek* his brother is.

    _____

2. Christopher is such a *hater* that we try to *ditch* him whenever we can.

    _____

3. Jesse finally *crashed* after *pulling an all-nighter* to finish his report.

    _____

CLICHÉS

Which of the following belongs in a nurse's daily report?

_____ The patient in 201 slept like a log until the crack of dawn.

_____ The patient in 201 slept deeply until 6:30 A.M.

A **cliché** is a commonplace, boring expression. Once, it might have been fresh, vivid, even funny. But too many people used it, so it has become stale. Don't be lazy and use other people's worn-out sayings. Find original ways to say what you mean.

Here are just a few of the many other clichés to avoid in your writing:

avoid like the plague	drive like a maniac	old as the hills
better late than never	easier said than done	pretty as a picture
busy as a bee	few and far between	scared to death
clear as a bell	in the nick of time	short and sweet
cold as ice	it goes without saying	sigh of relief
couldn't care less	last but not least	start from scratch
crazy like a fox	light as a feather	tried and true
dog-tired	needless to say	without a doubt

Practice 3

Rewrite the two clichés (printed in *italics*) in each sentence.

1. Hiroshi was *as sick as a dog* yesterday, but he looks *fit as a fiddle* today.

    _____

2. Since *time was of the essence*, I decided to *bite the bullet* and find a tutor to help me with my paper.

    _____

3. The news of the president's resignation, which came *like a bolt from the blue, spread like wildfire* across campus.

    _____

Note   Additional information about word choice appears on pages 226–227.

Name _____   Section _____   Date _____

Score: (Number right) _____ × 12.5 = _____ %

■ Word Choice: Test 1

Each sentence below contains one or two examples of ineffective word choice. Underline each error. Then, in the space provided, write *W, S,* or *C* to indicate wordiness, slang, or cliché. Finally, use the answer line to rewrite each faulty expression, using more effective language.

Note   To help you develop skill in choosing words effectively, suggestions are given for half of the corrections.

_____   1. I was stoked when I learned that our basketball team would be going to the playoffs.

_____

Correct the slang.

_____   2. Most of the critics trashed the new Will Smith film.

_____

_____   3. Due to the fact that it rained, the game was postponed until later.

_____

Correct the two cases of wordiness.

_____   4. Some students were late to class on account of their bus was delayed.

_____

_____   5. The course was supposed to be hard, but it was easy as pie.

_____

Correct the cliché.

_____   6. The explosion made enough noise to wake the dead.

_____

_____   7. In my opinion, I don't think there is any excuse for world hunger at this point in time.

_____

Correct the two cases of wordiness.

_____   8. Over fifty invitations were sent out in the mail, but only a total of twelve people responded.

_____

■ Word Choice: Test 2

Each sentence below contains one or more examples of ineffective word choice. Underline each error. Then, in the space provided, write *W, S,* or *C* to indicate wordiness, slang, or cliché. Finally, use the answer line to rewrite each faulty expression, using more effective language.

_____   1. The job applicant wore a suit that had seen better days.

_____

_____   2. I just found out that I won a cruise for two to the Bahamas. Sweet!

_____

_____   3. In the event that I'm not back by three o'clock, would you put the roast in the oven?

_____

_____   4. The actor gave a shout-out to his family when he won the Academy Award.

_____

_____   5. The contestants on *American Idol* were forced to sweat it out while the judges made their decision.

_____

_____   6. The new client has not called at this point in time but is expected to do so in the very near future.

_____

_____   7. When the computer screen went blank as I was writing my report, I realized I would have to start from scratch.

_____

_____   8. Jesse freaked when he found out that the deadline for the final paper was a week earlier than he had thought.

_____

_____   9. Owing to the fact of the teachers' strike, school has not yet opened.

_____

_____   10. Velma said her boyfriend treated her like dirt, so she told him to take a hike.

_____

Name _____   Section _____   Date _____

Score: (Number right) _____ × 10 = _____ %

■ Word Choice: Test 3

Each sentence below contains **two** examples of ineffective word choice. Underline each error. Then, in the space provided, write *W, S,* or *C* to indicate wordiness, slang, or cliché. Finally, use the answer line to rewrite each faulty expression, using more effective language.

Note   To help you develop skill in choosing words effectively, suggestions are given for the first correction in each group.

1. Shopping for hours and trying on dress after dress was a bummer, so she was on cloud nine when she finally found the perfect wedding dress.

    _____ a. _____   Correct the slang.

    _____ b. _____

2. It's too bad that dress is too large in size for Jen. The style and color both suit her to a T. I wonder if it could be taken in to fit her better.

    _____ a. _____   Correct the wordiness.

    _____ b. _____

3. There's never a dull moment in the Doyles' house! Yesterday the children emptied the sand that was in their sandbox onto the lawn, poured shampoo into the fish tank, and fed chocolate cake to the dog.

    _____ a. _____   Correct the cliché.

    _____ b. _____

4. Although Sheila's friends warned her that Mark was just a player, she didn't listen to them. She was head over heels about Mark. When he suddenly had no time for her, Sheila realized her friends were right.

    _____ a. _____   Correct the slang.

    _____ b. _____

5. Tired to the bone, the couple returned home after a long day's work. They were especially ticked to find a sink full of dirty dishes left by their children.

    _____ a. _____   Correct the cliché.

    _____ b. _____

Name _____   Section _____   Date _____

Score: (Number right) _____ × 10 = _____ %

■ Word Choice: Test 4

Each sentence below contains **two** examples of ineffective word choice. Underline each error. Then, in the space provided, write *W, S,* or *C* to indicate wordiness, slang, or cliché. Finally, use the answer line to rewrite each faulty expression, using more effective language.

1. Tyrell is playing with you when he says he can't be at your party. Don't listen to his teasing—he wouldn't miss that party for the world.

   ____ a. _____

   ____ b. _____

2. The last election proved that voters are sick and tired of politicians who aren't being real with them about the challenges facing the country.

   ____ a. _____

   ____ b. _____

3. Our city was psyched even before the World Series started. Local fans were excited due to the fact that it was our team's first appearance in the World Series in 28 years.

   ____ a. _____

   ____ b. _____

4. Linda was down in the dumps after learning that a large number of the guests wouldn't be able to attend the baby shower.

   ____ a. _____

   ____ b. _____

5. My uncle has been down on his luck lately. His situation took a turn for the worse when he got sick and then lost his apartment.

   ____ a. _____

   ____ b. _____

Name _____   Section _____   Date _____

Score: (Number right) _____ × 10 = _____%

■ Word Choice: Test 5

Each sentence in the following passage contains an example of wordiness, slang, or a cliché. Underline each error. Then, in the space provided, write *W, S,* or *C* to indicate wordiness, slang, or cliché. Finally, use the answer line to rewrite the faulty expression, using more effective language.

Note   To help you develop skill in choosing words effectively, suggestions are given for half of the corrections.

¹My sister, Elaine, never had good luck with her boyfriends, even though she's dated some hotties. ²She always broke up with them on account of the fact that all they cared about was their gorgeous selves. ³Then it dawned on her that she might get along better with very studious types. ⁴So she started going out with nerds. ⁵But she would return back home again from those dates complaining that the smart ones weren't much fun. ⁶I hated to see my sister in the dumps. ⁷I kept saying, "Don't lose hope—someday you'll find someone as awesome as Jeff." ⁸Jeff, my boyfriend, was good-looking, did well in school, and was as sweet as pie, too. ⁹During the time that Elaine was having boyfriend problems, Jeff and I often discussed her. ¹⁰Maybe I mentioned Jeff and Elaine to each other too often; anyway, they're getting hitched this June.

1. ____ _____   Correct the slang.

2. ____ _____

3. ____ _____   Correct the cliché.

4. ____ _____

5. ____ _____   Correct the wordiness.

6. ____ _____

7. ____ _____   Correct the slang.

8. ____ _____

9. ____ _____   Correct the wordiness.

10. ____ _____

Name _____ Section _____ Date _____

Score: (Number right) _____ × 10 = _____ %

■ Word Choice: Test 6

Each sentence in the following passage contains an example of wordiness, slang, or a cliché. Underline each error. Then, in the space provided, write *W, S,* or *C* to indicate wordiness, slang, or cliché. Finally, use the answer line to rewrite the faulty expression, using more effective language.

[1]Chocolate is one of the most awesome foods in the world. [2]People began consuming unsweetened chocolate as a beverage around three thousand years ago in time in the area that is now Mexico. [3]They thought it was to die for. [4]Explorer Hernando Cortez introduced chocolate to Spain in the early 1500s, but the Spanish kept the delicacy under wraps for nearly one hundred years. [5]Once revealed, chocolate spread like wildfire across Europe. [6]By that point in time, sugar was added to the chocolate beverage; however, chocolate candy was not invented until the nineteenth century. [7]In this day and age, chocolate is a main ingredient in many snacks and desserts. [8]A serving of chocolate can provide a shot in the arm. [9]Recent research has shown that dark chocolate can strengthen the ticker and also can prevent cancer. [10]Some scientists say, however, that consuming the amount of chocolate necessary for those benefits would be like cutting off your nose to spite your face.

1. ____ _____

2. ____ _____

3. ____ _____

4. ____ _____

5. ____ _____

6. ____ _____

7. ____ _____

8. ____ _____

9. ____ _____

10. ____ _____

15 Misplaced and Dangling Modifiers

Seeing What You Know

What do you think the writer was trying to say in each of the following sentences? Underline the part of each sentence that does not seem clear. Then read the explanations below.

1. We looked at twenty-five sofas shopping on Saturday.

2. Thrown in a heap on the closet floor, Jean found her son's dirty laundry.

3. Carrying in the main course, the roast slid off its platter.

4. While taking notes in class, Jerome's thoughts were elsewhere.

Understanding the Answers

1. *Twenty-five sofas shopping on Saturday* is the unclear part of the sentence. The intended meaning is that we saw twenty-five sofas while *we* (not the twenty-five sofas) were shopping on Saturday. A better way to say so would be *Shopping on Saturday,* we looked at twenty-five sofas.

2. *Thrown in a heap on the closet floor, Jean* is the unclear part of the sentence.
   It sounds as if *Jean* was thrown onto the closet floor when she found her son's laundry. The writer means, however, that Jean found *her son's dirty laundry* thrown in a heap on the closet floor.

3. *Carrying in the main course, the roast* is the unclear part of the sentence. The sentence seems to say that the *roast* was carrying in the main course. Actually, the roast *was* the main course; a person (not the roast) was carrying it. To make the intended meaning clear, rewrite the sentence to show who that person was: *As Stacy was* carrying in the main course, the roast slid off its platter.

4. *While taking notes in class, Jerome's thoughts* is the unclear part of the sentence.
   It sounds as if *Jerome's thoughts* were taking notes in class. The sentence needs to be rewritten like this: While *Jerome was* taking notes in class, *his* thoughts were elsewhere.

A **modifier** is one or more words that describe other words. Two common errors involving these descriptive words are misplaced modifiers and dangling modifiers.

MISPLACED MODIFIERS

When a modifier is in the wrong place, the reader may not know just what it is meant to describe. Misplaced modifiers can lead to misunderstandings—some of which are unintentionally humorous.

To correct a misplaced modifier, place it as close as possible to what it is describing, so that its meaning will be clearly understood.

Misplaced modifier:	The Bensons watched the parade of high school bands sitting in chairs on their lawn. (It sounds as if *the high school bands* were sitting in chairs, rather than the Bensons.)
Corrected version:	**Sitting in chairs on their lawn, the Bensons** watched the parade of high school bands.
Misplaced modifier:	Please take this book to Mrs. Bey's house which she lent to me. (Did Mrs. Bey lend her *house* to the speaker?)
Corrected version:	Please take **this book, which Mrs. Bey lent to me,** to her house.
Misplaced modifier:	The robber ran into the bank carrying a gun. (The *bank* was carrying a gun?)
Corrected version:	**The robber, carrying a gun,** ran into the bank.

Practice 1

Underline the misplaced modifier in each sentence. Then rewrite the sentence, placing the modifier where it needs to go to make the meaning clear.

1. The young man gave his driver's license to the officer with shaking hands.

   _____

2. We were surprised to hear a siren driving down the country road.

   _____

3. Gina got badly sunburned after spending a day at the beach on her face and back.

   _____

4. The registrar will post the schedule for final exams on the Web site.

   _____

5. Stan bought a sports car from a fast-talking salesman with wire wheels.

   _____

SINGLE-WORD MODIFIERS

Pay special attention to single-word modifiers, such as *almost, only, nearly, hardly,* and *even.* For their meaning to be correctly understood, they should be placed directly in front of the word they describe.

Misplaced modifier: Sean won the pole vault event when he almost jumped sixteen feet.
(Did Sean think about jumping sixteen feet, but then not jump at all?)

Corrected version: Sean won the pole vault event when he **jumped almost sixteen feet**.
(The intended meaning—that Sean's winning jump was not quite sixteen feet—is now clear.)

Misplaced modifier: Tanya nearly earned a thousand dollars last summer.
(Tanya had the chance to make a lot of money but didn't take advantage of it?)

Corrected version: Tanya **earned nearly a thousand dollars** last summer.
(Now we see—she earned close to a thousand dollars.)

Practice 2

Underline the misplaced single-word modifier in each sentence. Then rewrite the sentence, placing the modifier where it will make the meaning clear.

1. I only spent two hours studying for the French test; I hope that was enough.

   _____

2. Carlos must have almost answered a hundred ads before he found a job.

   _____

3. My sister nearly spends all evening on the telephone.

   _____

DANGLING MODIFIERS

A modifier that starts a sentence must be followed right away by the word it is meant to describe. Otherwise, the modifier is said to be dangling, and the sentence takes on an unintended meaning. Look at this example:

Staring dreamily off into space, the teacher's loud voice startled me.

The modifier *staring dreamily off into space* is followed by *the teacher's loud voice,* giving the impression that the voice was staring off into space. However, this is not what the author intended. The modifier was meant to describe a word that is missing: *I.*

There are two ways to correct a dangling modifier:

1   Add a subject and verb to the opening word group, and revise as necessary.

As I was staring dreamily off into space, the teacher's loud voice startled me.

2   Place the word or words being described immediately after the opening word group, and revise as necessary.

Staring dreamily off into space, **I was startled by** the teacher's loud voice.

Here are more examples of dangling modifiers and ways they can be corrected:

Dangling modifier:	When pulling out of the driveway, the hedge blocks Tracy's view. (Is the *hedge* pulling out of the driveway?)
Corrected versions:	**Whenever Tracy pulls** out of the driveway, the hedge blocks **her** view. *Or:* When pulling out of the driveway, **Tracy finds that** the hedge blocks **her** view.
Dangling modifier:	Delighted with the movie, conversation over coffee ended our evening. (Was the *conversation* delighted with the movie?)
Corrected versions:	**We were** delighted with the movie **and** ended our evening **with** conversation over coffee. *Or:* Delighted with the movie, **we** ended our evening **with** conversation over coffee.

Practice 3

In each sentence, underline the dangling modifier. Then, on the line provided, rewrite the sentence so that the intended meaning is clear. Use both methods of fixing dangling modifiers.

1. While taking a shower, a mouse ran across my bathroom floor.

    _____

2. Sitting on the front porch, mosquitoes became annoying.

    _____

3. While eating at the restaurant, Kareem's coat was stolen.

    _____

4. Breathing heavily, the finish line finally came into the runner's view.

    _____

5. Hoping to catch a glimpse of the band, the parking lot was full of fans.

    _____

Name _____   Section _____ Date _____

■ **Misplaced and Dangling Modifiers: Test 1**

In each sentence, underline the one misplaced or dangling modifier. (The first four sentences contain misplaced modifiers; the second four sentences contain dangling modifiers.) Then rewrite each sentence so that its intended meaning is clear.

Note   To help you correct misplaced and dangling modifiers, explanations are given for half of the sentences.

1. I have a photograph of the Golden Gate Bridge on my cell phone.

    _____

    The sentence suggests that the Golden Gate Bridge is on the cell phone. The modifier *on my cell phone* needs to be placed earlier in the sentence.

2. A group of students talked about fishing with live bait in shop class.

    _____

3. The shipwrecked sailors almost went without food and water for a week.

    _____

    The sentence suggests that the sailors were in danger of going without food and water but avoided this danger. The writer actually means that the sailors *did* go without food and water—for just under a week.

4. Invitations to graduation exercises were nearly sent out to five hundred people.

    _____

5. Jumping at a sudden noise, the razor nicked Dean's face.

    _____

    Dean, not the razor, was the one who jumped at a sudden noise.

6. Just before leaving for home, the secretary's telephone rang.

    _____

7. While hiking through the state park, many animals can be seen.

    _____

    People—not animals—are the ones who are hiking through the state park.

8. Tossing trash out the window, the teenagers' car was stopped by the police.

    _____

■ Misplaced and Dangling Modifiers: Test 2

In each sentence, underline the one misplaced or dangling modifier. (The first four sentences contain misplaced modifiers; the second four sentences contain dangling modifiers.) Then rewrite each sentence so that its intended meaning is clear.

1. I had a big lunch today, so I hardly ate anything for dinner.

   _____

2. The children placed their soup on the windowsill, which was too hot to eat.

   _____

   _____

3. The instructor told the students to sit down in a loud voice.

   _____

   _____

4. Residents of the burning house were carried out by firemen wearing only pajamas.

   _____

   _____

5. Involved in a noisy game of Monopoly, the summer evening together was enjoyable for us.

   _____

   _____

6. Growing thinner every day, Albert's diet is really working.

   _____

   _____

7. Whining and twitching, the dog's dream must have been about chasing rabbits.

   _____

   _____

8. Unable to read yet, my mother explained that the sign said, "No children allowed."

   _____

   _____

Name _____ Section _____ Date _____

■ Misplaced and Dangling Modifiers: Test 3

Each group of sentences contains one misplaced and one dangling modifier. Underline these errors. Then, on the lines provided, rewrite the parts of the sentences that contain the errors so that the intended meanings are clear.

Note   To help you correct misplaced and dangling modifiers, explanations are given for the first error in each group.

1. Waiting anxiously at the front door, Shari arrived to the cries and jumps of her beloved dog, Nick. With tail wagging, Nick raced ahead of her to the treat jar. Then, sitting, lying down, and rolling over, Shari rewarded him.

   a. _____
   Waiting anxiously at the front door seems to be describing Shari. Actually, it is describing Nick.

   b. _____

2. Lani stopped to watch the sidewalk artist with amazement. He was drawing a pencil portrait of a little girl. Sketching quickly, the portrait took shape under the artist's careful hand. "What remarkable talent," Lani commented.

   a. _____
   Lani, not the artist, is the one who is amazed.

   b. _____

3. I lost my raincoat last fall. I thought I'd looked everywhere for it. Then, yesterday, stuffed under the bed, I spotted it. Wrinkled and dusty, I was still delighted.

   a. _____
   The intended meaning is that the *raincoat*—not the speaker—was under the bed.

   b. _____

4. The sky was blue and clear when we arrived home. Only minutes later, though, there was a sudden crash of thunder. Rushing like mad, the windows in the bedrooms were closed. Staring out at the downpour, we were glad to be safe inside. Then we remembered our open car windows, groaning with dismay.

   a. _____
   Rushing like mad seems to be describing the windows.

   b. _____

Name _____   Section _____   Date _____

Score: (Number right) _____ × 12.5 = _____ %

■ Misplaced and Dangling Modifiers: Test 4

Each group of sentences contains one misplaced and one dangling modifier. Underline these errors. Then, on the lines provided, rewrite the parts of the sentences that contain the errors so that the intended meanings are clear.

1. Going to camp was a nightmare for me. Being afraid of water, swimming was a frightening experience. I got a terrible case of poison ivy all over my legs, which seemed to be everywhere at the camp. I always remembered my time at camp as the longest week of my life.

   a. _____

   b. _____

2. Lana watched her twin sons toss a baseball back and forth through her living-room picture window. It was almost dinnertime. Shouting happily to each other, she knew their game of catch would soon have to end.

   a. _____

   b. _____

3. When a senior in high school, my parents offered to buy me a car. They told me that they would also pay for a driver's education course at my school, which costs $35.00 an hour. But they said I would have to get a job and pay for the insurance on the car before they would give me the keys.

   a. _____

   b. _____

4. Cold and hungry, the street seemed a cruel place. People passing by ignored the homeless man completely. He watched them talking and laughing, sitting on the sidewalk in his thin sweater. "When I get out of this mess, I'm never going to ignore another street person again," he promised himself.

   a. _____

   b. _____

Name _____   Section _____   Date _____

■ Misplaced and Dangling Modifiers: Test 5

Eight of the sentences in the following passage contain a misplaced or dangling modifier. Underline each modifier you believe to be misplaced or dangling, and then rewrite the parts of the sentences that contain the errors so that the intended meanings are clear.

Note To help you correct misplaced and dangling modifiers, explanations are given for four of the sentences.

Ted and Linda decided to give their friend Garry a surprise birthday party that he would never forget. Working hard to make everything perfect, their menu was planned weeks in advance. They ordered a beautiful cake from a bakery with thirty-five candles. They bought five flavors of ice cream for the party, which they hid in the freezer. They scattered dozens of colorful balloons around the house, which they filled with helium. Finally, excited and pleased with all they had done, the guests were eagerly awaited. Linda saw people starting to arrive through the window. However, Garry was nowhere in sight. Suddenly, with a gasp, Ted realized that he had forgotten to bring the guest of honor. Rushing off in search of Garry, the party finally started—an hour late. "This party was supposed to only be a surprise for Garry," Ted said to the crowd, "but it turned out to be surprising for us as well."

1. _____
   The words *working hard to make everything perfect* apply to Ted and Linda, not to their menu.

2. _____

3. _____
   The writer means that the ice cream—not the party—was hidden in the freezer.

4. _____

5. _____
   Ted and Linda, not the guests, are the ones who were excited and pleased.

6. _____

7. _____
   The words *Rushing off in search of Garry* seem to be describing the party, but they really are about Ted.

8. _____

Name _____   Section _____   Date _____

Score: (Number right) _____ × 12.5 = _____ %

■ Misplaced and Dangling Modifiers: Test 6

Eight of the sentences in the following passage contain a misplaced or dangling modifier. Underline each misplaced or dangling modifier. Then rewrite the parts of the sentences that contain the errors so that the intended meanings are clear.

The Simpsons is the longest-running prime-time animated show in American television history. Presented for the first time on the Fox Network in 1989, millions of American homes have tuned in faithfully every Sunday evening for more than 20 years. *The Simpsons* is a satiric comedy about a dysfunctional family living in a small town of five members. Naming the characters after his own parents and siblings, Matt Groening's fictional Simpson family was originally created for a skit on *The Tracey Ullman Show*. Later, Groening gave the Simpsons their own series, in which he makes fun of many aspects of American society. Homer, the dim-witted father, works as a safety inspector at the Springfield Nuclear Power Plant. Playing the role of a stereotypical housewife, Marge's trademark is her large blue beehive hairdo. Bart, the oldest child, is the mischievous member of the family. At the beginning of each episode, he can be seen writing about his latest prank at the classroom chalkboard. He loves to annoy his serious sister Lisa by reacting to her good causes with insults. Always seen with a pacifier in her mouth, viewers wonder when they'll hear baby Maggie's first words. The show's success led to a full-length *Simpsons Movie* in 2007, which almost earned $600 million. In 2000, the Simpson family was honored with its own star on the Hollywood Walk of Fame.

1. _____

2. _____

3. _____

   _____

4. _____

5. _____

6. _____

7. _____

8. _____

16 Parallelism

Seeing What You Know

Underline the part of each sentence that is not balanced—because it does not match other parts of the sentence. Then read the explanations that follow.

1. The manager is competent, good-natured, and offers help.

2. To lick water off the shower curtain, climbing up the side of the house, and sleeping in the kitchen sink are some of my cat's strange habits.

3. The expensive restaurant served overcooked fish, clam chowder that was cold, and half-melted ice cream.

4. No matter what his doctor tells him, Grady still smokes cigars, drinks heavily, and is staying out late at night.

Understanding the Answers

1. *Offers help* is the unbalanced portion of the sentence.
   Change it to *helpful* to match *competent* and *good-natured*.

2. *To lick water off the shower curtain* is out of balance.
   Change it to *Licking water off the shower curtain* to match *climbing up the side of the house* and *sleeping in the kitchen sink*.

3. *Clam chowder that was cold* does not match the rest of the sentence.
   Change it to *cold clam chowder* to give it the same form as the other two dishes—*overcooked fish* and *half-melted ice cream*.

4. *Is staying out late at night* is the unbalanced portion of the sentence.
   Change it to *stays out late at night* so that it has the same form as the other two parts of the list: *smokes cigars* and *drinks heavily*.

Two or more equal ideas should be expressed in **parallel**, or matching, form. The ideas will then read smoothly and naturally.

CORRECTING FAULTY PARALLELISM

Faulty parallelism is jarring and awkward to read. Consider this example:

Not parallel: The bowl was filled with **crisp apples**, **juicy oranges**, and **bananas that were ripe**.

In *crisp apples* and *juicy oranges,* the descriptive word comes first and the word being described comes second. In *bananas that were ripe,* the order is reversed.

To achieve parallelism, give the nonparallel item the same form as the others:

Parallel: The bowl was filled with crisp apples, juicy oranges, and **ripe bananas**.

Now, the listed items are expressed in parallel form: *crisp apples, juicy oranges,* and *ripe bananas.*

Here are additional examples of problems with parallelism and explanations of how to correct them:

Not parallel: My neighbor likes **to plant a garden**, **watering it**, and even **to weed it**.

To plant a garden and *to weed it* are similar in construction, but *watering it* is not. For parallel construction, another *to* is needed.

Parallel: My neighbor likes to plant a garden, **to water it**, and even to weed it.

Not parallel: Would you prefer to spend the morning **playing basketball**, **watching television**, or **at the mall**?

The word groups *playing basketball* and *watching television* both are *-ing* constructions, so *at the mall* needs an *-ing* word.

Parallel: Would you prefer to spend the morning **playing basketball**, **watching television**, or **shopping at the mall**?

Not parallel: The moviegoers **talked** and **were rattling** popcorn boxes during the film.

Talked, an *-ed* construction, is not parallel to *were rattling.* The problem could be corrected by changing either word group.

Parallel: The moviegoers **talked** and **rattled** popcorn boxes during the film.

Also parallel: The moviegoers *were talking* and *were rattling* popcorn boxes during the film.

Practice 1

Cross out the one item in each list below that is not parallel in form to the other two items. Then, in the space provided, write the parallel form for that item.

1. to gather information
   to write several drafts
   printing the final copy

   _____

2. couple argued
   neighbors listened
   crying baby

   _____

3. wide-brimmed hat
   sunglasses that are dark
   protective sunscreen

   _____

4. managing an office
   sales representative
   telephone operator

   _____

5. selfish
   impatient
   lacking kindness

   _____

6. teaches social studies
   is coach of the track team
   runs the teachers' union

   _____

Practice 2

The part of each sentence that is not parallel is italicized. On the line, rewrite this part to make it match the other items listed.

1. My husband, who likes to help out around the house, is good at washing dishes, cleaning the oven, and *he knows how to fold laundry.* _____

2. The most popular items on the buffet table were *shrimp that were steamed,* barbecued wings, and marinated steak tips. _____

3. Fall styles include wide-legged pants, short-cropped jackets, and *boots with high heels.* _____

4. Their intelligence, playfulness, and *being friendly* make dolphins appeal to people of all ages. _____

5. The crane's claws cradled the telephone pole, lifted it high overhead, and *were depositing it in the deep hole.* _____

WHEN TO USE PARALLELISM

Parallelism always applies to two or more *equal* ideas. Here are some writing situations in which parallelism is appropriate:

1   Presenting a series of items.

Popular summer vacation activities include **visiting** relatives, **hiking** in state parks, and **spending** time at the beach.

2   Offering choices.

The instructor announced that each student in the class could either **write a ten-page report** or **take the final exam**.

3   Making a point effectively.

Many famous speeches and pieces of writing feature skillful parallelism. The balance of their words and phrases helps make them memorable. For example,

"**Ask not what** your country can do for you; **ask what** you can do for your country." *—President John F. Kennedy*

Would Kennedy's speech have had the same ring if he'd said, "Don't ask what your country can do for you. Instead, you should be asking what you can do for your country"?

In his famous "I Have a Dream" speech, Dr. Martin Luther King, Jr., said he hoped that someday America would judge his children not "**by the color of their skin** but **by the content of their character.**"

Dr. King's words gain power because they balance "the color of their skin" with "the content of their character." They would have been much less forceful if he had said instead, "Not by the color of their skin but according to how good a person each one is."

Practice 3

In the space provided, complete each list by adding a parallel item.

1. During the summer, when I am not taking classes, I like to paint pictures, play video games, and _____.

2. To get the best buy on an appliance, compare brands, visit several stores, and _____.

3. At the adult evening school, I could sign up for a course in ballroom dancing, aerobic exercising, or _____.

4. "I still need a number of volunteers," the park director said, "to rake leaves, pick up trash, and _____."

5. Members of the work crew spent their lunch break eating sandwiches, napping on the grass, and _____.

Name _____ Section _____ Date _____

■ **Parallelism: Test 1**

Underline the part of each sentence below that upsets the sentence's parallelism. Then, in the space provided, rewrite the nonparallel item so that it matches the other item or items listed.

Note   To help you master the technique of parallelism, directions are given for half of the sentences.

1. I am always on some kind of fad diet; instead, I should be eating fewer calories, watching my portion size, and I need to exercise more.

   _____

   I need to exercise more is the unbalanced part of the sentence. It needs to be changed to the same form as *eating fewer calories* and *watching my portion size.*

2. Before leaving for work, Teresa exercises, eats breakfast, and the dog is fed.

   _____

3. A wrecked car and breaking a collarbone were the results of the accident.

   _____

   Breaking a collarbone should be made parallel to *A wrecked car.*

4. Their father's gentleness and the sense of humor of their mother were two things that the children missed after they left home.

   _____

5. Although the boss is smart, has good looks, and wealthy, he is coldhearted.

   _____

   Has good looks upsets the sentence's parallelism. It needs to be changed to the same form as *smart* and *wealthy.*

6. Even though Laila and Omar both loved to dance, enjoyed similar movies, and they shared some of the same friends, their blind date was not a success.

   _____

7. Three remedies for an upset stomach are antacid pills, a diet that is bland, and flat ginger ale.

   _____

   A diet that is bland is out of balance. It needs to match *antacid pills* and *flat ginger ale.*

8. With her long legs, movements that are graceful, and pulled-back hair, the young woman looks like a ballerina.

   _____

■ Parallelism: Test 2

Underline the part of each sentence below that upsets the sentence's parallelism. Then, in the space provided, rewrite the nonparallel item so that it matches the other item or items listed.

1. At the International Food Festival, visitors tasted tortillas, snacked on suki-yaki, and were munching on manicotti.

   _____

2. As the students waited for their instructor to arrive for class, they rummaged through their backpacks, were silencing their cell phones, and talked quietly to each other.

   _____

3. The ragged woman said she needed a meal, to have warm clothes, and a job.

   _____

4. You'll always be happy if you have your health, a loving family, and your work is satisfying.

   _____

5. The Harborside Restaurant offers delicious food, good service, and prices that are reasonable.

   _____

6. Making promises is easy; to keep them is hard.

   _____

7. My sister was looking out the window, she was watching the children play, and listening to their laughter.

   _____

8. Because she missed her friend and wanting her to visit, Juanita telephoned her with an invitation.

   _____

9. Every year at the family barbecue, we choose teams and are playing touch football.

   _____

10. The professor suggested dropping the course or to get extra tutoring.

    _____

Name _____ Section _____ Date _____

Score: (Number right) _____ × 10 = _____ %

■ Parallelism: Test 3

Each group of sentences contains **two** errors in parallelism. Underline these errors. Then, on the lines below, rewrite the unbalanced portion to make it parallel with the other listed items in the sentence.

Note To help you master the technique of parallelism, directions are given for half of the sentences.

1. Online dating is enjoyable, and it is exciting, but there are also difficulties. First, applicants have to write an introduction; then they must find a suitable photo; and finally, a decision must be made about which responses to answer.

   a. _____ *There are also difficulties* must parallel

   b. _____ *enjoyable* and *exciting.*

2. Good teachers, a modern facility, and students who are hardworking have all given the high school an excellent reputation. The school replaced two smaller schools that were known as places where teachers were third-rate, shabby described the buildings, and students were frustrated.

   a. _____ (*Students who are hardworking* must parallel

   b. _____ *good teachers* and *a modern facility.*)

3. My sister is a terrific athlete. She enjoys tennis, plays volleyball, and even rock climbing. I, on the other hand, find it challenging enough to climb stairs, walk around the block, or running for a bus.

   a. _____ (*Plays volleyball* must parallel *tennis* and

   b. _____ *rock climbing.*)

4. With her long black hair, eyes that are sparkling and dark, and tall, slim body, Regina looks like a fashion model. But she worries that no one notices her intelligence and hard work. Regina wants people to know that a woman can have beauty, ambition, and be intelligent, too.

   a. _____ (*Eyes that are sparkling and dark* needs to

   b. _____ parallel *long black hair* and *tall, slim body.*)

5. Working conditions at the factory were poor: loud machinery, conversations that were shouted, and blaring radios. Workers also complained about the low pay and the hours were long.

   a. _____ (*Conversations that were shouted* must

   b. _____ parallel *loud machinery* and *blaring radios.*)

Name _____   Section _____   Date _____

Score: (Number right) _____ × 10 = _____%

■ Parallelism: Test 4

Each group of sentences contains **two** errors in parallelism. Underline these errors. Then, on the lines below, rewrite the unbalanced portion to make it parallel with the other listed items in the sentence.

1. Everything seemed to go wrong on Tuesday. My car broke down, my girlfriend not calling, and I locked myself out of my apartment. Besides, I had a sore throat, a headache, and my stomach ached.

   a. _____

   b. _____

2. I never spend money on fancy wrapping paper. When people get a present, they generally want to rip off the paper and be looking at what's inside. So I wrap my gifts in either plain brown grocery bags or Sunday comics that are colorful.

   a. _____

   b. _____

3. The symptoms of diabetes often include extreme thirst, hunger, and losing weight. The need to urinate frequently can also be a sign of the disease. If untreated, diabetes can lead to kidney and heart failure, the person going into a coma, and death.

   a. _____

   b. _____

4. My New Year's resolutions are to stop smoking, to study harder, and getting more involved in campus activities. On the other hand, my wife has resolved to eat more chocolate, exercising less, and to spend more time buying things on eBay.

   a. _____

   b. _____

5. The woman had ordered a large head of lettuce, green beans that were fresh, and ripe strawberries. The delivery man arrived with a head of cabbage that was tiny, frozen yellow beans, and sour red cherries.

   a. _____

   b. _____

Name _____   Section _____   Date _____

Score: (Number right) _____ × 10 = _____ %

■ Parallelism: Test 5

Ten of the sentences in the passage below contain errors in parallelism. Underline the errors and write in the numbers of the sentences that contain the errors. Then rewrite the nonparallel portion of each sentence in the space provided.

Note   To help you master the technique of parallelism, directions are given for half of the sentences.

¹One summer Lynn worked as a student intern at her city's newspaper. ²Although she was young, didn't have much experience, and nervous, she did well at her job. ³Her cheerful attitude, willingness to work hard, and having the ability to get along with her coworkers impressed her editor. ⁴Lynn did some of everything: she wrote up traffic accidents and weddings, was covering a few meetings, and even helped the photographer in the darkroom.

⁵One day her editor said, "Lynn, our police reporter needs an assistant. ⁶Why don't you spend a few days following him around and see how you like it?" ⁷Ozzie, the police reporter, explained to Lynn that he spent much of his time talking with police officers, visited crime scenes, and interviewing victims and witnesses. ⁸Since she had always been interested in police work and liking Ozzie, Lynn was pleased with her new assignment. ⁹At first she just trailed Ozzie around, took notes, and was asking a lot of questions. ¹⁰One evening at home, however, as Lynn was straightening up her apartment and her plants were watered, Ozzie appeared at her door. ¹¹"Grab your notebook and camera—we're going on a raid," he yelled.

¹²Lynn dropped everything and was racing for Ozzie's car. ¹³Soon they were speeding toward the address Ozzie had: a campground that had been closed for years. ¹⁴Expecting a drug raid, the reporters were surprised to find dozens of police officers there breaking up an illegal cockfight operation. ¹⁵Lynn and Ozzie began photographing the dead and wounded roosters and to question the gamblers. ¹⁶As they drove back to the newspaper office late that night, Lynn said to Ozzie, "My college courses can teach me how to write, how to take pictures, and interviewing people. ¹⁷But they could never prepare me for a crazy night like this."

1. *Sentence* ____: _____ (Parallel *young* and *nervous*)

2. *Sentence* ____: _____

3. *Sentence* ____: _____ (Parallel *wrote up* and *helped*)

4. *Sentence* ____: _____

5. *Sentence* ____: _____ (Parallel *she had always been interested*)

6. *Sentence* ____: _____

7. *Sentence* ____: _____ (Parallel *straightening up her apartment*)

8. *Sentence* ____: _____

9. *Sentence* ____: _____ (Parallel *photographing the dead and wounded roosters*)

10. *Sentence* ____: _____

■ Parallelism: Test 6

Ten of the sentences in the passage below contain errors in parallelism. Underline the errors, and write in the numbers of the sentences that contain the errors. Then rewrite the nonparallel portion of each sentence in the space provided.

[1]"Reduce, Reuse, Recycle" is a slogan that can help you conserve energy. [2]The slogan means that you should use as little as possible, use a product again if you can, and then recycling it. [3]You can apply the "Reduce, Reuse, Recycle" principle at home, in your community, and where you work.

[4]"Reuse" and "Recycle" should be self-explanatory, but "Reduce" needs explaining.[5]If you live where the weather is very hot or in a cold climate, good insulation can reduce the energy needed to maintain a comfortable temperature in your home. [6]You can also adjust your thermostat, especially for times when you are sleeping or on a trip. [7]You can further reduce energy usage if you unplug appliances, turn off lights, and by setting computers to go into sleep mode. [8]You can reduce the amount of water you use—and the energy to heat it—by taking short showers and wash your dishes or clothes only when you have a full load. [9]Better yet, you can wash dishes or clothes by hand. [10]You can use less gasoline if you walk, bike, carpool, or public transportation. [11]All these measures are likely to save you money as well as saving energy.

[12]Shopping provides added opportunities for conserving energy. [13]First, you will use less energy if you shop efficiently and making fewer trips to the store. [14]You can also support energy conservation by purchasing products that are grown or manufactured close to your home and from stores that follow sound energy conservation policies themselves.

1. *Sentence* ____: _____

2. *Sentence* ____: _____

3. *Sentence* ____: _____

4. *Sentence* ____: _____

5. *Sentence* ____: _____

6. *Sentence* ____: _____

7. *Sentence* ____: _____

8. *Sentence* ____: _____

9. *Sentence* ____: _____

10. *Sentence* ____: _____

Part Two
Extending the Skills

Preview

Part Two presents some topics not included in Part One:

It also includes additional information about many of the topics presented in Part One:

17 Paper Form

Your instructor will probably give you specific directions for how your paper should look. However, the following guidelines normally apply:

1 Use 8.5 × 11-inch white paper.

2 Write or type on only one side of the paper.

3 Leave margins on all four sides of each page.

4 Put your name, the date, the course number, and, if required, your instructor's name where you have been told to put them—either at the top of page 1 or on a separate title page.

5 Put your title on the top line of the first page. Center it. Do not use quotation marks or underline your title. Capitalize the first word of the title as well as its other important words. (In the middle of a title, do not capitalize *a, an, the,* or prepositions such as *of, in, on, for, from, about, between,* and so on.) Skip a line between the title and the first sentence of your paper.

6 Indent the first line of each paragraph one-half inch from the left-hand margin. Do not indent when starting a new page—unless you are also starting a new paragraph.

7 Make sure your pages are in the correct order, numbered (except for the title page), and fastened.

8 Proofread your paper carefully before handing it in. Neatly correct any errors you find. Recopy or print a new copy of the paper if you discover a great many errors.

A Model Paper

While the *MLA Handbook* does not require a title page or an outline for a paper, your instructor may ask you to include one or both. On the next page is a model title page, as well as two versions of the first page of a paper.

Model Title Page

Successful Families:

Fighting for Their Kids

by

Sonya Philips

English 101

Professor Lessing

5 May 2014

The title should begin about one-third of the way down the page.

Center the title.

Double-space the lines in the title and your name. Also center and double-space the instructor's name and the date.

Papers written in MLA style use the simple format shown below. There is no title page.

1 inch

1/2 inch

Philips 1

Sonya Philips
Professor Lessing
English 101
5 May 2014

Successful Families: Fighting for Their Kids

It's a terrible time to be a teenager, or even a teenager's parent.

That message is everywhere. Television, magazines, and …

Your last name and the page number should be typed one-half inch from the top of the page.

Center the title.

Double-space lines. Leave a one-inch margin on all sides.

Model first page if title page is included.

Philips 1

Successful Families: Fighting for Their Kids

It's a terrible time to be a teenager, or even a teenager's parent.

That message is everywhere. Television, magazines, and newspapers

are all full of frightening stories about teenagers and families. They…

Header with your last name and page number.

Double-space lines of the text.

Leave a one-inch margin all around.

18 Spelling

The following hints will help even a poor speller become a better one.

1   **Use spelling aids.** These include a dictionary, a spelling-checker on a computer or electronic typewriter, and pocket-size electronic spell-checkers.

2   **Keep a personal spelling list.** Write down every word you misspell. Include its correct spelling, underline the difficult part of the word, and add any hints you can use to remember how to spell it. You might even want to start a spelling notebook that has a separate page for each letter of the alphabet. Here's one format you might use (another is on the inside back cover of this book):

How I spelled it	Correct spelling	Hints
recieve	rec*ei*ve	I before E except after C.
seperate	sep*a*rate	There's A RAT in sepARATe.

Study your list regularly, and refer to it whenever you write or proofread a paper.

3   **Learn commonly confused words.** Many spelling errors result from confusing words like *to* and *too, its* and *it's, where* and *were.* Study carefully the pairs of words on pages 144–146 and 223–225.

4   **Apply basic spelling rules.** Here are four rules that usually work. The first rule will help you spell *ie* and *ei* words. The last three rules refer to adding endings.

I before E rule: I before E except after C
                     Or when sounded like A, as in *neighbor* and *weigh.*

    Examples: bel**ie**ve, ch**ie**f, rec**ei**ve, c**ei**ling, th**ei**r
  Exceptions: **ei**ther, l**ei**sure, s**ei**ze, sc**ie**nce, soc**ie**ty, for**ei**gn

Silent E rule: If a word ends in a silent (unpronounced) *e,* drop the *e* before an ending that starts with a vowel. Keep the *e* before an ending that begins with a consonant.

    Examples: hope + ed = ho**ped**   guide + ance = gui**da**nce
                     confuse + ing = confu**sing**   love + ly = lov**ely**
                     fame + ous = fa**mous**   care + ful = car**eful**

  Exceptions: peac**ea**ble, tr**u**ly, arg**um**ent, jud**gm**ent

Y rule: Change the final *y* of a word to *i* when

    a The last two letters of the word are a consonant plus *y.*
    b The ending being added begins with a vowel or is *-ful,* *-ly,* or *-ness.*

> ***But:*** Keep a *y* that follows a vowel. Also, keep the *y* if the ending being added is -*ing*.
>
> *Examples:* fly+ es = fl**ies**   happy + ness = happ**i**ness
> try + ed = tr**ied**   destroy + s = destro**ys**
> beauty + ful = beaut**iful**   display + ed = displa**yed**
> lucky + ly = luck**ily**   carry + ing = carr**ying**
>
> Exceptions: paid, said, laid, daily
>
> ***Doubling rule:*** Double the final consonant of a word when
>
> **a** The last three letters of the word are a consonant, a vowel, and a consonant (CVC).
> **b** The word is only one syllable (for example, *stop*) or is accented on the last syllable (for example, *begin*).
> **c** The ending being added begins with a vowel.
>
> *Examples:* stop + ed = sto**pped**   hot + er = ho**tter**
> begin + ing = begi**nning**   red + est = re**ddest**
> control + er = contro**ller**   occur + ence = occu**rrence**

Note   With amazing frequency, students misspell the words *a lot* and *all right*. In each case they incorrectly combine the words to form one word: *alot* and *alright*. Remember that both *a lot* and *all right* are two words!

Practice

Use the preceding rules to spell the ten words that follow.

1. (Add the ending)   deny + s =   _____
2. (Add the ending)   skip + ing =   _____
3. (Add the ending)   write + ing =   _____
4. (Add the ending)   definite + ly =   _____
5. (Write *ie* or *ei*)   dec____ve
6. (Add the ending)   employ + er =   _____
7. (Add the ending)   admit + ance =   _____
8. (Add the ending)   marry + ing =   _____
9. (Write *ie* or *ei*)   fr____ndly
10. (Add the ending)   pity + ful =   _____

19 Pronoun Types

Personal Pronouns

Subject Pronouns

Subject pronouns function as subjects of verbs. These are the subject pronouns:

I	you	he	she	it	we	they

Here are some examples of subject pronouns in sentences:

He can resolve the problem. (*He* is the subject of the verb *can resolve*.)

You and **she** had a fight. (*You* and *she* are the ones who had a fight.)

It was **I** who called you.
(Use a subject pronoun after a form of the verb *be—am, are, is, was, were, has been,* etc.)

I'm as hungry as **they**.
(This means, "I'm as hungry as they *are*." *They* is the subject of the suggested verb *are*.)

Object Pronouns

Object pronouns serve as the objects of verbs (receivers of the verbs' action) or of prepositions (the last words in prepositional phrases). Here are the object pronouns:

me	you	him	her	it	us	them

Here are examples of object pronouns in sentences:

The children had wandered away, but their father finally found **them**. (*Them* receives the action of the verb *found*.)

The teacher gave a retest to José and **me**. (*Me* is the object of the preposition *to*.)

Hint   If a sentence is about two people and you aren't sure which pronoun to use, try using each pronoun by itself. Then choose the pronoun that sounds correct. For example, you would say, "The teacher gave a retest to me," not "to I."

Possessive Pronouns

Possessive pronouns show ownership or possession. Here are the possessive pronouns:

Singular:	**my, mine**	**your, yours**	**his**	**her, hers**	**its**
Plural:	**our, ours**	**your, yours**		**their, theirs**	

189

Here are examples of possessive pronouns in sentences:

José got an A on **his** retest, but I got only a B on **mine**. (*His* refers to José's test; *mine* refers to my test.)

There are two points to remember about possessive pronouns:

1   Possessive pronouns never contain an apostrophe.

The book Alice lent me is missing **its** cover (not *it's cover*).

2   Do not use a subject or object pronoun where a possessive is needed.

Could I borrow **your** notes (not *you notes*) before the exam?
My refrigerator (not *me refrigerator*) is out of order.

Relative Pronouns

Relative pronouns refer to someone or something already mentioned in the sentence. Relative pronouns include the following:

who   **whose**   **whom**   **which**   **that**

Here are some examples of relative pronouns in sentences:

A cousin **whom** I've never met is coming to visit me. (*Whom* refers to *cousin.*)

The drill **that** you want is in the basement. (*That* refers to *drill.*)

Dick saw an old classmate **whose** name he had forgotten. (*Whose* refers to *classmate.*)

Here are some rules to remember about relative pronouns:

1   *Whose* means *belonging to whom.* Don't confuse it with *who's,* which means *who is.* (See page 146.)

2   The pronouns *who* and *whom* refer to people. *Whose* usually refers to people but often refers to things ("The tree **whose** branches damaged our roof belongs to our neighbor"). *Which* refers to things. *That* can refer to either people or things.

3   *Who* is a subject pronoun; *whom* is an object pronoun.

I wonder **who** is at the door. (*Who* is the subject of the verb *is.*)

The clerk **whom** I asked couldn't help me. (*Whom* is the object of *asked.*)

Note   To determine whether to use *who* or *whom,* find the first verb after the place where the *who* or *whom* will go. Decide whether that verb already has a subject. If it lacks a subject, use the subject pronoun *who.* If it does have a subject, use the object pronoun *whom.*

My parents will accept any person (who, whom) I choose to marry.

Look at the verb *choose.* Does it have a subject? Yes: the subject is *I.* Therefore, the object pronoun *whom* is the correct choice: My parents will accept any person *whom* I choose to marry.

Demonstrative Pronouns

Demonstrative pronouns are used to point out one or more particular persons or things. These are the demonstrative pronouns:

Singular: **this**   **that**   *Plural:* **these**   **those**

This and *these* generally refer to things that are near the speaker; *that* and *those* refer to things farther away.

I like **this** better than **those**.

Don't ever say **that** to me again.

Note 1 Demonstrative pronouns can also be used as adjectives: **this** cake, **those** cookies, **that** word.

Note 2 Do not use *them, this here, that there, these here,* or *those there* to point out.

Reflexive and Intensive Pronouns

Singular: **myself**   **yourself**   **himself, herself, itself**
Plural: **ourselves**   **yourselves**   **themselves**

(Remember that the plural of *-self* is *-selves*. There is no such word as *ourself* or *themself*.)

A **reflexive pronoun** is the object of a verb or preposition in sentences in which that object is the same as the subject.

I gave **myself** a birthday present.
(The subject of the verb, *I,* is the same as the object of the verb, *myself.*)

In the shower, Dad talks out loud to **himself**.
(The subject of the sentence, *Dad,* is the same as the object of the preposition *to, himself.*)

An **intensive pronoun** emphasizes a noun or another pronoun.

I **myself** will tell the police what happened.

She has to do her schoolwork **herself**.

Interrogative Pronouns

Interrogative pronouns are used to ask questions. Here are common interrogative pronouns:

who   **whose**   **whom**   **which**   **what**

Here are examples of interrogative pronouns in sentences:

Who is downstairs?   **Which** road should we take?   **What** is the matter?

There are two points to remember about interrogative pronouns:

1   Choose *who* or *whom* in the same manner as you would for relative pronouns.

Whom should I pick for the team?
(*I* is the subject of *should pick,* so use *whom.*)

Who tries hardest?
(The verb after *who* is *tries,* which does not have a subject. Therefore, use the subject form of the word, *who.*)

2   *Whose* is the possessive form of *who. Who's* means *who is.*

Whose turn is it?   **Who's** bringing the sodas?

Indefinite Pronouns

Indefinite pronouns do not refer to specific persons or things. Most of them are singular:

one	**none**	**each**	**either**
anyone	**someone**	**everyone**	**no one**
anybody	**somebody**	**everybody**	**nobody**
anything	**something**	**everything**	**nothing**

Some are plural:

both	**several**	**few**	**many**

Some can be either singular or plural:

all	**any**	**more**	**most**	**some**	**none**

Here are examples of indefinite pronouns in sentences. (See also pages 41–42.)

Somebody ate the last piece of chocolate cake. **None** of the cake is left.

Both of my sisters want to become police officers.

Most of the house has been painted. (*Singular; refers to one thing—the house*)

Most of the rooms need painting, too. (*Plural; refers to several things—the rooms*)

Practice

Underline the correct pronoun in each pair in parentheses.

1. Are those (you, your) car keys on the kitchen table?

2. All those dirty clothes on the closet floor are (hers, her's).

3. Today the manager warned two coworkers and (I, me) about personal use of the copy machine.

4. (He, Him) and (I, me) haven't seen each other in months.

5. Everyone else in my family is taller than (I, me).

6. (Them, Those) eggs are rotten.

7. (Who, whom) is going to get a bonus this year?

8. Are you going to eat (these, these here) corn chips?

9. It is (they, them) who will be sorry for what they (themself, themselves) have done.

10. All the people (who, whom) we asked for directions turned out to be just as lost as we were.

11. Michelle was pointing to (these, these here) shoes, not the ones with the pointed toes and four-inch heels.

12. I really like Connie, but between you and (me, I), she seems almost too nice sometimes.

13. (Her, She) and I have been friends ever since we were in Ms. Martin's kindergarten class.

14. (Whoever, Whomever) she chooses will have to be willing to work overtime.

15. Diana is a lot more competitive than (he, him).

16. I painted my home office by myself, so my children want to paint their bedrooms by (themselfs, themselves).

17. (Me, I) and two of my friends volunteered to feed the homeless last Christmas.

18. The bird injured (it's, its) wing when the dog chased it off the lawn.

19. Did we ever find out (who, whom) was responsible for the accounting error?

20. The manager of the theater ejected (them, those) boys because they were laughing loudly and throwing popcorn at people during the movie.

20 Adjectives and Adverbs

Identifying Adjectives

Adjectives are words that describe nouns (names of people, places, or things). An adjective can be found in two places in a sentence:

1   An adjective comes before the word it describes (a **loud** noise, a **wet** dog, the **oldest** child).

2   An adjective that describes the subject of a sentence may also come after a linking verb (see pages 6 and 19). The linking verb may be a form of the verb *be* (they are **delicious**, she is **pleased**, I am **sure**). Other linking verbs include *feel, look, sound, smell, taste, appear, seem, grow, remain,* and *become* (it seems **strange**, I feel **sick**, you look **happy**, it tastes **awful**).

Adjectives in Comparisons

Adjectives change form when they are used to make a comparison. Add *-er* to a short (usually one-syllable) adjective when you are comparing two things. Add *-est* when you are comparing three or more things.

This green chili pepper is **hot**, but that red one is **hotter**.

Of all the chili peppers I've ever tasted, that red one is the **hottest**.

With most adjectives that have two or more syllables, however, do not change the form of the adjective at all. Instead, use the word *more* when comparing two things and *most* when comparing three or more things.

To me, David Letterman is **more entertaining** than Jay Leno, but Johnny Carson was the **most entertaining** of all.

Note 1   Do not use both an *-er* ending and *more,* or both an *-est* ending and *most.*

Incorrect: "This is the most happiest day of my life," Denise said.

Correct: "This is the **happiest** day of my life," Denise said.

Note 2   Certain short adjectives have irregular forms:

	Comparing two	*Comparing three or more*
bad	worse	worst
good, well	better	best
little	less	least
much, many	more	most

In my opinion, David Letterman's show is **better** than Jay Leno's, but Johnny Carson's was the **best**.

Identifying Adverbs

Adverbs are words that describe verbs, adjectives, and other adverbs. Most adverbs end in the letters *ly*. The following examples show how adverbs are used:

The clerk spoke to me **rudely**. (The adverb *rudely* tells how the clerk spoke.)

Colleen is **truly** sorry for her angry remark. (The adverb *truly* describes the adjective *sorry*; it tells how sorry Colleen is.)

The canary sings **very** sweetly. (The adverb *very* describes the adverb *sweetly*; it tells how sweetly the canary sings.)

Using Adverbs

Be careful to use an adverb—not an adjective—after an action verb. Compare the following:

Incorrect	*Correct*
The car runs good. (*Good* is an adjective, not an adverb)	The car runs **well**.
Listen careful to the directions. (*Careful* is an adjective)	Listen **carefully** to the directions.
She went to sleep quick. (*Quick* is an adjective.)	She went to sleep **quickly**.

Pay particular attention to the difference between the words *good* and *well*. *Good* is an adjective that often means "talented" or "positive":

Zoe is a **good** guitarist.
We had a **good** time.
Do you feel **good** about yourself?

As an adverb, *well* often means "skillfully" or "successfully":

She plays the guitar **well**.
He does his job **well**.
I did **well** on that project.

As an adjective, *well* means "healthy," as in the question "Are you feeling **well**?"

Practice

Cross out the incorrect adjective or adverb in each of the following sentences. Then write the correction on the line provided.

1. _____ Is psychology a more harder subject than sociology?

2. _____ To stay in good shape, exercise regular.

3. _____ Those three students did real well on the last exam.

4. _____ The most greatest challenge in my life is working and going to school at the same time.

5. _____ Of the two computers I tried last week, the Macintosh was easiest for me to use.

6. _____ Brenda spoke soft to the frightened puppy.

7. _____ I use lesser butter and sugar in my cooking than I used to.

8. _____ Always proofread the last version of your paper careful before handing it in.

9. _____ Cara didn't go to class today because she didn't feel good.

10. _____ After she took aspirin and cold medicine, Cara felt more better than she had before.

11. _____ Of all of the candidates, Damon proved to be the most good for the job.

12. _____ Overall, Anita did very good on all her final exams, except for biology.

13. _____ The hardest part of my diet plan is learning to eat more small portions.

14. _____ Suzanne did the littlest possible to help out during her sister's wedding.

15. _____ Although Sid was nervous, he sang his solo beautiful.

21 Numbers and Abbreviations

Numbers

Here are some guidelines to follow when writing numbers:

1 Spell out a number if it can be written in one or two words. Otherwise, write it in numerals.

The new high school has **three** vice principals, **ninety-five** teachers, and **two thousand** students.

There are **15,283** books in its library.

2 Spell out any number that begins a sentence.

Four hundred ninety-three people were in the first graduating class.

3 Be consistent when you write a series of numbers. If one or more numbers in the series need to be written as numerals, write *all* the numbers as numerals.

The carpenter bought **150** nails, **12** bolts, and **2** drill bits.

4 Use numerals to write dates, times, addresses, percentages, portions of a book, and exact amounts of money that include change.

The attorney asked the witness where she was on September **12, 2013**.

Set the alarm for **5:45** A.M. (When the word *o'clock* is used, however, the time is spelled out, as in *I get up at five o'clock.*)

The cabdriver took me to **418** East **78th** Street.

Only **30** percent of the students voted in the mock presidential election.

The test will cover Chapters **1**, **2**, and **3** in your textbook, pages **5–74**.

My monthly car payment is **$348.37**.

Abbreviations

In general, avoid using abbreviations in papers you write for class. The following are among the few abbreviations that are acceptable in formal writing.

1 Titles that are used with proper names (for example, *Mr., Mrs., Dr., Jr., Sr.*):

Mrs. Richardson   **Dr.** Bell   Edwin Sacks, **Jr.**   **Prof.** George Smith

2 Initials in a person's name:

J. Edgar Hoover   Edgar **A.** Poe

3   Time references (A.M., P.M., B.C., A.D.):

After the party, we didn't get to bed until 4 **A.M.**

4   Organizations, technical words, and trade names referred to by their initials. These are usually written in all capital letters and without periods:

FBI   CIA   IRS   AIDS   NAACP   UNICEF   YMCA

Practice

Cross out the mistake in number or abbreviation in each of the following sentences. Then write the correction on the line provided.

1. _____ This semester, Amahl is taking 5 classes and two labs.

2. _____ If only twenty-five percent of every paycheck didn't get taken out for taxes!

3. _____ The co. is taking job applications from 8:00 to 11:00 A.M.

4. _____ 150 members of the marching band spelled out "Victory!" in front of fifty thousand cheering fans.

5. _____ To earn my degree, I went to coll. for 4 years, took 40 courses, and wrote a 125-page thesis.

6. _____ Why are you setting the alarm for six A.M. if your first class isn't until eight o'clock?

7. _____ My dr. just told me that I had to lose fifteen pounds.

8. _____ On June seventh, 2016, Rasheed will finally be discharged from military duty.

9. _____ That prof. doesn't give you an A unless you score 94 percent or above.

10. _____ When Rachel opened the used book she had purchased, she saw that Chapter Ten (pages 89 through 102) had been torn out.

22 Usage

Here are some common incorrect expressions, together with their correct forms:

Incorrect	Correct
anyways, anywheres	anyway, anywhere
being as, being that	because, since
can't help but, cannot hardly, cannot scarcely (*double negatives*)	can't help, can hardly, can scarcely
could of, may of, might of, must of, should of, would of	could have, may have, might have, must have, should have, would have
had ought	ought
irregardless	regardless
kind of a	kind of
nowheres	nowhere
off of	off
suppose to, use to	supposed to, used to
sure and, try and	sure to, try to
the reason is because	the reason is that (See page 201.)
ways (meaning "distance")	way

Practice

Cross out the incorrect expression in each sentence. Then, on the line provided, rewrite that part of the sentence to eliminate the error in usage.

1. Every time I see the movie *Titanic,* I can't hardly keep from crying.

   _____

2. Joanne's boss asked her to try and finish two huge projects before leaving for vacation.

   _____

3. Verna used to live a long ways from here, but now she's renting an apartment a few blocks away.

   _____

4. Since no one in this course understands the textbook, the instructor had ought to assign a different one.

   _____

5. Nobody could of known ahead of time how different college is from high school.

   _____

6. "Regardless of what you think," the counselor said, "you should of gone to class more often."

   _____

7. I couldn't help but notice that you're wearing a different kind of cologne.

   _____

8. Being that he has spent at least ten winters in Indiana, Bob ought to be used to cold weather.

   _____

9. "Take your muddy feet off of my sofa this minute!" Juanita screamed at her son. "You certainly should have known better than to do that!"

   _____

10. The driver pulled over to the curb and asked, "Is there a convenience store anywheres nearby?"

    _____

11. Irregardless of how much you think you know, there's always more to learn.

    _____

12. I have never seen that kind of a dog before.

    _____

13. The police searched the entire neighborhood, but the missing child was nowheres to be found.

    _____

14. My brother's current wife use to be married to a professional skydiver.

    _____

15. The reason that I can't lose weight is because I never met a dessert I didn't like.

    _____

23 Mixed Constructions

Sometimes, by the time they reach the end of a sentence, writers forget how they started it. In these cases, the sentence can end up in a very different—and confusing—grammatical form. Sentences whose parts do not logically fit together are called **mixed constructions**.

To correct a mixed construction, do one of the following:

1 Turn the first part of the sentence into something that can be the subject.
Mixed: By practicing six hours a day helped Sasha become a champion skater.
Corrected: **Practicing six hours a day** helped Sasha become a champion skater.

2 Turn the second part of the sentence into a complete statement.
Mixed: Just because you got your learner's permit does not automatically give you permission to drive the car.
Corrected: Just because you got your learner's permit, **you do not automatically get permission to drive the car**.

Three Word Groups That Lead to Mixed Constructions

is when	is where	reason is because

Is (along with other forms of *to be*) is a linking verb. It needs to be followed by a subject complement (a noun), not a dependent word like *where, when,* or *because*. In definitions, or when giving examples, avoid using *is when* or *is where*.

Mixed: An approach-avoidance conflict is when someone is both attracted to and repelled by the same goal.
Corrected: An approach-avoidance conflict is **a situation in which** someone is both attracted to and repelled by the same goal.
Corrected: An approach-avoidance conflict **occurs when** someone is both attracted to and repelled by the same goal.

Mixed: Hawaii is where I have always wanted to go for a vacation.
Corrected: **I have always wanted to go to Hawaii** for a vacation.
Corrected: Hawaii is **the place where** I have always wanted to go for a vacation.

To correct *reason is because,* eliminate either *reason* or *because:*

Mixed: The reason Tanya was promoted is because she is a hard worker.
Corrected: **Tanya was promoted because** she is a hard worker.
Corrected: The reason Tanya was promoted is **that** she is a hard worker.

Practice

Rewrite each of the following sentences to eliminate the mixed construction.

1. The reason I got an A on the exam is because I studied all my class notes.

   _____

   _____

2. Although that dog is ten years old, but he still runs around like a puppy.

   _____

   _____

3. By healthy eating and reducing portion sizes helped me lose twenty pounds.

   _____

   _____

4. When a recent immigrant applies for citizenship can take a long time.

   _____

   _____

5. For people who live alone often become depressed during the holiday season.

   _____

   _____

6. Revision is where a writer improves a paper by finalizing details, organizing clearly, and correcting spelling and grammar.

   _____

   _____

7. Kaylin set a new track record at her high school is why she was offered a scholarship.

   _____

   _____

8. At the beginning of the year is when students register for classes.

   _____

   _____

24 More about Subjects and Verbs

Sentences with More Than One Subject

A sentence may have a compound subject—in other words, more than one subject.

Ellen and **Karla** have started their own part-time business.

Sentences with More Than One Verb

A sentence may have a compound verb—in other words, more than one verb.

They **plan** parties for other people and also **provide** all the refreshments.

Sentences with More Than One Subject and Verb

A sentence may have both a compound subject and a compound verb.

In the last two weeks, **Ellen** and **Karla arranged** a wedding reception, **catered** a retirement dinner, and **earned** more than five hundred dollars.

Practice

In the sentences below, cross out any prepositional phrases. Then underline each subject once and each verb twice.

1. The catcher's mitt, skateboard, and pile of dirty laundry in the closet belong to my teenage son.

2. The car's motor coughed once and refused to start.

3. Accounting and computer science are very practical majors but require a lot of work.

4. Lisa tore the wrapping off the present, lifted the lid of the box, and gasped in delight.

5. The author of the popular children's book and her husband attended the book signing, sipped coffee, and chatted with visitors.

25 Even More about Verbs

Tense

Tense refers to time. The tenses of a verb tell us when the action of the verb took place. The twelve major tenses in English for the regular verb *look* are shown in the box that follows.

<table>
<tr><td colspan="3" align="center">Twelve Verb Tenses</td></tr>
<tr><td>Tense</td><td>Time Referred To</td><td>Example</td></tr>
<tr><td>Present</td><td>Happens now or happens habitually</td><td>I look good today. Miguel looks like his father.</td></tr>
<tr><td>Past</td><td>Already happened</td><td>Students looked the word up in the dictionary.</td></tr>
<tr><td>Future</td><td>Is going to happen</td><td>Things will look better for you in a few days.</td></tr>
<tr><td>Present perfect</td><td>Began in past and now completed or continuing in present</td><td>Corinne has looked much more relaxed since she changed jobs.
Corinne has looked for a new job before.</td></tr>
<tr><td>Past perfect</td><td>Happened before another past action</td><td>She had looked very tired before she quit her old job.</td></tr>
<tr><td>Future perfect</td><td>Is going to happen before some other future action</td><td>Her former boss will have looked at 350 job applications by the end of the month.</td></tr>
<tr><td>Present progressive</td><td>Is in progress</td><td>Eli is looking for a new apartment right now. His parents are looking, too.</td></tr>
<tr><td>Past progressive</td><td>Was in progress</td><td>He was looking in their old neighborhood, but they were looking downtown.</td></tr>
<tr><td>Future progressive</td><td>Will be in progress</td><td>With rents so high, they probably will be looking for quite a while.</td></tr>
<tr><td>Present perfect progressive</td><td>Was in progress and still is</td><td>Flora has been looking at soap operas for the last two hours.</td></tr>
<tr><td>Past perfect progressive</td><td>Was in progress until recently</td><td>She had been looking at her study notes.</td></tr>
<tr><td>Future perfect progressive</td><td>Will be in progress until a set time in the future</td><td>Unless she gets back to work, she will have been looking at television until dinnertime.</td></tr>
</table>

Voice

Voice refers to the active or passive form of a verb. In the **active voice**, the action of the verb is done *by* the subject:

Active: A police officer **took** the lost child home. (The police officer performed the action.)

In the **passive voice**, the action is done *to* the subject:

> *Passive:* The lost child **was taken** home by a police officer. (The police officer performed the action, which was done to the child.)

In your own writing, you should normally use active verbs, which are more powerful than passive verbs. Use the passive voice, however, in situations where the doer of the action is not known or not important:

> *Passive:* On the morning of Chen's wedding day, his car **was stolen**.

> *Passive:* I **was promoted** last week.

Verbals

Verbals, formed from verbs, are used to name or describe people, places, and things. The three kinds of verbals are shown below.

Verbal	How Formed	Example and Comment
Infinitive	*To* plus a verb	The lost child began **to cry**. (Infinitives are used as adjectives, adverbs, or nouns. In the sentence above, *to cry* functions as a noun—the direct object of the verb *began.*)
Participle	Present: verb plus *-ing* Past: verb + *-ed* or irregular form	The **crying, frightened** child could not be comforted. (Participles are used as adjectives to describe a noun; here the adjectives *crying* and *frightened* describe the child.)
Gerund	verb plus *-ing*	**Crying** is sometimes very healthy. (Gerunds are used as nouns; here the noun *crying* is the subject of the sentence.)

Practice 1

On the line, write the indicated form of each verb in parentheses.

1. (gerund)   *(See)* _____ is *(believe)* _____.

2. (infinitive)   Peter Pan was determined never *(grow)* _____ up.

3. (present perfect) My mother *(take)* _____ the same bus at the same time from the same bus stop for the past forty years.

4. (future progressive) In early October, many tourists *(travel)* _____ through New England, just when the trees *(display)* _____ their most magnificent fall colors.

5. (passive) Since the couple wanted to keep wedding costs low, the bride's gown was homemade, and the groom's tuxedo *(borrow)* _____ from his uncle.

Three Troublesome Pairs of Irregular Verbs

	Basic Form	Past Tense	Past Participle
lie / lay	*Lie* means *rest* or *recline.*	lay	lain
	Lay means *put* or *place* something down.	laid	laid

My father likes to **lie** down and take an afternoon nap. Yesterday he **lay** on the living-room couch for two hours. He has sometimes **lain** there all afternoon without getting up.

Rico **lays** his wet towel anywhere in the house. This morning he **laid** it on a hot radiator. After he **had laid** it there, the towel began to steam.

	Basic Form	Past Tense	Past Participle
sit / set	*Sit* means *rest* or *take a seat.*	sat	sat
	Set means *put* something down or *prepare* something for use.	set	set

LaToya never **sits** down at a table to eat. Monday she **sat** at her desk to eat lunch. She **has sat** in front of the television to eat dinner every night this week.

My sister is the one who **sets** the family dinner table every day. She **has set** it in various ways, depending on what's for dinner. For instance, when we had Chinese food last week, she **set** the table with just napkins and chopsticks.

	Basic Form	*Past Tense*	*Past Participle*
rise / raise	*Rise* means *go up.*	rose	risen
	Raise means *lift* something up or *increase* it.	raised	raised

The sun **rises** every morning. Today it **rose** at 6:12 A.M. As soon as it **had risen**, trash trucks began clattering down the street.

Justine **raises** her hand a lot in class. This week, she **raised** her hand every time the instructor asked a question. Maybe she **has raised** her grade this way.

Practice 2

Underline the correct form of each verb in parentheses.

1. You look tired. Why don't you (sit, set) down and rest for a while?

2. Those old magazines have (lain, laid) in piles in our garage for years.

3. The accident victim was in such pain that she couldn't (rise, raise) her head.

4. Everyone in the stadium (rose, raised) to sing the national anthem.

5. The restaurant customer (lay, laid) a five-dollar bill on the table and said to the waiter, "This is yours if you can bring me my food in five minutes."

6. I was so tired after mowing both the front and back lawns that I decided to (lay, lie) down in the hammock for a few minutes.

7. "Just (set, sit) the vase of flowers in the middle of that long table," the funeral director said.

8. In my opinion, the sun (raises, rises) in the eastern sky far too early in the morning.

9. Aunt Cathy always (sat, set) in the chair by the window so she could watch the neighborhood children playing in the street.

10. (Laying, Lying) across my bed was the beautiful quilt my husband had found in his grandmother's attic.

26 More about Subject-Verb Agreement

When compound subjects are joined by *or, nor, either . . . or, neither . . . nor,* or *not only . . . but also,* the verb agrees with the closer subject.

> Either clams or lobster **is** the featured special every Friday at the restaurant. (*Lobster,* a singular subject, is closer to the verb, so the singular form *is* is required.)

> Either lobster or clams **are** the featured special every Friday at the restaurant. (*Clams,* a plural subject, is closer to the verb, so the plural verb *are* is used.)

While most indefinite pronouns are always singular (*each, everyone, one, somebody,* etc.—see page 41), a few are not. The pronouns *both, several, many,* and *a few* are always plural and require plural verbs:

> Both of my uncles **play** the piano and **sing** professionally. A few of my cousins **are** also performers.

The pronouns *all, any, some, more, most,* and *none* are either singular or plural, depending on the words that follow them. If the words after them are singular, they are singular. If the words after them are plural, however, they are plural. Notice the examples.

> Some of the birthday cake **is** still on the table. (Since *cake* is singular, *some* is singular in this sentence. A singular verb, *is,* is needed.)

> Some of the party guests **are** not having any dessert. (*Guests* is plural, making *some* plural in this sentence. The plural verb *are* is appropriate here.)

Practice

Underline the subject or subjects of each sentence. Then fill in the verb in parentheses that agrees with the subject or subjects.

1. *(tastes, taste)* A few of the chocolates in the box _____ funny.

2. *(stays, stay)* Either Thelma or her mother _____ at home to care for Thelma's grandmother.

3. *(is, are)* Not only Carl but also his friends _____ working at the neighborhood food bank this weekend.

4. *(was, were)* All of the students in the course _____ glad when it was over.

5. *(has, have)* Neither the head coach nor his assistant coaches _____ yet been fired for supplying bodybuilding drugs to players.

6. *(needs, need)* Both of my good shirts _____ to be ironed.

7. *(has, have)* Either the professor's lectures or the textbook _____ to be updated.

8. *(Is, Are)* _____ any of the lemon chiffon pie still in the refrigerator?

9. *(Is, Are)* _____ any of the other desserts still available?

10. *(seems, seem)* Since all of the desserts _____ to be gone, I'm going out for ice cream.

11. *(looks, look)* Most of the children _____ more interested in the turtle than in what the teacher is saying about it.

12. *(was, were)* When the accident victim asked for witnesses, none of the bystanders _____ willing to step forward.

13. *(has, have)* Some of the pages in this used textbook _____ writing on them.

14. *(appears, appear)* Many of the pages in this used textbook _____ to be missing.

15. *(is, are)* All of the material in the textbook _____ going to be on the final exam.

27 More about Run-Ons and Comma Splices

Other Methods of Correcting a Run-On or a Comma Splice

Run-ons and comma splices may be corrected by putting a **semicolon** (**;**) between the two complete thoughts. A semicolon is a stronger mark of punctuation than a comma; it can therefore be used to connect two complete thoughts.

Run-on:	Carmen has a broken foot she won't be doing any hiking this summer.
Corrected:	Carmen has a broken foot**;** she won't be doing any hiking this summer.
Comma splice:	Our history professor has the flu, half the class is sick as well.
Corrected:	Our history professor has the flu**;** half the class is sick as well.

Note Use the semicolon only when the connection between the two complete thoughts is obvious.

Or you can use a **semicolon plus a transitional word** (also called an **adverbial connective** or a **conjunctive adverb**) **and a comma** to make the connection between the two complete thoughts even clearer:

Carmen has a broken foot**; therefore,** she won't be doing any hiking this summer.

Our history professor has the flu**; in fact,** half the class is sick as well.

Here are some other transitional words that may be used to correct a run-on or a comma splice:

Transitional Words		
afterward	however	nevertheless
also	in addition	now
as a result	indeed	on the other hand
besides	instead	otherwise
consequently	meanwhile	then
furthermore	moreover	thus

Words That May Lead to Run-Ons and Comma Splices

Pay special attention to your punctuation when you use the following two types of words. Since they often begin a new complete thought, they can be a signal to help you avoid writing a run-on or a comma splice.

1 Personal pronouns—*I, you, he, she, it, we, they.*

Run-on: We were tired of studying we took a break.
Corrected: We were tired of studying, **so** we took a break.

2 Transitional words such as *therefore, in fact,* and the words in the box above.

Comma splice: The air conditioning wasn't working, as a result, many customers left the store.

Corrected: The air conditioning wasn't working**;** as a result, many customers left the store.

Note When the transitional word occurs in the middle of one complete thought, it is an interrupter and is set off by commas:

The air conditioning wasn't working; many customers**, as a result,** left the store.

Practice

Correct each of the following run-ons or comma splices by adding a semicolon. In some cases, the semicolon will take the place of a comma.

1. Traffic leaving the concert was horrible we finally squeezed out of the parking lot at midnight.

2. Working from home saves time and money however, it can be very lonely.

3. The family made sure all doors and windows were locked moreover, they turned the thermostat down before leaving the house.

4. Pedestrians are treated like royalty in London cars and buses stop to allow them to cross the street.

5. Many ads talk about new and improved products nevertheless, the label on the box is often all that is new.

6. Jenny couldn't afford to pay her rent consequently, she advertised in the paper for a roommate.

7. The waiters served soft drinks to the children, they offered wine to the adults.

8. Chipmunks have dug many holes in our yard now it looks like a miniature golf course.

9. We will have to leave for the game within ten minutes, otherwise, we will miss the kickoff.

10. Our dog barks too much, as a result, the landlord has refused to renew our lease.

28 More about the Comma

Short Introductory Material

Short introductory material need not be followed by a comma.

> On my return I found the children had cooked dinner.
>
> Next to the computer a pot of coffee was leaking.
>
> Afterward Martin was glad he had gotten the tattoo.

More about Interrupters

A word group that identifies another word in the sentence is actually not an inter-rupter. It is needed to make the sentence clear and should not be set off with commas.* For instance, look at the boldfaced words in the following sentences:

> The woman **who lives next door to me** just won a million dollars in the lottery.
>
> Alice Adams**, who lives next door to me,** just won a million dollars in the lottery.

In the first sentence, the boldfaced words are needed to identify the woman. Without them, we would not know who just won a million dollars. Since the words do not interrupt the sentence, we do not use commas. In the second sentence, however, we already know who won the million dollars. (It was Alice Adams.) In that case, the boldfaced words are not essential to the main message of the sentence. So, in the second sentence, *who lives next door to me* is an interrupter and should be set off by commas.

To find out whether a word group is an interrupter and should be set off by commas, try reading the sentence without it. The first sentence above would then read, "The woman just won a million dollars in the lottery." This version makes us ask, "Which woman?" The boldfaced words are needed to give us that information. If we read the second sentence without the boldfaced words, we would not be omitting essential information: "Alice Adams just won a million dollars in the lottery."

Other Joining Words

You already know that when two complete thoughts are combined into one sentence by a joining word like *and, but,* or *so,* a comma is used before the joining word. *Or, nor, for* (which means *because*), and *yet* (which means *however*) are also joining words. Put a comma before each of these words when it joins two complete thoughts.

---

*Grammar books sometimes refer to interrupters as "nonrestrictive elements" and essential descriptions as "restrictive elements."

Buyers may pay in advance, **or** they may choose the easy-payment plan.

Alonso did not want to read his paper aloud, **nor** did he want anyone else to read it for him.

All the houseplants died, **for** they hadn't been watered in weeks.

The home team was behind by seven runs, **yet** the fans remained in the stadium.

Other Uses of the Comma

1   Use a comma to set off short expressions (*yes, no, well,* and the like) at the beginnings or ends of sentences.

No, you may not borrow the car.

Would you step aside, please?

2   Use a comma to set off the name of a person spoken to.

Can't you sleep, Barry?

Mom, your skirt is too short.

Hey, mister, you forgot your change.

3   Use commas within a date or an address.

Friday, May 16, 2014, will be the last day of final exams. (Place commas after the day of the week, the date, and the year.)

Send your comments about *English Brushup* to McGraw-Hill, 2 Penn Plaza, New York, NY 10121.

Note   When you write an address in a sentence, place commas after the name (if included), the street address, and the city. Do not place a comma between the state and the ZIP code.

4   Place a comma after the opening and closing of an informal letter.

Dear Aunt Ruth,   Dear Mr. Ellis,   With love,   Sincerely,

Note   A colon is used after the opening of a business letter.

5   Place a comma between two descriptive words when they are interchangeable (in other words, when reversing their order would make sense).

Many people dream about taking a vacation from their stressful, demanding jobs. (We could just as easily say "demanding, stressful jobs," so a comma is needed.)

For some people, a fantasy vacation spot is a small tropical island. (We wouldn't say "a tropical small island," so the words are not reversible. No comma is used.)

Note   Another way to tell if two descriptive words need a comma is to see if the word *and* can be put between them. If so, a comma is used. "Stressful and demanding jobs" makes sense, so the comma is appropriate. "Small and tropical island" does not, so no comma is used.

Practice 1

Insert commas where needed in each of the following sentences.

1. Vanessa are you ready to give your report?

2. The letter was mailed on Monday morning yet it did not arrive until the following Saturday.

3. The official-looking form dated March 8 2014 said to report for jury duty to the Glendale Courthouse Front and Orange Streets Glendale CA 91208.

4. The confused angry man seemed to be yelling at nobody.

5. The man who came to the party with Joy says he was kidnapped by aliens.

6. Harvey who came to the party with Joy says he was kidnapped by aliens.

7. No you do not need an appointment to get a haircut.

8. Please wear your dark blue suit to the reception Sam.

9. I'm going to ask Alice for a loan for she has plenty of money to spare.

10. Dear Rhett

    I can't wait to see you! I'll be there to greet you when you step off the plane.

    > With love
    > Scarlett

When Not to Use a Comma

If no clear comma rule applies, it's better not to use a comma—"when in doubt, leave it out." Do not use a comma in the following situations:

Between a subject and verb:
A fast-moving storm, dumped a foot of snow onto our town last night.

Between a verb and its object:
The snow that fell completely covered, every road and bridge.

Before a prepositional phrase:
Salting crews and snowplow operators battled the storm, throughout the night.

Before *and* in a compound subject or compound verb:
Today workers, and shoppers reluctantly got up extra early, and tried to uncover their cars.

Before *that* (unless an interrupter follows):
The children happily slept late because they knew, that they had a day off from school.

Practice 2

In each sentence, cross out the **one** comma that does not belong there. Do not add any commas.

1. In the middle of the night, my cat jumped on the bed, and woke me up, but I went back to sleep again.

2. Yes, my friend, I can see, that you've lost a lot of weight.

3. Although taking the bus, which stops right at her corner, saves her money, Delia, prefers driving to work.

4. On Saturday, June 4, 2015, I will finally graduate, from community college.

5. Whenever I see, the commercial about the beautiful weather in Florida, I want to grab the TV, carry it to the window, and throw it onto my icy sidewalk.

6. Just ten years ago, there were over ten soap operas, on daytime television, but only four of them are still on the air today.

7. No matter how hard I study, I fail every test, that I take in my Spanish I class.

8. Next Wednesday, the man who rear-ended my van, and the witness who saw the accident will appear at my court hearing.

9. My best friend, has moved more than 2,500 miles away, but she has promised to e-mail and text me every day.

10. Two cups of nonfat milk, one half cup of unsweetened cocoa powder, one quarter cup of sugar, and a tablespoon of cornstarch, make the richest hot chocolate anyone will ever taste.

29 More about the Apostrophe

Apostrophes in Special Plurals

Use an apostrophe and *s* to make each of the following plural:

Letters. Bert usually gets **C's** in math and science and **A's** in everything else. How many **e's** are there in *cemetery*?

Words used as words. The instructor told us not to use so many **and's** in our papers.

But To make a number plural, add only an *s*:

There are three **7s** in the store's telephone number.

Today's reality TV shows actually originated in the **1940s** and **1950s**.

When Not to Use an Apostrophe: Possessive Pronouns

Do not put an apostrophe in any of these possessive pronouns: *his, hers, its* (meaning *belonging to it*), *ours, yours, theirs*. Since they are already possessive, they do not need an apostrophe.

Incorrect	*Correct*
The baseball jackets are theirs'.	The baseball jackets are **theirs**.
One can sometimes tell a book by it's cover.	One can sometimes tell a book by **its** cover.
Are those car keys his' or your's?	Are those car keys **his** or **yours**?

Practice

Insert apostrophes where needed in each of the following sentences. (Not all of the sentences require the addition of apostrophes.)

1. When I write quickly, my 4s, 7s, and Ts look exactly alike.

2. Those packages are ours, but the shopping bags in the corner are hers.

3. Does a student need to have all As and Bs to graduate with honors?

4. Until the freshly varnished table has completely dried, its surface will be sticky.

5. What this world needs is more *pleases* and *thank-yous*.

30 More about Quotation Marks

Other Uses of Quotation Marks

1   Use single quotation marks to indicate a quotation within a quotation.

You've learned to use quotation marks to indicate someone's exact words or the title of a short work. When a second group of exact words or the title of a short work appears within a quoted passage, use single quotation marks to set it off.

Cal's boss told him, "If I hear you say 'That's not my job' one more time, you're not going to have any job at all."

"Let's join together and serenade our guest of honor with 'Happy Birthday,'" Enrique said.

2   Use quotation marks to set off words used in a special sense or words used as words.

The "major hurricane" we had all worried about turned out to be just a little rain and breeze.

Many people misspell the word "separate" as "seperate."

Note   In printed matter, *italics* are often used to indicate a word used as a word: The word *separate* contains the words *a rat*.

Quotation Marks and Other Punctuation

Periods and commas at the end of a quotation always go *inside* the quotation marks.

"Unless you're downstairs in three minutes," Lila said, "I'm leaving without you."

Semicolons and colons at the end of a quotation always go *outside* the quotation marks.

The speaker quoted the famous line from Langston Hughes's poem "Harlem": "What happens to a dream deferred?"

Question marks and exclamation points at the end of a quotation normally go *inside* the quotation marks. They go *outside* the quotation marks only if they apply to the entire sentence, not just the quoted part.

Lila asked, "How much longer are you going to take?" (The question mark applies only to what Lila said.)

Did Lila say, "I'm leaving without you"? (The question mark applies to the entire sentence.)

Practice

On the lines provided, rewrite each sentence, inserting quotation marks where needed.

1. For our next class, please read the short story The Yellow Wallpaper and write a journal entry about it, the instructor said.

   _____

   _____

2. I can't believe it—they just scored the winning basket with half a second remaining! the announcer gasped.

   _____

   _____

3. In which of Shakespeare's plays does a character say, To thine own self be true?

   _____

   _____

4. One of the longest words in the English language is antidisestablish-mentarianism.

   _____

   _____

5. Whenever I'm feeling depressed, my father always makes me smile by saying, Life is far too important to be taken seriously, Joanne said.

   _____

   _____

31 More about Punctuation Marks

Semicolon

Use a semicolon to set off items in a series when the items themselves contain commas.

> At the family reunion I spent time talking with Uncle Ray, who is a retired train engineer; my cousin Cheryl, who works in publishing; and my nephew Walt, who plays violin in his high-school orchestra.

> The radio station invited listeners to choose which of three songs should be named the greatest rock-and-roll classic of all time: "Hey, Jude," by the Beatles; "Satisfaction," by the Rolling Stones; or "Heartbreak Hotel," an Elvis Presley song.

Hyphen

1 Put a hyphen between the two parts of a fraction: one-half, two-thirds.

2 Hyphenate compound numbers from twenty-one to ninety-nine.

> Hassan pays his parents eighty-seven dollars, one-fourth of his weekly salary, for room and board.

3 Use a hyphen after the prefixes *all-, ex-,* and *self-.*

> Leaders should be self-confident, but they should never think they are all-powerful.

> My ex-husband has started therapy to raise his self-esteem.

Dash

Use a dash to signal the end of a list of items.

> A three-mile run, forty minutes of weight lifting, and seventy-five push-ups— that's how Grandfather starts his day.

Parentheses

Place parentheses around numbers that introduce items in a list within a sentence.

> Grandfather's exercise program consists of (1) jogging, (2) weight lifting, and (3) push-ups.

Underline and Italics

Underline (or italicize) the titles of long works: books, magazines, newspapers, movies, plays, television series, CDs, and albums. (Remember, though, that titles of short works are placed in quotation marks. See page 116.)

Students in the current events class must skim <u>USA Today</u> every morning, read both <u>Time</u> and <u>Newsweek</u>, and watch <u>60 Minutes</u> and <u>Meet the Press</u>.

Note   Printed material uses *italics* instead of underlining. Also, if you are writing on a computer, use italics instead of underlining.

Practice

Insert semicolons, hyphens, dashes, parentheses, or underlines where needed in each of the following sentences.

1. Callie's thirtieth birthday was six months ago, but she's still telling people, "I'm only twenty nine."

2. A jar of mustard, a bottle of beer, and half a can of cat food these were the contents of the refrigerator.

3. The latest issue of Reader's Digest includes some interesting articles: "The Town That Wouldn't Die," the story of a Texas suburb that survived an epidemic "Work Out at Work," a guide to starting an exercise club at the office and "Fatal Distraction," a first-person account of one man's battle against television addiction.

4. A new couple's budget should cover items such as 1 rent or mortgage, 2 food, 3 car expenses, 4 clothing, 5 entertainment, and, of course, 6 miscellaneous.

5. The most frightening book I ever read was Stephen King's The Tommy-knockers, and the most frightening movie I ever saw was The Fly.

6. If you'd like to receive a printed brochure about the all inclusive vacations advertised on the TV show Fantasy Islands, just send a self addressed stamped envelope to the address on the screen.

7. The requirements for the grammar course are as follows: 1 buy the textbook, English Brushup 2 complete the "Seeing What You Know" exercises, which are on the first page of each chapter and 3 score at least 80% on the chapter tests.

8. Creating their own presidential libraries, building homes for people living in poverty, and leading disaster relief efforts worldwide these are some of the projects that American ex presidents have supported.

32 More about Capital Letters

Other Rules for Capital Letters

1   Capitalize the names of geographic locations.

The **S**outhwest is known for its hot, dry climate, while **N**ew **E**ngland is famous for cold winters.

People from the **S**outh have a reputation for hospitality.

Note   Do not, however, capitalize words that mean directions (not places).

The mountains are **s**outh and slightly **w**est of here.

Drive six blocks **e**ast on Walnut Street and then turn **n**orth onto 23d Street.

2   Capitalize the names of historical periods and well-known events.

The **R**enaissance is a period famous for the art it produced.

The **M**y **L**ai **M**assacre was one of the ugliest incidents of the **V**ietnam **W**ar.

3   Capitalize all words in the opening of a letter and the first word in the closing.

Dear **P**rofessor **C**ross: **D**ear **M**s. **H**ill: **V**ery truly yours,   **W**ith all my love,

4   Capitalize common abbreviations made up of the first letters of the words they represent.

FBI   NAACP   NASA   IBM   NBC   UFO   AIDS

Note   Periods are usually not used in these abbreviations.

Practice

Capitalize words as necessary in the following sentences.

1. After serving in the korean war, my grandfather worked for the cia.

2. Although we've lived in the northeast for fifteen years, our neighbors do not consider us natives because we were born in the midwest.

3. The aids epidemic is often compared to a plague that killed millions during the period known as the dark ages.

4. On our pbs channel, we saw a nature program about the animals of Tanzania, a country located just south of Kenya.

5. dear sir or madam:

   Please have your store send me a replacement for the defective dvd player I bought from you last week.

   yours truly,

   Wanda Stern

6. Most of my favorite prime-time television programs are on cbs, but during the day, I watch the talk shows on nbc.

7. "Operation desert storm" was the code name of the us-led un military action to liberate Kuwait from Iraq.

8. The roaring twenties is a period in our nation's history, after world war I, when Americans enjoyed new technologies, like the automobile, and flappers danced to the new music called jazz. It ended with the crash of the stock market and the beginning of the great depression.

9. After the United States civil war, both the south and the north went through economic, political, and social changes during the period known as reconstruction.

10. Dear president smith,

   This is to inform you that members of the Davis High School pta wish to address district officials at the May meeting about the possibility of raising teachers' salaries.

   respectfully submitted,

   Michael Browsen

33 More about Homonyms

Other Homonyms

all ready   *completely prepared*

already   *previously* or *before*

Those cans of tuna have **already** been stacked too high; they appear **all ready** to fall on an unlucky shopper.

coarse   (1) *rough;* (2) *crass* or *rude*

course   (1) *a unit of instruction;* (2) *a part of a meal;* (3) *certainly* (with *of,* as in *of course*)

The telephone operators are required to take a **course** in phone etiquette to ensure that they do not treat even irritating customers in a **coarse** manner.

lead   *a metal*

led   (past tense of *lead*) (1) *influenced* or *persuaded;* (2) *guided*

The children's poor health **led** the doctor to suspect they were being poisoned by **lead**-based paint in their home.

pair   *a set of two*

pear   *a fruit*

The **pear** tree in the backyard is home this spring to a **pair** of nesting doves.

principal   (1) *main;* (2) *the person in charge of a school*

principle   *a guideline* or *rule*

The **principal** lectured incoming students about drugs. "Our **principle** is a simple one: if you bring drugs to school, you're out of school," she said.

Hint   A trick to remembering one meaning of *principal* is that, ideally, a principal should be a **pal**—the last three letters in the word.

Other Confusing Words

Here are more words that people often have trouble telling apart.

a   *one*—used before a consonant

an   *one*—used before a vowel sound (*a, e, i, o, u,* or silent *h*)

a book	**a** degree	**a** mistake	**a** surprise	**a** yard	**a** hero
an assignment	**an** egg	**an** instructor	**an** orange	**an** uncle	**an** honor

Note   The *h* in *hero* is pronounced, but the *h* in *honor* is silent. (The word *honor* is pronounced "ON-er.") Since *honor* begins with a vowel sound, *an* is correct.

accept   (1) *to receive (willingly)*; (2) *to agree to*

except   (1) *to leave out*; (2) *but*

> All the workers **except** the part-timers voted to **accept** the new contract.

advice   (rhymes with *nice*) *a suggestion* or *suggestions*

advise   (rhymes with *size*) *to give advice or suggestions to*

> Most fortune-tellers' **advice** is pretty worthless; fortune-tellers **advise** their clients to become more and more dependent on them for guidance.

affect   *to influence* or *to have an effect on*

effect   (1) *to cause*; (2) *a result*

> The heavy rain the night before did not **affect** the success of the picnic; in fact, the rain had the **effect** of clearing the air and producing a beautiful day.

among   used with three or more

between   used with two

> A contest **among** eight candidates who campaigned for the presidency finally came down to a choice **between** two persons—a man and a woman.

desert   (pronounced DEZ-ert) *a dry and sandy place*

desert   (pronounced de-ZERT) *to leave behind*

dessert   (also pronounced de-ZERT) *the final course of a meal*

> Lost in the wasteland of the **desert**, the stranded man dreamed of gallons of ice water and of a cool, refreshing **dessert**, such as orange sherbet.

does   (rhymes with *fuzz*) present tense of *do*

dose   (rhymes with *gross*) *a measured amount of medicine*

> **Does** a double **dose** of cold medicine cure a cold twice as fast?

fewer   *smaller in number*—used with plurals (more than one thing)

less   *smaller in degree, value, or amount*—used with singular words (one thing)

> If you work **fewer** hours, you will earn **less** money.

loose   (rhymes with *juice*) (1) *not tight*; (2) *free* or *not confined*

lose   (rhymes with *blues*) (1) *to misplace*; (2) *to get rid of*

> It's easy to **lose** a ring that is too **loose** on one's finger.

Hint   Here's one way to remember which is which: *Loose* and *tight* both have five letters; *lose* and *find* both have four letters.

quiet   *silent*

quit   (1) *to give up;* (2) *to stop doing something*

quite   *very*

"This house is **quite** noisy," said the babysitter to the children. "If you don't become **quiet** soon, I'm going to **quit** being so patient."

were   (rhymes with *fur*) past tense of *are*

where   (rhymes with *air*) *in what place* or *to what place* (see page 146)

Where did the movie director get all the thousands of people who **were** hired for that immense crowd scene?

Practice

Underline the correct word or words in each group in parentheses.

1. The cocky young man had (all ready, already) decided to (quit, quite, quiet) school, and he refused to (accept, except) his family's (advise, advice) to reconsider.

2. The rich (desert, dessert) had the (effect, affect) of giving several guests a stomachache, so their host gave them each a (does, dose) of Pepto-Bismol.

3. If I'm going to (lose, loose) ten pounds, I'll just have to eat (fewer, less) fattening food, but it'll be worth it for (a, an) opportunity to wear the (pair, pear) of size ten designer jeans that's been hanging in my closet for (a, an) year.

4. To protect themselves from heat and sand, people who live in the (desert, dessert) wear (loose, lose) robes made of (coarse, course) material.

5. I was (all ready, already) to put my groceries on the counter when I saw the sign reading "Ten Items or (Fewer, Less)."

6. "It's (quiet, quit, quite) difficult to (quiet, quit, quite) smoking," the doctor said, "but I (advice, advise) you to give up cigarettes at once—smoking will (affect, effect) your life span."

7. "Please don't (desert, dessert) me," Kim begged her brother. "I don't know anyone at this party (accept, except) you."

8. In her American Government (coarse, course), Sarita is learning the (principal, principle) of the balance of power—how decision-making is divided (among, between) the three branches of the federal government.

9. Jameer walked up to the desk and said in a (quiet, quit, quite) voice, "What time (does, dose) the library close?"

10. The parents couldn't remember (were, where) the Christmas decorations (were, where) stored until their six-year-old (lead, led) them to the Christmas box stacked (among, between) many other boxes in the attic.

34 More about Word Choice

Inflated Words

Keep your writing simple. Overly fancy words may confuse (or unintentionally amuse) a reader. Look at the following example:

> The outdoor repast was deferred because of precipitation.

The sentence would communicate more effectively if it were written like this:

> The picnic was postponed because of rain.

Here are a few other inflated words and simple replacements for them:

Inflated	Simple	Inflated	Simple
ascertain	learn, find out	facilitate	help
assert	say	finalize, culminate	finish
commence	begin	inquire	ask
commend	praise	manifest	show
compensate	pay	parameters	limits
elucidate	explain	prior to	before
embark upon	begin	replenish	refill
endeavor	try	subsequent to	after

Practice

Cross out the two inflated expressions in each of the sentences below. Then rewrite the faulty expressions on the lines provided, using simpler language. Feel free to consult a dictionary to find the meanings of any of the inflated words.

1. Students must remit 50 percent of their tuition prior to the first day of classes.

   _____   _____

2. Nobody had ascertained when the next bus would depart.

   _____   _____

3. Working conditions in that store are good, but the remuneration is insufficient.

   _____   _____

4. Since the children were being vociferous, the babysitter endeavored to quiet them.

   _____   _____

5. Subsequent to the heavy rains, people piled sandbags to keep the river from inundating the nearby city.

   _____   _____

6. As soon as the game commenced, it was clear that the home team would be victorious.

   _____   _____

7. "I simply cannot believe any more of your justifications," Marva told Rodney. "You've prevaricated entirely too often."

   _____   _____

8. At a fine restaurant, someone will replenish your glass of water as soon as you deplete it.

   _____   _____

9. "As soon as you return to your domicile," my father said, "please transmit word that you arrived safely."

   _____   _____

10. On Thanksgiving, everyone in my family enjoys a delectable repast at Cousin Miriam's house.

    _____   _____

11. "Were you planning to compensate me for the four hours I just spent mowing your lawn?" my son inquired.

    _____   _____

12. "No, but I do commend you for your diligence," I answered.

    _____   _____

13. Every year, the NFL finalizes its season with an athletic competition known as the Super Bowl.

    _____   _____

14. "I cannot comprehend anything in this chapter," the student told her tutor. "Can you elucidate?"

    _____   _____

15. To facilitate students' understanding of proper classroom behavior, instructors often provide a list of regulations such as "No eating in class" and "No texting once class has begun."

    _____   _____

Part Three

Applying the Skills

Preview

Part Three contains twelve combined mastery tests and ten editing tests:

Name _____ Section _____ Date _____

Score: (Number right) _____ × 10 = _____ %

VERBS

■ **Combined Mastery Test 1**

Each sentence contains a mistake involving (1) standard English or irregular verb forms, (2) subject-verb agreement, or (3) consistent verb tense. Cross out the incorrect verb, and write the correct form in the space provided.

_____ 1. Each of the sisters in that family have a tattoo.

_____ 2. The artist picked up a brush, stared hard at the model, and begins to paint.

_____ 3. To everyone's surprise, the newest member of the track team breaked the school record for the five-hundred-yard dash.

_____ 4. Because so many uninvited people came to the party, we runned out of food.

_____ 5. Three enormous bags of money was sitting in the trunk of the arrested man's car.

_____ 6. On Saturdays, Jeremy mows the grass, raked the leaves, and pulls the weeds.

_____ 7. Just as she was thinking about buying new shoes, Tanya sees a "Sale" sign in the shoe-store window.

_____ 8. Sleeping on the sunny windowsill is two black-and-white cats.

_____ 9. When George first met Lana, he thinks she was the most beautiful girl in the world.

_____ 10. I went to my favorite pizza parlor, where I ran into my ex-boyfriend, who pretends he didn't see me.

Name _____   Section _____ Date _____

Score: (Number right) _____ × 10 = _____ %

VERBS

■ Combined Mastery Test 2

Each sentence contains a mistake involving (1) standard English or irregular verb forms, (2) subject-verb agreement, or (3) consistent verb tense. Cross out the incorrect verb, and write the correct form in the space provided.

_____   1. Although Charlene be teasing you, she doesn't mean to hurt your feelings.

_____   2. Several trees in our backyard needs to be cut down.

_____   3. At the first game of our baseball team's season, the oldest man in town throwed the opening pitch.

_____   4. Yvonne opened the refrigerator door, looked hungrily at the chocolate pudding inside, and closes the door again.

_____   5. The chickens roosting in the hen house squawks loudly every morning and evening.

_____   6. The sign said "Beware of the Dog," but the dog laying under the sign did not look very fierce.

_____   7. Is there any bagels left for breakfast?

_____   8. At the party Donny flirted with all the girls, tells all his best jokes, and danced up a storm.

_____   9. I was amazed when my friends described how far they had rode on their bicycles.

_____   10. My little cousin is only eleven, but she already play the piano better than I ever will.

Name _____   Section _____   Date _____

FRAGMENTS, RUN-ONS, AND COMMA SPLICES

■ Combined Mastery Test 3

In the space provided, indicate whether each item below contains a fragment (F), a run-on (R-O), or a comma splice (CS). Then correct the error.

_____ 1. The little boy liked his new glasses he thought they made him look grown-up. He wanted to wear them all the time, even while he slept.

_____ 2. Forest fires destroy thousands of acres of woodland every year. Many of them are started through acts of carelessness. Such as tossing a cigarette onto dry leaves.

_____ 3. Snow piled up in great drifts outside the door. Making it impossible to open. The family actually had to leave the house through a window.

_____ 4. A terrifying scream pierced the night, the friends screamed too and hugged each other. They all agreed it was the best haunted house they'd ever been to.

_____ 5. Matthew had never been called for jury duty before. He was very nervous as the trial started. But soon found the process fascinating.

_____ 6. The king's daughter stared in horror at the slimy green frog. How could she ever bring herself to kiss it? Even if it was an enchanted prince.

_____ 7. The juice of the aloe plant is very soothing, it can help heal burns and scrapes. Just break open a piece of the plant and rub the cool juice across your skin.

_____ 8. How can you eat that chili? It is so hot it made my eyes water I couldn't eat more than a spoonful.

_____ 9. Christmas comes earlier each year. Because merchants like to stretch out the buying season. Right after Halloween this year, store owners hung colored lights and filled their windows with Christmas decorations.

_____ 10. Darlene walked into the living room. She sat down next to her boyfriend, she held his hand. Then she gently said, "I can't marry you."

Name _____   Section _____   Date _____

Score: (Number right) _____ × 10 = _____ %

FRAGMENTS, RUN-ONS, AND COMMA SPLICES

■ Combined Mastery Test 4

In the space provided, indicate whether each item below contains a fragment (F), a run-on (R-O), or a comma splice (CS). Then correct the error.

_____   1. My mother insists that I look good wearing light yellow clothes. I think when I wear yellow, I look as though I had died. Several days ago.

_____   2. As darkness began to fall, the searchers grew more anxious, they called the missing child's name again and again. To their great relief, they finally heard the child answer them.

_____   3. Americans spend millions of dollars each year on bottled water, critics say that tap water is just as good. There are no plastic bottles to dispose of, and tap water is equally safe to drink.

_____   4. When scientists found ancient seashells buried high on the mountain, they became very excited. They realized that the mountain had been below sea level. Many years ago.

_____   5. Mrs. Morris gazed at her lazy son. Asleep on the couch for the fourth afternoon in a row. She decided the time had come for him to get a job.

_____   6. I don't understand why you won't answer the telephone you're sitting closer to it than I am. Am I the only one who hears it?

_____   7. *Gone with the Wind* was Vivica's favorite book when she was younger. For a few months, she even began speaking with a Southern accent. In imitation of Scarlett O'Hara.

_____   8. For years, there have been reports of a strange manlike creature living in northern climates. The creature, whose existence has never been proved, has various names. Such as the Yeti, the Sasquatch, and the Abominable Snowman.

_____   9. Garlic may smell bad it tastes delicious. It has other good qualities as well. Garlic helps lower cholesterol and is also supposed to keep vampires away.

_____   10. There are no clocks in Las Vegas gambling casinos. If gamblers don't know what time it is. They'll stay longer and lose more money.

Name _____   Section _____ Date _____

Score: (Number right) _____ × 10 = _____ %

PRONOUNS

■ **Combined Mastery Test 5**

Each sentence contains a mistake involving (1) pronoun agreement, (2) pronoun reference, (3) pronoun point of view, or (4) pronoun form. Cross out each incorrect pronoun, and write the correction in the space provided.

_____   1. If I have an "A" average, does that mean that you don't have to take the final exam?

_____   2. Each of the football players had the team's name printed on the back of their jersey.

_____   3. The police officer told Omar that he would get a fine for parking in a handicapped space.

_____   4. Between you and I, that restaurant does not serve food fit for humans.

_____   5. If them seats aren't taken, could we sit there?

_____   6. We wanted to order a hot meal after 10 P.M., but they said the kitchen was closed.

_____   7. Our instructor was disappointed when nobody in the class volunteered to read their paper out loud.

_____   8. I don't like the new movies even though every reviewer has praised it.

_____   9. When our union called for a strike, all of us had to stay home from work, even if they didn't want to.

_____   10. If anyone is going to the convenience store, would they bring me a bag of potato chips?

Name _____ Section _____ Date _____

Score: (Number right) _____ × 10 = _____ %

PRONOUNS

■ Combined Mastery Test 6

Each sentence contains a mistake involving (1) pronoun agreement, (2) pronoun reference, (3) pronoun point of view, or (4) pronoun form. Cross out each incorrect pronoun, and write the correction in the space provided.

_____ 1. Neither of my brothers likes their job.

_____ 2. Heather and me are having a contest to see who can lose more weight.

_____ 3. Last night, Elena hung her new dress in the closet, and now she can't find it.

_____ 4. If we can't find our voter registration card, will you be stopped from voting?

_____ 5. This here microwave must be broken—all it does is buzz.

_____ 6. When my neighbors bought new tires, they were very cheap.

_____ 7. I like eating at that restaurant because the servers always bring you free refills for drinks.

_____ 8. Both of my sisters get her hair done at the same salon.

_____ 9. One of the classroom buildings is having their roof repaired.

_____ 10. Nearly every day, several people call my home office, wanting me to participate in a survey or offering a free vacation. I wish this would stop so I could get some work done!

Name _____   Section _____ Date _____

Score: (Number right) _____ × 10 = _____ %

CAPITAL LETTERS AND PUNCTUATION

■ **Combined Mastery Test 7**

Each of the following sentences contains an error in capitalization or punctuation. Refer to the box below and, in the space provided, write the letter identifying the error. Then correct the error.

a.	missing capital letter
b.	missing apostrophe
c.	missing quotation marks
d.	missing comma

_____ 1. During my haircut, it made me very nervous to hear my barber say, Oops.

_____ 2. Most of the towns citizens agree that the mayor is doing a fine job.

_____ 3. My math class is not too difficult, but my english class is driving me crazy.

_____ 4. "Please close your books and put away your notes" said Mrs. Shoup. "It is time for a quiz."

_____ 5. If you know you cant keep a secret, you should warn your friends not to tell you any.

_____ 6. Everyone knows that my uncles hair isn't real, but we all pretend to think it is.

_____ 7. "I tell you, my whole life has been tough," said the comedian. When I was a kid, I had to tie a pork chop around my neck so the dog would play with me."

_____ 8. Even though we told him the four o'clock party began at three o'clock my brother still showed up two hours late.

_____ 9. If you drive forty miles north of here, you will reach the michigan line.

_____ 10. *Rebecca*, a wonderful novel by Daphne du Maurier is about a woman who is haunted by her husband's former wife.

Name _____ Section _____ Date _____

Score: (Number right) _____ × 10 = _____ %

CAPITAL LETTERS AND PUNCTUATION

■ Combined Mastery Test 8

Each of the following sentences contains an error in capitalization or punctuation. Refer to the box below and, in the space provided, write the letter identifying the error. Then correct the error.

a.	missing capital letter
b.	missing apostrophe
c.	missing quotation marks
d.	missing comma

_____ 1. If youve got time before school, would you take the trash out to the curb?

_____ 2. Almost nine hundred people showed up to audition for a part in the movie but only two were chosen.

_____ 3. My mother always insisted on using crisco shortening in her pie crust, but I use any brand I happen to have on hand.

_____ 4. "On my first date with your mother, my father told me, "her little brother came along to make sure I behaved myself."

_____ 5. A real banana split should contain a banana three scoops of ice cream, whipped cream, peanuts, and a cherry.

_____ 6. As I carefully eased open the front door, I heard my mother's stern voice say, "you missed your curfew."

_____ 7. For the Bradshaw family, it's a tradition to watch the movie *It's a wonderful Life* at least once during the holiday season.

_____ 8. Although Jimmy claims to hate tomatoes he loves spaghetti sauce and pizza.

_____ 9. My sisters boyfriend gave her a ring that quickly turned her finger green.

_____ 10. "I'm giving you three weeks to work on this project," announced Mrs. Smithfield, so I don't expect anyone to ask for extra time."

Name _____   Section _____ Date _____

Score: (Number right) _____ × 5 = _____ %

HOMONYMS AND WORD CHOICE

■ Combined Mastery Test 9

Each of the following groups of sentences contains two errors. The errors involve either homonym mistakes or ineffective word choices: slang, clichés, or wordy expressions. Underline the two errors. Then write the corrections in the spaces provided.

_____
_____
1. Why do I have to take algebra? I couldn't care less about it. In addition, I don't see how a math course will lead me too a decent job.

_____
_____
2. At the county fair, we saw the fattest pig in size you can imagine. We also walked threw a barn where cows were being milked.

_____
_____
3. Wear my sister is going, the weather will be warm, so she is packing light. She is taking just two pears of shorts, two T-shirts, and a sweatshirt.

_____
_____
4. Brad eagerly excepted his aunt's offer of a summer job. He knew he'd really lucked out to get it, and he was determined to make the most of it.

_____
_____
5. Although Maria and Teresa are the best of friends, there personalities are very different. Maria is quite and shy, while Teresa is talkative and outgoing.

_____
_____
6. I am constantly loosing my house key. I guess I'm just to absentminded. Maybe I should tie it on a string around my neck.

_____
_____
7. Is the knew movie "one of the most exciting ever made" or "a waste of two hours"? It depends on weather you believe one critic or another.

_____
_____
8. The girl that Paul is beginning to date seems to really like him. She has all ready invited him to hang out with her family at Thanksgiving.

_____
_____
9. I can't believe that you spent fifteen dollars to have you're fortune told. If you ask me, a fortune-teller's advise is just a waste of money.

_____
_____
10. "I worked my fingers to the bone preparing the desert for tonight's dinner," Hannah laughingly told her guests. "I had to drive all the way to the bakery and all the way back again."

Name _____   Section _____   Date _____

Score: (Number right) _____ × 5 = _____ %

HOMONYMS AND WORD CHOICE

■ Combined Mastery Test 10

Each of the following groups of sentences contains two errors. The errors involve either homonym mistakes or ineffective word choices: slang, clichés, or wordy expressions. Underline the two errors. Then write the corrections in the spaces provided.

_____
_____   1. If its sunny tomorrow, we are going to go for a long bike ride. But if the whether is bad, we're going to rent videos and watch them all day.

_____
_____   2. Nobody knows what the man next door dose for a living. He never seems to go to work, but he has the best wheels in the neighborhood.

_____
_____   3. At the school's annual costume party, everyone was amazed too see the most serious teacher of them all arrive. He hopped into the room, dressed as a huge rabbit that was pink in color.

_____
_____   4. Although many children believe in Santa Claus, it's quiet unusual to find an adult who thinks Santa is real. My sister's boyfriend, however, is an unusual dude.

_____
_____   5. Larry thinks the secret of happiness is being rich. Coming into the possession of money is more important to him then anything else in the world.

_____
_____   6. Sarah looked as pretty as a picture at the awards banquet. She was wearing a very plane black dress, but she'd dressed it up with a new silver necklace and earrings.

_____
_____   7. Don't you hate it when someone says, "Oh, I don't want dessert," but then wants a peace of whatever you order? In my opinion, their just being rude in doing that.

_____
_____   8. Our star player sprained his ankle, but fortunately, he didn't brake it. We need him back in the lineup soon, or we'll have know chance in the playoffs.

_____
_____   9. The Taylors are to protective of there children. They won't let them ride bicycles, play softball, or roller-skate, believing that they're going to get badly hurt.

_____
_____   10. Didn't anyone else here that loud party going on last night? I was already to call the police when it finally quieted down at 3 A.M.

Name _____   Section _____   Date _____

Score: (Number right) _____ × 10 = _____ %

FAULTY MODIFIERS AND PARALLELISM

■ Combined Mastery Test 11

In the spaces at the left, indicate whether each sentence contains a misplaced modifier (MM), a dangling modifier (DM), or faulty parallelism (FP). Then correct the errors in the space between the lines.

_____   1. Forgetting that it was due, my English paper was turned in late.

_____   2. My father always said coffee should be strong as sin, sweet as love, and it should be as hot as blazes.

_____   3. Making a loud grating sound, Michelle stopped the car to see what was wrong.

_____   4. Bob noticed a police officer driving behind him with a sense of dread.

_____   5. Hitting the "snooze" button on my alarm clock, my eyes just wouldn't open.

_____   6. Playing cards, to watch football, and working in the garden are my grandfather's favorite activities.

_____   7. While trying on an old pair of blue jeans, Marvin's waistband wouldn't close.

_____   8. Gina uses her computer to send e-mail, get school papers written, and search the Internet.

_____   9. "Don't you feel well? You're hardly eating anything!" June said to her teenage son.

_____   10. I couldn't find my car keys, even though I searched in my coat pockets, on the kitchen shelf, and looked inside every drawer in the house.

Name _____   Section _____ Date _____

Score: (Number right) _____ × 10 = _____ %

FAULTY MODIFIERS AND PARALLELISM

■ Combined Mastery Test 12

In the spaces at the left, indicate whether each sentence contains a misplaced modifier (MM), a dangling modifier (DM), or faulty parallelism (FP). Then correct the errors in the space between the lines.

_____   1. Cleaning the bathroom, doing the laundry, and to scrub the kitchen floor are among my least favorite chores.

_____   2. Glaring angrily at each other, it was easy to tell that Ron and Helen's argument was serious.

_____   3. The little boy stared in wonder at the elephant sitting on his father's shoulders.

_____   4. Bending almost double in the strong wind, I was surprised the trees didn't break.

_____   5. Without a word of good-bye, the car sped off with Teron at the wheel.

_____   6. High fever, a hacking cough, and muscles that ache are all symptoms of the flu.

_____   7. Denzel almost received fifty e-mails yesterday.

_____   8. In my dreams, I am often a star athlete, a scientist who is brilliant, or a talented rock musician.

_____   9. We enjoyed the delicious barbecue that our neighbors had prepared with hearty appetites.

_____   10. Clicking all the buttons on the remote control, my search for something good to watch on TV was unsuccessful.

Name _____   Section _____ Date _____

Score: (Number right) _____ × 20 = _____ %

EDITING TEST 1

Identify the sentence-skills mistakes at the underlined spots in the selection that follows. From the box below, choose the letter that describes each mistake and write it in the space provided. Then, in the spaces between the lines, correct each mistake.

a.	comma splice
b.	fragment
c.	missing capital letter
d.	missing apostrophe
e.	missing comma

Every year, on the third Sunday in May, the world's largest footrace is held, it takes
                                                                                    1
place in San Francisco, California. As many as 100,000 runners participate in the Bay
        1
to Breakers Run, a twelve-kilometer run that begins at the San Francisco Bay and ends

at the Pacific ocean. Although some of the worlds best runners participate in the race,
               2   3
many others are less serious about winning. Costumed runners dress up as almost anything

imaginable. Including human tacos, palm trees, and even the Golden Gate Bridge. Groups
           4
of thirteen runners tied together compete as human centipedes. Waiters jog along, trying

to balance glasses of champagne resting on trays. The race which has been held annually
                                                            5
since 1912, is as much fun to watch as it is to participate in.

1. _____   2. _____   3. _____   4. _____   5. _____

Name _____   Section _____ Date _____
                                          Score: (Number right) _____ × 20 = _____ %

EDITING TEST 2

Identify the sentence-skills mistakes at the underlined spots in the selection that follows. From the box below, choose the letter that describes each mistake and write it in the space provided. Then, in the spaces between the lines, correct each mistake.

a.	faulty parallelism
b.	inconsistent verb tense
c.	fragment
d.	run-on
e.	missing comma

If you know the name of Leonardo da Vinci, it is probably as an artist. Leonardo produced some of the world's most famous paintings, including the *Mona Lisa* and *The Last Supper.* But Leonardo was not only an artist. He also deserves to be known as an inventor, a scientist, <u>and he worked in engineering too</u>. Leonardo was born in 1452. He
1
<u>goes</u> to Florence, Italy, to study art when he was a teenager. Although he became an official
2
"court artist," he also found time to dream up dozens of inventions. <u>Some became realities</u>
3
<u>in his lifetime others were left for the future</u>. Among the many designs that Leonardo came
3
up with were those for flying machines, <u>parachutes submarines</u>, and underwater breathing
4
devices. Although he was a gentle vegetarian, Leonardo also designed many new weapons. By the time he died in 1519, Leonardo was recognized as a genius. <u>One of the greatest the</u>
5
<u>world had ever produced</u>.
5

1. _____   2. _____   3. _____   4. _____   5. _____

Name _____ Section _____ Date _____

Score: (Number right) _____ × 20 = _____ %

EDITING TEST 3

Identify the sentence-skills mistakes at the underlined spots in the selection that follows. From the box below, choose the letter that describes each mistake and write it in the space provided. Then, in the spaces between the lines, correct each mistake.

a.	fragment
b.	run-on
c.	inconsistent verb tense
d.	homonym mistake
e.	missing quotation mark

I'm only sixty-three, but something happened recently that made me feel like a human dinosaur. I was taking care of my eight-year-old niece for the afternoon. I said I wanted to talk to an old friend of mine who lives in another state. Kate <u>says,</u> "Why don't you e-mail
₁
her?" I answered, "Because I don't have a computer, and I don't know how to use e-mail, anyway." Kate stared at me. <u>As if I'd just said I didn't know how to tie my shoes.</u> <u>"How can
₂
anybody not know how to use e-mail?" she said she really didn't seem able to believe it.</u> The
₃
next week Kate came over to visit again. This time she had her friend Paige with her. "Paige wanted to meet you," she said. Feeling flattered, I said, "Well, hello, Paige." "Hi," Paige said. <u>I've</u> never met anyone who couldn't use e-mail before. My brother said you must be one of
₄
those people who lives in the <u>passed.</u>" I gave them cookies and sent them home. I guess it
₅
could be worse. At least Kate didn't take me to school for show-and-tell.

1. _____   2. _____   3. _____   4. _____   5. _____

Name _____   Section _____   Date _____

Score: (Number right) _____ × 20 = _____ %

EDITING TEST 4

Identify the sentence-skills mistakes at the underlined spots in the selection that follows. From the box below, choose the letter that describes each mistake and write it in the space provided. Then, in the spaces between the lines, correct each mistake.

a.	fragment
b.	comma splice
c.	inconsistent verb tense
d.	homonym mistake
e.	missing apostrophe

Do you have a memory that makes you burn with shame, even years after the event? I do. A boy I didn't know very well had walked up to me in the lunchroom. <u>And asked me</u> [1] <u>for a date.</u> [1] I was so surprised that I automatically said yes. Later, though, <u>I start to have</u> [2] second thoughts. <u>I didnt</u> [3] think I would have any fun. I began to wish I had said no. And so, a few hours before our date, I called him. Trying to sound miserable, I said I was <u>to</u> [4] sick to go out. He politely said that was all right. Feeling much better, I instantly called a girlfriend and arranged to go out for pizza. When we arrived, there in the pizza parlor was the boy I had stood up. I'll never forget the disappointed look he gave me. Over the next few years, I realized that he was a really great guy and that I'd been an idiot not to go out with him. <u>But by then, of course, I'd lost my chance, he never spoke to me again.</u> [5]

1. _____   2. _____   3. _____   4. _____   5. _____

Name _____   Section _____   Date _____

Score: (Number right) _____ × 20 = _____ %

EDITING TEST 5

Identify the sentence-skills mistakes at the underlined spots in the selection that follows. From the box below, choose the letter that describes each mistake and write it in the space provided. Then, in the spaces between the lines, correct each mistake.

a.	missing capital letter
b.	faulty parallelism
c.	homonym mistake
d.	comma splice
e.	fragment

My great-aunt was an unusual woman, she liked animals at least as much as she
<u>1</u>

liked humans. She lived in a house with a big backyard that faced a forest. Over the years,
<u>1</u>

she took in dozens of wounded or orphaned animals. Visitors never <u>new</u> what they would
<u>2</u>

find when they stopped by her house. I remember seeing broken-legged blue jays, bullet-

wounded squirrels, and <u>owls with one eye</u> living there. She once raised a family of baby
<u>3</u>

foxes, feeding them from a bottle. <u>And then returned them to the woods.</u> When my aunt
<u>4</u>

died, she left the little bit of money she had to the Society for the <u>prevention</u> of Cruelty to
<u>5</u>

Animals.

1. _____   2. _____   3. _____   4. _____   5. _____

Name _____ Section _____ Date _____

Score: (Number right) _____ × 10 = _____ %

EDITING TEST 6

Identify the sentence-skills mistakes at the underlined spots in the selection that follows. From the box below, choose the letter that describes each mistake and write it in the space provided. Then, in the spaces between the lines, correct each mistake. (The number in parentheses indicates how many of each mistake occur in the selection.)

a.	fragment (2)
b.	pronoun mistake (2)
c.	apostrophe mistake (2)
d.	homonym mistake (1)
e.	mistake in subject-verb agreement (1)
f.	missing quotation mark (1)
g.	unnecessary comma (1)

Many of us are annoyed by <u>telemarketer's</u> who call <u>you</u> day and night, trying to sell
1   2

everything from magazine subscriptions<u>, to</u> vacation homes. These electronic intruders
3

<u>dont</u> seem to care how much they are inconveniencing us. <u>And refuse to take "no" for an</u>
4   5

<u>answer.</u> However, nuisance callers can be stopped if we take charge of the conversation.
5

<u>As soon as one of them asks how we are doing.</u> We should respond, "Fine, and are you
6

a telephone <u>solicitor?</u> This technique puts the caller on the defensive. We then have an
7

opening to say that we do not accept solicitations over the phone, only <u>threw</u> the mail. <u>This</u>
8   9

puts a quick end to the conversation. Of course, anyone who <u>prefer</u> not to be called at all
10

can sign up at the National Do Not Call Registry at **www.donotcall.gov** and be safe from

annoying calls forever.

1. _____   2. _____   3. _____   4. _____   5. _____

6. _____   7. _____   8. _____   9. _____   10. _____

Name _____ Section _____ Date _____

Score: (Number right) _____ × 10 = _____ %

EDITING TEST 7

Identify the sentence-skills mistakes at the underlined spots in the selection that follows. From the box below, choose the letter that describes each mistake and write it in the space provided. Then, in the spaces between the lines, correct each mistake. (The number in parentheses indicates how many of each mistake occur in the selection.)

a.	fragment (2)
b.	run-on (1)
c.	missing comma (2)
d.	homonym mistake (2)
e.	mistake in subject-verb agreement (1)
f.	dangling modifier (1)
g.	comma splice (1)

Millions of people in this country <u>is</u> terrified of going to the dentist. If you are one
    1
of them, you should know that some dentists specialize in treating people. <u>Who are very
                                                                            2
fearful of dental work.</u> These dentists encourage patients to discuss <u>there</u> fears and will
         2   3
answer questions in an honest, understanding manner. Even if your dentist does not have

such a <u>specialty you</u> can arrange to use a <u>signal such</u> as raising your right hand, if you
         4   5
experience too much pain. <u>This will give you a feeling of control it will also guarantee that
                                                                      6
the pain—if any—will not go beyond what you can tolerate.</u> You can also try a relaxation
                           6
technique. <u>Breathing deeply before and during appointments,</u> your fears will subside. <u>A
                                 7   8
last good idea is to bring an iPod, you can then listen to your favorite music in the dental
                                        8
chair.</u> <u>Its</u> hard for the brain to register pain. <u>When your favorite song is filling your head.</u>
 8   9   10

1. _____   2. _____   3. _____   4. _____   5. _____

6. _____   7. _____   8. _____   9. _____   10. _____

Name _____ Section _____ Date _____

Score: (Number right) _____ × 10 = _____ %

EDITING TEST 8

Identify the sentence-skills mistakes at the underlined spots in the selection that follows. From the box below, choose the letter that describes each mistake and write it in the space provided. Then, in the spaces between the lines, correct each mistake.

a. fragment	f. pronoun mistake
b. comma splice	g. missing comma
c. irregular verb mistake	h. missing apostrophe
d. mistake in subject-verb agreement	i. missing quotation mark
e. inconsistent verb tense	j. misplaced modifier

When President Theodore "Teddy" Roosevelt visited the South in 1902. He was
                                                    1
invited to a hunting party. The organizers of the hunt was eager for the President to have a
                                                    2
successful hunt. They tied a bear cub to a stake so that the President could not miss it. After
                                                                                        3
he realized that the bear could not escape Roosevelt refused to fire. A political cartoon was
                                            4
printed in a number of newspapers based on the incident. The cartoon, with a drawing of
                                    5
the small bear, was seen by a shop owner in Brooklyn. The shop owner then maked up a
                                                                                6
window display version of the little bear in a soft plush material. Before offering the bear
to customers, the shop owner asks Roosevelt for permission to sell the new toy as "Teddys
                                7   8
Bear." The President gave his approval but wrote, I don't think my name is worth much to
                                                9
the toy bear cub business." He was clearly wrong, a bear-buying frenzy swept the country.
                                    10
The teddy bear has been popular ever since.

1. _____   2. _____   3. _____   4. _____   5. _____

6. _____   7. _____   8. _____   9. _____   10. _____

Name _____   Section _____   Date _____

Score: (Number right) _____ × 10 = _____ %

EDITING TEST 9

See if you can locate and correct the ten sentence-skills mistakes in the selection that follows. The mistakes are listed in the box below. As you locate each mistake, write the number of the word group containing it in the space provided. Then, in the spaces between the lines, correct each mistake.

1 fragment _____	2 homonym mistakes _____
1 run-on _____	_____
1 missing comma _____	1 misplaced modifier _____
1 unnecessary comma _____	1 dangling modifier _____
1 apostrophe mistake _____	1 faulty parallelism _____

[1]Some people believe the superstition that cats have nine lives because they can fall with few, if any, injuries from high places. [2]They may have minor injuries, such as a bloody nose or cracked teeth or ribs but they recover. [3]Cats are able to survive long falls because they possess several advantages. [4]For one thing, there small size and body weight that is low soften the impact. [5]As they make contact with the ground. [6]Also, cats have highly developed inner ears these give them a keen sense of balance. [7]Quickly adjusting themselves in the air and landing on all four feet, the impact is absorbed by their legs. [8]Additionally, cats bend their legs when they land. [9]This ability cushions and spreads the impact, not only through bones that might brake otherwise, but through a cats joints, and muscles as well.

Name _____   Section _____   Date _____

Score: (Number right) _____ × 10 = _____ %

EDITING TEST 10

See if you can locate and correct the ten sentence-skills mistakes in the selection that follows. The mistakes are listed in the box below. As you locate each mistake, write the number of the word group containing it in the space provided. Then, in the spaces between the lines, correct each mistake.

1 fragment _____	1 missing comma _____
1 run-on _____	1 missing quotation mark _____
1 inconsistent verb tense _____	1 missing hyphen _____
1 mistake in subject-verb agreement _____	1 homonym mistake _____
1 missing capital letter _____	1 faulty parallelism _____

[1]One of the top April fool's Day hoaxes of all time was created by Burger King. [2]On April 1, a few years ago, Burger King placed a full-page advertisement in *USA Today*. [3]The ad stated that an item were being added to their menu it was a "Left-Handed Whopper" specially designed for the 32,000,000 left-handed Americans. [4]The knew sandwich included the same ingredients as the original Whopper (lettuce tomato, a patty made of hamburger, etc.), but all the condiments are rotated 180 degrees for the benefit of their left-handed customers. [5]Burger King issued a follow-up press release the next day. [6]According to the press release, although the Left-Handed Whopper was a hoax, thousands of customers had gone into restaurants. [7]To order the new sandwich. [8]The release went on to add, "Many others requested their own right handed version.

Limited Answer Key

Important Note   To strengthen your grammar, punctuation, and usage skills, you must do more than simply find out which of your answers are right and which are wrong. You also need to figure out (with the help of this book, the teacher, or other students) *why* you missed the items you answered incorrectly. By using each of your wrong answers as a learning opportunity, you will strengthen your understanding of the skills. You will also prepare yourself for the chapter tests, for which answers are not given here.

ANSWERS TO THE PRACTICES IN THE INTRODUCTION

Practice 1 (p. 3)

Note   Answers will vary.
Below are some possibilities.

1. package
2. Donovan
3. paper
4. tree
5. job

Practice 2 (p. 3)

1. hawk, tree, yard
2. end, game, teams
3. sister, dancer, class
4. boys, car, garage
5. workers, jobs, hours

Practice 3 (p. 4)

1. She . . . it
2. They . . . her
3. I . . . your
4. He (*or* She) . . . them
5. him . . . his

Practice 4 (p. 6)

Note   Answers will vary.
Below are some possibilities.

1. cut
2. walks
3. asked

4. mows
5. graded

Practice 5 (p. 7)

1. were
2. am
3. look
4. is
5. feel

Practice 6 (p. 7)

1. should
2. could
3. must
4. has been
5. does

Practice 7 (p. 8)

1. with
2. in
3. Without
4. of
5. by

Practice 8 (p. 9)

Note   Answers will vary.
Below are some possibilities.

1. hungry . . . large
2. old . . . torn
3. dark . . . lonely

4. wilted . . . overripe
5. slight . . . sore

Practice 9 (p. 10)

Note   Answers will vary.
Below are some possibilities.

1. quickly
2. carefully . . . slowly
3. softly
4. happily
5. rarely . . . very

Practice 10 (p. 11)

1. or
2. but
3. so
4. and

Practice 11 (p. 13)

1. when
2. Because
3. Even though
4. Before
5. until

Practice 12 (p. 13)

1. Either . . . or
2. both . . . and
3. neither . . . nor

253

ANSWERS TO THE PRACTICES IN PART ONE

1 SUBJECTS AND VERBS

Practice 1 (p. 19)

1. *Subject:* Nikki   *Verb:* waited
2. *Subject:* dog   *Verb:* padded
3. *Subject:* One   *Verb:* is
4. *Subject:* kittens   *Verb:* need
5. *Subject:* I   *Verb:* have

Practice 2 (p. 20)

1. *Subject:* Everyone
   Verb: is working
2. *Subject:* list
   Verb: will be posted
3. *Subject:* siren
   Verb: began
4. *Subject:* shirt
   Verb: should have been put
5. *Subject:* you
   Verb: must remember

2 MORE ABOUT VERBS

Practice 1 (p. 29)

1. began
2. broken
3. eaten, drunk
4. driven, saw
5. read, written, taken

Practice 2 (p. 30)

1. dresses
2. dropped
3. looked
4. hate
5. manages

Practice 3 (p. 31)

1. did
2. has
3. were
4. doesn't
5. was

Practice 4 (p. 32)

1. realized
2. disappears
3. discovered
4. want
5. yelled

3 SUBJECT-VERB AGREEMENT

Practice 1 (p. 40)

1. *Subject:* workers
   Verb: like
2. *Subject:* women
   Verb: score
3. *Subject:* noise
   Verb: hurts
4. *Subject:* bag
   Verb: contains
5. *Subject:* instructions
   Verb: are

Practice 2 (p. 41)

1. *Subject:* keys
   Verb: are
2. *Subject:* hundreds
   Verb: live
3. *Subject:* people
   Verb: were
4. *Subject:* dogs
   Verb: do
5. *Subject:* boxes
   Verb: are

Practice 3 (p. 42)

1. *Subject:* Everything
   Verb: is
2. *Subject:* Neither
   Verb: works
3. *Subject:* No one
   Verb: is
4. *Subject:* Each
   Verb: deserves
5. *Subject:* Everybody
   Verb: knows

Practice 4 (p. 42)

1. *Subject:* cats, dog
   Verb: stay
2. *Subject:* CDs, DVDs
   Verb: Are
3. *Subject:* sister, friend
   Verb: drive
4. *Subject:* scratches, dents
   Verb: were
5. *Subject:* course, course
   Verb: require

4 SENTENCE TYPES

Practice 1 (p. 50)

Note   Answers will vary. Below are some possibilities.

1. car
2. threw
3. Roast beef . . . Swiss cheese
4. Sylvia . . . jog
5. My aunt . . . uncle . . . ate

Practice 2 (p. 51)

1. I turned in my paper early, but it was on the wrong topic.
2. All my clothes were dirty this morning, so I'm wearing my husband's shirt.
3. Virginia has learned karate, and she carries a can of self-defense spray.

Practice 3 (p. 52)

1. As the familiar "Wedding March" played, the bride and her father walked down the aisle.
2. Jeff broke out in red blotches after he walked through a bank of poison ivy.
3. Although the chocolate cake was delicious, everyone at the dinner party was dieting.

5 FRAGMENTS

Note   Methods of correction may vary.

Practice 1 (p. 61)

1. <u>When I sat down to answer the exam questions,</u> my mind went completely blank.
2. <u>Because smoke detectors are so important to a family's safety,</u> their batteries should be checked often.
3. <u>After the children washed the family car,</u> they had a water fight with the wet sponges.
4. Please hang up the damp towel <u>that you just threw on the floor.</u>

Practice 2 (p. 62)

1. Police officers stood near the corner. They were <u>directing people around the accident.</u>
2. The magician ran a sword through the box <u>to prove no one was hiding inside.</u>
3. <u>Sitting quietly on the couch,</u> the dog didn't look as if he'd eaten my sandwich.
4. Kaylin walked quickly down the street and up the hill. <u>She wanted to meet her boyfriend on time at the restaurant.</u>

Practice 3 (p. 63)

1. Television censors watch out for material that viewers might find offensive, <u>such as sexual or racial jokes.</u>
2. The children's toys were everywhere <u>except in the toy chest.</u>
3. All applicants at that company must take a skills assessment test. They must <u>also</u> take <u>a personality profile test.</u>
4. The film class saw every Dustin Hoffman film, <u>including his first one, *The Graduate*.</u>

Practice 4 (p. 64)

1. Our instructor seems strict <u>but is actually friendly and helpful.</u>
2. A mouse's face popped out of a hole near the sink. <u>Then it disappeared quickly.</u>
3. The nurse brought the patient an extra pillow and a glass of water. <u>But she forgot his pain medication.</u>
4. The pot of coffee sat on the burner for hours <u>and became too strong and bitter to drink.</u>

6 RUN-ONS AND COMMA SPLICES

Note   Methods of correction may vary.

Practice 1 (p. 73)

1. It's easy to begin smoking, but it's much harder to quit.
2. Because some people at the office have gotten raises, the other workers are jealous.
3. That color isn't right for you. The style is wrong as well.

Practice 2 (p. 74)

1. Hakim was talking on the phone, and he was switching TV channels with his remote control at the same time.
2. I chose the shortest checkout line at the supermarket. Then the one customer in front of me pulled out dozens of coupons.
3. Since the electricity at Jasmin's house went out, she had to write her paper by candlelight.

7 PRONOUNS

Practice 1 (p. 83)

1. she
2. their
3. he or she
4. it
5. him

Practice 2 (p. 83)

1. his father
2. the maintenance people
3. the sugar
4. cheating
5. the stores

Practice 3 (p. 84)

1. I
2. his
3. They
4. we
5. you

8 COMMA

Practice 1 (p. 92)

1. newspapers, cardboard, glass, aluminum,
2. Walking, bicycling,
3. kids, loaded the van,
4. insomnia, inability to concentrate,

Practice 2 (p. 92)

1. course,
2. on,
3. doorway,
4. hours,

Practice 3 (p. 93)

1. Beatles, who originally called themselves the Quarrymen,
2. yogurt, a dessert that is relatively low in calories,
3. dieters, on the other hand,
4. building, forty stories high,

Practice 4 (p. 94)

1. help, but
2. glasses, so
3. quickly, but
4. family, and

Practice 5 (p. 94)

1. replied,
2. ends,"
3. you," said the math instructor,
4. do,"

9   APOSTROPHE

Practice 1 (p. 102)

1. What's, that's
2. you'll, it's
3. I'd, who's
4. aren't, isn't
5. didn't, they're

Practice 2 (p. 103)

1. It's, its
2. They're, their
3. Who's, whose
4. your, your
5. It's, their, whose, your

Practice 3 (p. 104)

2. mail carrier's job, that man's vicious dog
3. Everyone's assignment, Monday's class
4. Ben Franklin's inventions, people's ideas
5. Doris's grades, her brothers' grades

Practice 4 (p. 105)

1. Lucy's
   texts—verb
2. storefront's
   years—plural
3. manager's
   gives—verb
   assignments—plural
4. year's
   shows—plural
   programs—plural
   seasons—plural

5. son's
   coughs—verb
   wheezes—verb
   starts—verb
6. Theo's
   failings—plural
   conclusions—plural
7. Dieters—plural
   glasses—plural
   water's
8. dozens—plural
   elephants—plural
   water holes'
   edges—plural

10   QUOTATION MARKS

Practice 1 (p. 114)

1. "My throat is so sore I can't talk,"
2. "Life's a tough proposition, and the first hundred years are the hardest."
3. "Don't go in that door!"
4. "If you can't help me, I'll have to find someone else who can,"
5. "If at first you don't succeed," . . . "you should read the directions."

Practice 2 (p. 115)

2. Coach Hodges told Lori, "You played an outstanding game."
3. Manuel insisted, "My new glasses haven't improved my vision one bit."
4. The detective exclaimed, "I know the murderer's identity!"
5. "Study well because you can't use the book or your notes on the test," our instructor told us.

Practice 3 (p. 116)

1. The Good Food Book . . . "How to Eat More and Weigh Less."
2. "The Red Wheelbarrow."
3. The Sound of Music, . . . "Climb Every Mountain"
4. "All Gamblers Lose" . . . Newsweek . . . Time.
5. "Will the Circle Be Unbroken?" . . . The Atlantic Monthly

11   OTHER PUNCTUATION MARKS

Practice 1 (p. 124)

1. close?
2. today.
3. birth!
4. run.
5. bins.

Practice 2 (p. 126)

1. red-haired
2. (I think I've mentioned her to you before)
3. all—if
4. attachments:
5. diet;

12   CAPITAL LETTERS

Practice 1 (p. 135)

1. As, Doug, Don't
2. St. Mary's, Seminary, Baltimore, Maryland, Catholic
3. We, Professor, Henderson, Florentine, Italian, Lake, Street
4. Some, Rodeo, Drive, Beverly, Hills, California
5. When, Rodney, Dangerfield, I

Practice 2 (p. 136)

1. Caucasian, African-American, Hispanic, Asian
2. All, Shook, Up, Pepsi
3. Introduction, Statistics
4. Monday, October, Columbus, Day
5. Mommy, Solarcaine

13 HOMONYMS

Practice (p. 145)

1. It's, it's, its
2. There, their, they're
3. to, two, too
4. You're, you're, your

14 WORD CHOICE

Note   Wording of answers may vary.

Practice 1 (p. 155)

1. Because the judge's hair is prematurely gray, people think she is much older than thirty-eight.
2. The company is now taking many steps to reduce environmental pollution.
3. If the weather is bad, the baseball game will be postponed.

Practice 2 (p. 156)

1. talking . . . genius
2. negative person . . . get away from
3. fell asleep . . . working all night

Practice 3 (p. 156)

1. very sick . . . healthy
2. there wasn't much time left . . . accept the situation
3. unexpectedly . . . traveled quickly

15 MISPLACED AND DANGLING MODIFIERS

Note   Wording of answers may vary.

Practice 1 (p. 164)

1. With shaking hands, the young man gave his driver's license to the officer.
2. Driving down the country road, we were surprised to hear a siren.
3. Gina got badly sunburned on her face and back after spending a day at the beach.
4. The registrar will post on the Web site the schedule for final exams.
5. Stan bought a sports car with wire wheels from a fast-talking salesman.

Practice 2 (p. 165)

1. I spent only two hours studying for the French test; I hope that was enough.
2. Carlos must have answered almost a hundred ads before he found a job.
3. My sister spends nearly all evening on the telephone.

Practice 3 (p. 166)

1. While I was taking a shower, a mouse ran across my bathroom floor.
2. Sitting on the front porch, we were annoyed by mosquitoes.
3. While Kareem was eating at the restaurant, his coat was stolen.
4. Breathing heavily, the runner finally saw the finish line come into view.
5. Hoping to catch a glimpse of the band, fans filled the parking lot.

16 PARALLELISM

Practice 1 (p. 175)

1. to print the final copy
2. baby cried
3. dark sunglasses
4. office manager
5. unkind
6. coaches the track team

Practice 2 (p. 175)

1. folding laundry
2. steamed shrimp
3. high-heeled boots
4. friendliness
5. deposited it in the deep hole

Practice 3 (p. 176)

Note   Answers will vary. Below are some possibilities.

1. watch television
2. wait for sales
3. creative writing
4. plant flowers
5. reading newspapers

ANSWERS TO THE PRACTICES IN PART TWO

18 SPELLING

Practice (p. 188)

1. denies
2. skipping
3. writing
4. definitely
5. deceive
6. employer
7. admittance
8. marrying
9. friendly
10. pitiful

19 PRONOUN TYPES

Practice (p. 192)

1. your
2. hers
3. me
4. He, I
5. I
6. Those
7. Who
8. these
9. they, themselves
10. whom
11. these
12. me
13. She
14. Whomever
15. he
16. themselves
17. I
18. its
19. who
20. those

20 ADJECTIVES AND ADVERBS

Practice (p. 195)

1. harder
2. regularly
3. really
4. greatest
5. easier
6. softly
7. less
8. carefully
9. well
10. better
11. best
12. well
13. smaller
14. least
15. beautifully

21 NUMBERS AND ABBREVIATIONS

Practice (p. 198)

1. five
2. 25
3. company
4. One hundred fifty
5. college
6. 6
7. doctor
8. 7
9. professor
10. 10

22 USAGE

Practice (p. 199)

1. ~~can't hardly~~ can hardly
2. ~~try and~~ try to
3. ~~ways~~ way
4. ~~had ought~~ ought
5. ~~could of~~ could have
6. ~~should of~~ should have
7. ~~couldn't help but notice~~ couldn't help noticing
8. ~~Being that~~ Since (*or* Because)
9. ~~off of~~ off
10. ~~anywheres~~ anywhere
11. ~~Irregardless~~ Regardless
12. ~~kind of a~~ kind of
13. ~~nowheres~~ nowhere
14. ~~use to~~ used to
15. ~~is because~~ is that

23 MIXED CONSTRUCTIONS

Practice (p. 202)

1. I got an A on the exam because I studied all my class notes.

    (*Or:* The reason I got an A on the exam is that I studied all my class notes.)

2. That dog is ten years old, but he still runs around like a puppy.

    (*Or:* Although that dog is ten years old, he still runs around like a puppy.)

3. Eating healthy foods and reducing portion sizes helped me lose twenty pounds.

    (*Or:* By eating healthy foods and reducing portion sizes, I was able to lose twenty pounds.)

4. A recent immigrant's application for citizenship can take a long time.

    (*Or:* When a recent immigrant applies for citizenship, the process can take a long time.)

5. People who live alone often become depressed during the holiday season.

    (*Or:* For people who live alone, the holiday season is often depressing.)

6. Revision is a process in which a writer improves a paper by finalizing details, organizing clearly, and correcting spelling and grammar.

   (*Or:* During revision, a writer improves a paper by finalizing details, organizing clearly, and correcting spelling and grammar.)

7. Because Kaylin set a new track record at her high school, she was offered a scholarship.

   (*Or:* Kaylin set a new track record at her high school; therefore, she was offered a scholarship.)

8. At the beginning of the year, students register for classes.

   (*Or:* The beginning of the year is the time when students register for classes.)

24 MORE ABOUT SUBJECTS AND VERBS

Practice (p. 203)

1. *Subjects:* mitt, skateboard, pile
   Verb: belong
2. *Subject:* motor
   Verbs: coughed, refused
3. *Subjects:* Accounting, computer science
   Verbs: are, require
4. *Subject:* Lisa
   Verbs: tore, lifted, gasped
5. *Subjects:* author, husband
   Verbs: attended, sipped, chatted

25 EVEN MORE ABOUT VERBS

Practice 1 (p. 205)

1. Seeing . . . believing
2. to grow
3. has taken
4. will be traveling . . . will be displaying
5. was borrowed

Practice 2 (p. 207)

1. sit
2. lain
3. raise
4. rose
5. laid
6. lie
7. set
8. rises
9. sat
10. Lying

26 MORE ABOUT SUBJECT-VERB AGREEMENT

Practice (p. 208)

1. *Subject:* few
   Verb: taste
2. *Subjects:* Thelma, mother
   Verb: stays
3. *Subjects:* Carl, friends
   Verb: are
4. *Subject:* All
   Verb: were
5. *Subjects:* coach, coaches
   Verb: have
6. *Subject:* Both
   Verb: need
7. *Subjects:* lectures, textbook
   Verb: has
8. *Subject:* any
   Verb: Is
9. *Subject:* any
   Verb: Are
10. *Subject:* all
    Verb: seem
11. *Subject:* Most
    Verb: look
12. *Subject:* none
    Verb: were
13. *Subject:* Some
    Verb: have
14. *Subject:* Many
    Verb: appear
15. *Subject:* All
    Verb: is

27 MORE ABOUT RUN-ONS AND COMMA SPLICES

Practice (p. 211)

1. horrible;
2. money;
3. locked;
4. London;
5. products;
6. rent;
7. children;
8. yard;
9. minutes;
10. much;

28 MORE ABOUT THE COMMA

Practice 1 (p. 214)

1. Vanessa,
2. morning,
3. March 8, 2014, Courthouse, Streets, Glendale,
4. confused,
5. no commas needed
6. Harvey, Joy,
7. No,
8. reception,
9. loan,
10. Rhett, . . . With love,

Practice 2 (p. 215)

1. bed,
2. see,
3. Delia,
4. graduate,
5. see,
6. operas,
7. test,
8. van,
9. friend,
10. cornstarch,

29   MORE ABOUT THE APOSTROPHE

Practice (p. 216)

1. T's
2. no apostrophes needed
3. A's . . . B's
4. no apostrophes needed
5. *please's . . . thank-you's*

30   MORE ABOUT QUOTATION MARKS

Practice (p. 218)

1. "For our next class, please read the short story 'The Yellow Wallpaper' and write a journal entry about it," the instructor said.
2. "I can't believe it—they just scored the winning basket with half a second remaining!" the announcer gasped.
3. In which of Shakespeare's plays does a character say, "To thine own self be true"?
4. One of the longest words in the English language is "antidisestablishmentarianism."
5. "Whenever I'm feeling depressed, my father always makes me smile by saying, 'Life is far too important to be taken seriously,'" Joanne said.

31   MORE ABOUT PUNCTUATION MARKS

Practice (p. 220)

1. twenty-nine
2. food—
3. Reader's Digest ... epidemic; ... office;
4. (1) ... (2) ... (3) ... (4) ... (5) ... (6)

5. The Tommyknockers . . . The Fly
6. all-inclusive . . . Fantasy Islands . . . self-addressed
7. (1) . . . English Brushup; (2) . . . chapter; . . . (3)
8. worldwide— . . . ex-presidents

32   MORE ABOUT CAPITAL LETTERS

Practice (p. 221)

1. Korean War . . . CIA
2. Northeast . . . Midwest
3. AIDS . . . Dark Ages
4. PBS
5. Dear Sir . . . Madam . . . DVD . . . Yours
6. CBS . . . NBC
7. Desert Storm . . . US . . . UN
8. Roaring Twenties . . . World War . . . Great Depression
9. Civil War . . . South . . . North . . . Reconstruction
10. President Smith . . . PTA . . . Respectfully

33   MORE ABOUT HOMONYMS

Practice (p. 225)

1. already . . . quit . . . accept . . . advice
2. dessert . . . effect . . . dose
3. lose . . . less . . . an . . . pair . . . a
4. desert . . . loose . . . coarse
5. all ready . . . Fewer
6. quite . . . quit . . . advise . . . affect
7. desert . . . except
8. course . . . principle . . . among
9. quiet . . . does
10. where . . . were . . . led . . . among

34   MORE ABOUT WORD CHOICE

Practice (p. 226)

1. ~~remit~~ pay
   ~~prior to~~ before
2. ~~ascertained~~ found out
   ~~depart~~ leave
3. ~~remuneration~~ pay
   ~~insufficient~~ too low
4. ~~vociferous~~ noisy
   ~~endeavored~~ tried
5. ~~Subsequent to~~ After
   ~~inundating~~ flooding
6. ~~commenced~~ began
   ~~be victorious~~ win
7. ~~justifications~~ excuses
   ~~prevaricated~~ lied
8. ~~replenish~~ refill
   ~~deplete~~ empty
9. ~~domicile~~ home
   ~~transmit~~ send
10. ~~delectable~~ delicious
    ~~repast~~ meal
11. ~~compensate~~ pay
    ~~inquired~~ asked
12. ~~commend~~ praise
    ~~diligence~~ hard work
13. ~~finalizes~~ finishes
    ~~an athletic competition~~ a game
14. ~~comprehend~~ understand
    ~~elucidate~~ make it clear
15. ~~facilitate~~ help (*or* make easier)
    ~~regulations~~ rules

Index